International Business

International Business

Institutions and the Dissemination of Knowledge

Edited by
Brian Toyne
and
Douglas Nigh

UNIVERSITY OF SOUTH CAROLINA PRESS

© 1999 Brian Toyne and Douglas Nigh

Published in Columbia, South Carolina, by the
University of South Carolina Press

03 02 01 00 99   5 4 3 2 1

Manufactured in the United States of America

Library of Congress Cataloging-in-Publication Data

International business : institutions and the dissemination of knowledge / edited by
Brian Toyne and Douglas Nigh.
   p.   cm.
Papers presented at a conference held at the University of South Carolina in May 1992.
Includes bibliographical references.
ISBN 1-57003-256-4
   1. Business education—United States—Congresses.   2. Business education—Congresses.
3. International economic relations—Study and teaching (Higher)—United States—Congresses.
4. International economic relations—Study and teaching (Higher)—Congresses.   I. Toyne,
Brian.   II. Nigh, Douglas William.
HF1131 .I582   1999
658'.049—dc21   98-40226

*I dedicate this book to the many doctoral students in the
University of South Carolina's International Business program
who constantly challenged me with their probing questions
and lively arguments, particularly Nicholas Athanassiou,
Steven Barnett, Thomas Hench, and Alan William Wallace.*
—Brian Toyne

To Linda, Kassie, and Jessamyn
—Douglas Nigh

Contents

It is safer to have a whole people respectably enlightened than a few in a high state of science and the many in ignorance.

—Thomas Jefferson (from *The Vocation of A Teacher*)

A university will have ceased to exist when its learning has degenerated into what is now called research, when its teaching has become mere instruction and occupies the whole of an undergraduate's time, or when undergraduates come with no understanding of the manners of conversation but desire only a qualification for earning a living or a certificate to let them in on the exploitation of the world.

—from *The Idea of a University*

Preface

During the past two and a half decades that we have been intimately involved in International Business (IB) education, we have been struck by the tremendous strides made by our colleagues in establishing the legitimacy, and, perhaps more correctly, centrality of IB for today's business training. Partly as a consequence of efforts by such acclaimed IB scholars as John Fayerweather, Lee Nehrt, Dick Robinson, and "Rusty" Root, and partly as a consequence of geopolitical and geoeconomic changes, IB education is increasingly viewed as an integral, if not central, part of business programs. Thus, for some, the work undertaken by four decades of IB scholars is on the threshold of being completed. Unfortunately, the work has not yet been finished, it has only begun, particularly in those countries, such as the United States, where business education has traditionally been housed in universities.

It is true that for some—those who only sought to persuade the functional disciplines of the virtues of IB research and education—the work is about to be completed. Most, if not all, business academic associations and academies now recognize the importance of the international dimensions for their particular specializations.

But today there is a new debate; a debate that is centered on the relative merits of business training versus business education. As noted in the opening chapter, training is viewed here as preparing someone for a known "present" or anticipated future (such as, emphasis is placed on acquiring skills and the regurgitation of "temporal facts.") On the other hand, education is viewed as preparing that person for an unknown, uncertain future by providing her or him with a fundamental, liberal, broad-based understanding of human endeavor, the ability to think critically, and the ability to modify his or her learned behavior when circumstances change.

The increased emphasis by the AACSB–International Association for Management on the liberal arts, for example, is in response to the circumstances of, and trends in, the world of business today. By raising the lower limit on the number of humanities and social sciences courses, the AACSB has clearly come down on the side arguing for business education.

The challenges facing IB scholars today are not the same as yesterday. Today, they are at the vanguard of business educational change. Because of their "worldview," their acceptance of the humanities and social sciences, and an anthropology of business, they can be expected to be called upon to lead and transform yesterday's business training into tomorrow's business education. In contrast, yesterday's IB scholars were challenged to persuade an already established and well entrenched assembly of functional specialists to incorporate a worldview into the training of future business graduates.

As noted in our preface to this book's companion volume, *International Business: An Emerging Vision*, IB inquiry is evolving into an academic discipline that holds out considerable promise for the United States, its business community and its people in the years ahead. Yet this potential has gone unrecognized by most academia outside the area. The research and teaching implications that the development of this area has for business research and the education of future managers have also gone unrecognized by those responsible for its integration into institutions of higher learning.

This does not mean that attempts have not been made to alert higher education to the international trend of the economic interdependence and interconnectedness of nation-states. To the contrary, many efforts have been made over the years to focus attention on the importance and need for the "international" dimension of business research and education. For example, in the 1950s and 1960s, Indiana University held two widely attended meetings that focused on IB education. In the 1950s, the participants gathered to discuss the proper development of an educational program that would offer rigorous academic work for young people interested in careers in "global corporations." In 1964, the second Indiana University meeting was to share the experiences and plans of faculty members interested in the development (refinement) of international business programs.

These two meetings were subsequently followed by others. For example, four meetings during 1975 and 1976 was held by the Task Force on Business and International Education, Government/Academic Interface Committee, International Education Project, American Council on Education. The results of these meetings and the subsequent reflections of the task force were published in 1977 in a report, *Business and International Education*.

Also, the AACSB has long recognized that IB needs to be an integral part of business programs. Unfortunately, no decisive attempt was made to make IB such a requirement using specific pedagogical approaches. Instead, the decision as to how the "international" dimension was to be incorporated into business programs was left in the hands of a primarily uninterested, and parochial business faculty.

Despite these limitations, the major reason for the failure of the field of IB to gain recognition can be traced to the field's hesitancy, if not unwillingness, to make clear what its purpose was in words understandable to the business disciplines and business schools. Unlike the functional disciplines that very early in their development established clearly articulated statements concerning their domains of inquiry and their research priorities as first steps in making others aware of what was needed and to some extent what might be possible, those interested in IB as a topic of research and education felt no pressure to provide such a clarifying definition of IB, what it was and where it could and should be going in terms of both teaching and research.

It was this failure to articulate such a statement that led to this volume of collected papers and to the conference at which they were first presented and discussed. Although IB as a subject of research and education has made considerable progress in the last forty years, it has been thwarted to some extent by its lack of direction, coherence, legitimacy, and recognition. Thus, the primary purpose of the conference was to establish the domain of IB, and to establish its legitimacy as a distinct and viable area for research and education.

The conference had two goals that get to the core issues that we believe will shape the scope, content, and direction of IB research and education in the immediate years ahead. One goal was to demonstrate that IB is a distinct and creditable field of scientific inquiry and education by providing a timely report on the theoretical and research frontiers of the field. The second goal was to examine what institutional arrangements can best insure that we meet our full responsibilities as IB scholars. Thus, it was hoped that a set of guidelines would be generated for the institutional housing of IB within schools and colleges of business that will foster and stimulate the growth of the field's theory-building, research and educational activities.

To meet these challenges, the conference was designed to address the following four objectives:

1. To define the domain, phenomena, and relationships that constitute the field of IB inquiry, and to identify constructs that hold promise for integrating the field and for encouraging theory-building and theory-testing in the future.
2. To identify opportunities that exist for research in the field, to explore the limitations imposed by, and the benefits derived from, various research methodologies and their embedded paradigms, and to suggest directions that seem particularly fruitful for future research.
3. To help institutional administrators better understand the emerging importance of IB as a unified systematic body of knowledge, and to acquaint them with the unique research and educational issues and problems confronting the field.
4. To identify and explore the implications of current institutional arrangements and incentives as they relate to our ability to fulfill our responsibilities as scholars, researchers and educators, and to suggest ways that these institutional arrangements and incentives can be modified to encourage the field's advancement.

The conference was organized by the editors of this book and held at the University of South Carolina in May 1992. To achieve the four objectives, twelve topic sessions were organized that addressed issues related to domain, lines of inquiry, and education. In addition, three panels were assembled to address the following questions:

1. Can (should) IB develop into a viable and distinct field of inquiry given its lack of a unifying definition and its current and foreseeable dependency on the paradigms, theories and constructs of economics, political science, sociology, and the business disciplines?
2. How should the IB dimension be institutionally housed in order to simultaneously satisfy its theory-building, research, and educational responsibilities?
3. What are the most effective and efficient teaching and learning forms for insuring that the IB dimension is adequately and properly covered in everything from formal degree programs to small, in-house executive training programs?

This book contains the papers presented at three of the twelve sessions and the last two panels. They address issues that are of direct and immediate concern to institutions and organizations associated with higher education, including accreditation organizations, educational consortia, and universities and colleges offering business education programs at the undergraduate, graduate, and advanced degree levels. Together, the three sessions explore the historical and current institutional attempts that have been made and are being made to encourage IB research and education. Also explored are the advantages and disadvantages of these attempts as they relate to the encouragement of IB theory-building, research, and educational activities. In our judgment, they constitute the foundation on which future IB education will be based.

Three internationally renowned scholars were asked to write original papers for each topic. Two additional and equally well-known scholars were asked to critique these papers for their content, rigor, and logic. This was done to insure that the dimensions of each topic were adequately and comprehensively covered. The topics include a historical, worldview of IB from an institutional perspective, the institutional structuring of IB research, and the institutional structuring of IB education. In addition, the two panels consisting of distinguished scholars who contributed papers "for the record" and jointly addressed the institutional and educational implications of IB.

The remaining nine topics and one panel are considered central to a better understanding of the scope, content, and intricacies of IB inquiry. Collectively, the nine topics sessions and one panel explore the domain of IB inquiry, the political and economic environment of IB inquiry, and the functional frontiers of IB inquiry. The papers for these nine sessions and one panel appear in a companion volume entitled *International Business: An Emerging Vision.*

For all fifteen sessions over the four days of the conference, we sought maximum engagement and discussion among all participants. Since most papers were distributed in advance and available for a complete review by the participants prior to the sessions, the authors of the papers generally took only a short time to reiterate their major points. Consequently, a substantial portion of the formal sessions consisted of a lively conversation among all in attendance. In addition, the discussion and debates carried over into the coffee breaks and lunches and beyond into the evenings.

At any one time, only one session was scheduled. There were no concurrent sessions—again, to promote maximum engagement of IB issues among the participants. Although the participants had in common a strong interest in some aspect of international business, they came from quite disparate academic backgrounds. During the conference those with a finance background, for example, listened, thought about, and commented on the issues and perspectives presented by those with an organizational behavior background; and vice versa. We believed that such contact and communication held out the promise of real progress for the field of IB.

This book and its companion volume reflect the intellectual energy of the conference in a number of ways. First, the authors had the opportunity to revise their papers to reflect and to update their thinking as a result of the happenings at the conference. Second, some authors drafted replies to the critiques of their papers, thus bringing into print some of the back-and-forth debate occurring during the conference. Third, the two of us have made our own sense of what went on at the conference and used this as one component in our synthesis of the issues addressed in the entire research project.

At the conference, people who cared about the future of international business got together, wrestled with some tough issues usually left unexamined, agreed about some things, and disagreed sharply about others. The conversation continues and we invite the reader to take part.

In concluding this preface, we need to express our most sincere appreciation to the many individuals and organizations that made possible the conference and consequently this book and its companion volume. First we thank the authors whose work appears in the books. They were not given the easiest of specifications or deadlines within which to work. Our special thanks for their patience, tolerance, and willingness to share their experience and expertise. To the participants of the conference who made substantial contributions to the discussions and subsequent development of everyone's thought must also go our gratitude, for the conference results exceeded our highest expectations. We thank the conference session chairs, who managed to keep the sessions focused on the major topics and yet reflective of all the participants' ideas.

The highest compliment we can pay those involved with the accommodations and arrangements for the conference is to state that we all had a great time and the two of us never had to worry about them. We thank Colette Gauthier, then administrative assistant of USC's Center for International Business Education and Research (CIBER), for doing her usual excellent job of handling all the administrative tasks before, during, and after the conference. We also thank Michael Shealy, current CIBER managing director for carrying this project to the publication of the two conference books. To Christine Carson and the rest of the staff of the Daniel Management Center, we say thanks for providing an atmosphere in which such a fruitful exchange could take place and, in particular, for such imaginative and fun events as world-class jazz at the Townhouse and dinner at the Columbia Zoo. In addition, we thank the USC doctoral students (our IB scholars of the future) who pitched in and helped out with all the administrative and logistical tasks.

Our gratitude also goes to several individuals and organizations who were especially instrumental in making this conference a reality. First to be acknowledged and thanked is Professor W. R. Folks, Director, CIBER, University of South Carolina. Without his personal encouragement and the financial support provided by CIBER, the conference and the resulting books would still be a dream rather than a reality. The then dean of the University of South Carolina, Dean James F. Kane, must also be recognized and applauded for providing the College of Business Administration's support for this effort. We also gratefully acknowledge ARCO Chemical Company, Phillips Petroleum Foundation, and the U.S. Department of Education whose financial support was crucial to the conference and research project. In particular, Jack Johnson of ARCO Chemical and Thomas Lambrix receive our thanks for believing in the worth of our project and conference.

A special note of appreciation and thanks is owed to Michael Shealy, Amy Lantz and Jill Olney for their editorial assistance. Likewise our gratitude goes to the USC Press staff for their expertise and patience in making our ideas a tangible reality.

Brian Toyne
Douglas Nigh

International Business

1

The Challenge: Internationalized Business Education

Brian Toyne and Douglas Nigh

INTRODUCTION

International business (IB) education is an inheritance of the 1950s. It emerged from U.S. business education's failure to address the many peculiarities associated with the crossing of national borders in order to conduct business in strange lands.[1] In other words, a few business scholars concluded that U.S. business education was simply too parochial. It did not address the needs of an emerging cadre of international managers; at least for a few business students, business, as examined and taught in the United States, needed to be broadened and made more universal.

In the following decades these champions of the embryonic field of IB education offered a wide variety of purposes and techniques that would save the field from being viewed merely as an educational supplement charged with awakening students to the diversity of business interpretations and practices. More pointedly, those of us involved in IB education were asked to employ our knowledge and research for the mature task of building a progressive political movement within our business schools. We were to be the defenders of a truly universal science and art of business. Using "scientifically established," yet U.S.-based principles, concepts, and theories of the various business disciplines, we were to teach business students the art of discerning when and how business activities were to be ad-

justed or adapted to differences in the business environment encountered as a consequence of crossing national borders. We were to discover, and thus reveal, the principles that makes business work wherever, and whenever undertaken by "strangers in strange lands." We were to discover the architectonic vision that shows how all variants of business at the national level are simply alternative expressions of a universal form of business. We were to develop and teach new business courses—"comparative marketing," "international accounting," "international finance," "international management," "international marketing," "international production."

More recently we have been urged to accept both a new perspective on IB and a new educational role. We are now asked to accept as our core a study of the global management of human-created diversities: the study of how multinational and global corporations "manage" sociocultural diversity, technological diversity, and political diversity (for example, Bartlett and Ghoshal 1992; Bartlett, Doz, and Hedlund 1990; Hedlund 1986; Toyne and Nigh 1997). In addition, we are to help our parochial colleagues become internationally and scientifically expansive and tolerant in their thinking, research and teaching; to have them recognize, in effect, that business practice may indeed vary across nation-states since it is both an interactive consequence of societal forces and a producer of some of these forces (see, for example, Boyacigiller and Adler 1991 and Toyne 1997).

We have no interest in attacking these commendable efforts to develop a distinct field of inquiry and education. What we do want to underline, however, is the obvious point that ultimately, these efforts depend for their success on our learning to teach and practice the art of what we term liberated business thinking. From an educational perspective, for example, we would like our business students to arrive at a level of intellectual understanding of their craft that is above, even apart from, the business practices that are predicated on their sociocultural heritages. From a research perspective, we would like our colleagues to liberate themselves from their parochial perspectives when developing and testing theories that have to do with business and business practice.

We also want to underline a less obvious, but still important point. The paradigms implicit in the IB educational efforts championed by IB scholars since the 1950s have been augmented with other, increasingly more complex and inclusive paradigms that have a direct bearing on the future of IB education in particular, and business education in general. Initially, it was assumed that business is business regardless of where practiced, and thus IB was viewed merely as an extension of domestic business (albeit adjusted for environmental differences) (Vernon 1964). During the 1980s, as an increasing number of companies of various nationality became established world competitors, IB was viewed as a more complex, yet still parochial phenomenon; the crossborder management of business activities affected by both environmental and human resource diversity. More recently, however, as companies of various nationalities continue the arduous task of evolving into truly global organizations that seek to bring together sociocultural differences rather than isolate these differences, IB is seen by some as a socially-embedded, evolving, multilevel, hierarchical system of interactions (Toyne and Nigh 1997, ch. 1).

As will be discussed in more detail in chapter 7, this "emerging interaction" paradigm requires fundamental changes in the way business is viewed, examined, and thus taught.

The point of all of this by way of an introduction is to suggest that efforts to disseminate the experience, knowledge and wisdom accumulated over the years on the socio-politico-economic activity known as international business involves more than just recommending a few changes or additions to the business programs already offered by U.S. and foreign schools of business. As a minimum, for example, U.S. schools of business seriously intent on internationalizing their business programs need to recognize that they must contend in many cases with (1) a highly specialized, yet provincial faculty (Toyne 1993), (2) a college-destined group of students who are, in general, ill-prepared to absorb an intellectually liberating business education,[2] and (3) a body of accumulated business knowledge, experience, and wisdom that is, at best, Anglo-American in orientation and substance or, at worst, even more narrowly parochial (Boyacigiller and Adler 1991).

EDUCATIONAL CHALLENGES OF THE TWENTY-FIRST CENTURY

The changing demands of the marketplace for business education can no longer be ignored, or treated in an incremental, departmentalized, or insular way. Globalization, the rapid—even radical—changes in technology and its use by society in general, and business in particular, and the growing demographic and cultural diversity of the workforce all point to a need for fundamental change in the way we view business and educate future business owners and managers (see, for example, GMAC 1990). Thus, the first challenge confronting schools of business is to inculcate their faculties with a new vision, a new paradigm, that energizes them as individuals and as groups that are functional, crossfunctional, and crossdisciplinary in scope to creatively meet the educational challenge posed by these environmental changes.[3]

Business students, regardless of their lifetime aspirations and career goals, will have to be prepared for a future that has become highly uncertain and geographically and culturally expansive. To prosper in such a future, academic excellence is not enough. They must also be freed from their parochial constraints. That is, business education steeped in parochialism, whether defined in geographic, experiential, or knowledge terms, can no longer be justified. Thus, the second challenge confronting schools of business is to insure that their students learn to think in a liberating way that is ethical, logical, analytical, integrative, historical, and holistic. Nor can these students just be well *trained* in current business skills and practices. They must also be *educated* in ways that will enable them to appreciate, enter into, and enjoy the benefits of lifelong learning, and to respond in positive ways to the rapidly changing challenges that will confront them in the years ahead.[4]

Lastly, as the papers included in this book clearly demonstrate, business schools in increasing numbers are beginning to emulate the actions taken by successful companies when faced with new environmental threats and opportunities. They are becoming more creative, more flexible, and certainly more sensitive and responsive to the implications and demands that environmental change may have for the qualifications, interests, and educational and research activities of their faculties and the future career needs of their graduates. At a minimum, they are recognizing that their mission statements, strategies, and governance structures may have to be modified, perhaps frequently, and their faculties periodically re-trained and their activities refocused. They are also responding to the possibility that their educational programs may have to be modified in ways that encourage crossdisciplinary learning, and reflect new, perhaps even radical, pedagogical approaches such as crossdisciplinary, and crossnational learning.[5]

Organizations, such as the AACSB–International Association for Management have changed or are changing their accreditation requirements to reflect the new emerging reality. Business schools across the country are responding in increasing numbers to the mandate to internationalize and liberalize their missions, programs, and faculties. Many of these responses are laudable, original, and daring; however, many lack vision, and are mere copies of what others have done, or are doing. These business schools, however, are faced with a future in which more business schools are seeking AACSB accreditation, are seeking to maintain a stable share of a shrinking pool of students, and are faced with a possible decline in federal and state support (for example, educational programmatic support, research support, student loans and grants). Thus, the third challenge confronting individual schools of business requires that they not be emulators, but rather educational innovators.

FACTORS INFLUENCING THE INTERNATIONALIZATION EFFORT AND THE EDUCATION-RESEARCH RELATIONSHIP

A business school's ability to respond to, and successfully meet the global changes impacting not just the content of business programs but also the educational process itself depends on several institutional factors not easily changed in the short-term: (1) the faculty's dominant form of scholarship, (2) the institution's dominant position on the research-teaching continuum, and (3) the assumptions made by the faculty concerning the educational role played by IB scholarship.[6] The first two factors create an institutional culture that has proven to be highly impervious and unresponsive to change (see, for example, O'Reilly 1994). The third factor has a direct bearing on the material selected and the interpretation given the selected material by those faculty who are willing to include the international dimensions in their courses.

As both Nehrt (1993) and Toyne (1993)

point out, a business school's faculty are central to its ability to internationalize its business programs. Nehrt (1993, 35) notes that it is the faculty who control the curriculum, and that they "lack the knowledge and motivation to incorporate the international dimensions into the core of the curriculum." Avoiding the issue of motivation, he suggests that the knowledge deficiency can be alleviated by the AACSB and the twenty-three Centers for International Business Education and Research (CIBERs) offering workshops to internationalize business school faculties, and by modifying AACSB accreditation standards to include the requirement that all graduates, particularly at the M.B.A. level, take at least one course in international business and have a thorough understanding of the international dimensions of their fields of specialization (such as, a specific course in their specialty). Toyne (1993, 48–49) takes a different tack. He suggests that the non-IB business faculty constitute a "bottleneck" to any internationalization effort because of the increasingly specialized training and socialization they receive as Ph.D. students, and the departmental structuring of business schools. Put more strongly, "[t]he specialization and socialization of faculty members and the emergence of strong, narrowly focused functional departments have resulted in an internationally illiterate faculty." In addition to recommending that doctoral business programs need to be modified, he also suggested that the governance structure of schools of business need to be changed, and incentives used that encourage faculty to include the international dimension first in their research and then in their courses.

A faculty's dominant form of scholarship, and the institution's dominant position regarding the research and teaching emphasis limit the number of options—at least in the near term—that can be chosen from when seeking to internationalize the business school's faculty and programs. More specifically, these options, as illustrated in figure 1.1, are defined by (1) the

relative emphasis placed on teaching and research, (2) the type of research emphasized; and (3) the type of teaching emphasized.[7] These constraints are briefly examined in the next three subsections.

A more extensive discussion of the model and the various internationalization options are presented in the concluding chapter. At this point, it is sufficient to note that we believe that there is neither an ideal internationalization approach, nor a single, universal set of internationalization recommendations. The approach used and the programmatic recommendations followed must be tailored to the somewhat unique characteristics of each institution. Thus, when reading the papers included in this book, it is recommended that the reader keep in mind the influence that the three factors identified in figure 1.1 may have on the internationalization effort. For example, the relative emphasis place on teaching and research will have a direct bearing on the approaches to be used to ignite an interest of non-IB faculty in the international dimensions of their specialties (for example, self-learning). Also, in addition to having a bearing on the methods used to stimulate faculty interest in the international dimensions of their specialties, the type of research and type of teaching will also have a bearing on the programmatic initiatives that can be undertaken.

BOYER'S SCHEMA OF SCHOLARSHIP

Boyer (1990, 16) has classified scholarship in the United States as having "four separate, yet overlapping functions." These are (1) the scholarship of discovery, (2) the scholarship of integration, (3) the scholarship of application, and (4) the scholarship of teaching. Although elements of these four forms of scholarship are found in all business schools, they are not necessarily given equal attention or importance. Importantly, the dominant form of scholarship will have a pronounced influence on the internationalization approaches that can be successfully used (such as, the means used to motivate non-IB faculty). It will also have

Figure 1.1 Classification Schema for Institutions Examing the Internationalization of Their Business Programs

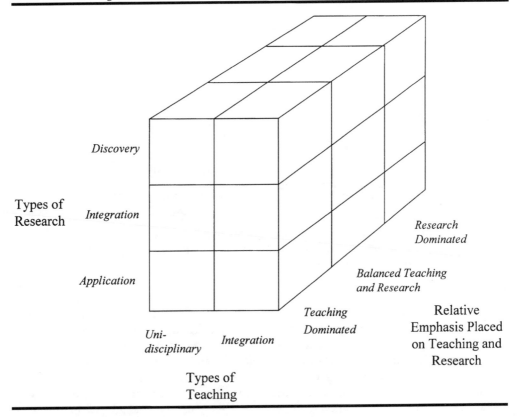

Discovery

Types of
Research

Integration

*Research
Dominated*

Application

*Balanced Teaching
and Research*

*Teaching
Dominated*

Relative
Emphasis Placed
on Teaching and
Research

*Uni-
disciplinary*

Integration

Types of
Teaching

an influence (albeit smaller) on the types of internationalized courses offered (for example, conceptual, concrete), the international content of these courses (for example, theories and concepts, description, anecdotes), and the pedagogical techniques employed (for example, didactic instruction, cases, lectures, Socratic questioning).

Scholarship of Discovery

The scholarship of discovery is closest to what is often called "research" by today's business academics. It is a commitment to the production of knowledge (for its own sake). The parenthetical statement is deliberate and necessary for this is what distinguish those who seek to understand for the sake of understanding and those who seek to understand for the sake of application or as a consequence of application. Even within academic circles, even within indi-

vidual researchers, the two views often stand against one another. Thus, we often speak of basic and applied research as if they are distinct, even mutually exclusive, and attach greater "value" to one or the other depending on our philosophical inclinations. Importantly, "cultures" differ on the relative importance placed on basic and applied research, and this will have an impact of the thrust and content of educational programs. For example, Boyer (1990, 22) points out that the British and Germans tend to regard scholarship as "an end in itself," and people in the United States tend to view it as "equipment for service."

It is also important to recognize that the scholarship of discovery can be uni-, multi, or inter-functional or disciplinary. For our purposes, unifunctional research is the study of business phenomena from a single functional perspective (such as, accounting, finance, information systems, management, marketing, and so on). Multifunctional research is the study of a specific business phenomenon from two or more functional perspectives simultaneously. Interfunctional research is the study of business phenomena from a functionally integrated perspective (for example, the conjoining of strategic management and marketing at some higher level of abstraction).[8]

The Scholarship of Integration

The scholarship of integration, defined by Boyer as interdisciplinary, interpretive, and integrative, is the "bringing together" of knowledge across the physical sciences, the social sciences and the business functions; that is, the placing of specialties in a larger context (for example, placing the findings of marketing management and financial management scholars within the field of sociology and within a greater, more complex context than the firm, such as a socially embedded business process). In contrast to the "renaissance man" of yesteryear, the scholarship of integration for today's scholar means the "serious, disciplined work that seeks to interpret, draw together, and bring new insights to bear on original research" (Boyer 1990, 19).

Such scholarship is important because of the call for relevance by the business community and by such representatives of the business education community as Porter and McKibbin (1988), the AACSB, and the Graduate Management Admission Council (GMAC) (1990). In addition, if the various business functions continue to become even more specialized (see, for example, Toyne 1993), it will be increasingly necessary for unifunctional scholarship of discovery to be interpreted within the greater, more generalized body of business knowledge.

The Scholarship of Application

In contrast to the investigative and synthesizing traditions of discovery and integration, respectively, the scholarship of application shows how knowledge can be applied to important problems and how important problems can define an agenda for scholarly investigation. Like the scholarship of discovery, the scholarship of application can be categorized as uni-, multi-, or interfunctional or disciplinary.

The implications of the scholarship of application go beyond the issue of research. For example, the GMAC report (1990, 17) specifically calls for "a new synthesis between rigorously developed knowledge and managerial practice." This call, of course, is at the heart of Boyer's fourth function of scholarship, teaching.

The Scholarship of Teaching

Boyer (1990, 23) also observed that teaching becomes scholarship when it educates and entices others to further discovery, integration, and application. Thus, the last of the four functions of scholarship, teaching, is simultaneously the means by which the results of the other three functions are disseminated, and the inducement to further discovery, integration, and application. Again, for an internationalization effort to be successful, it is important to note that what we learn depends on what we have learned, why we have learned it, and how we have learned it. That is, for truly liberated business learning to occur, it needs to be recognized that current and future learning is influenced by cultural, historical, situational, and philosophical factors that vary from one locale to another, or one "culture" to another. Moreover, the student entering college has been socialized to a set of values and norm of behavior that is generally the consequence of a culture-bound educational process (for example, the interpretation and meaning given to historical facts). Collectively, learning and socialization ultimately have a pronounced effect on how students see (conceptualize) and question reality, and what body of knowledge they draw upon when seeking solutions to problems.

ALUTTO'S SCHEMA OF SCHOOLS

While Boyer's schema recognizes that scholarship involves four functions, it is silent on those institutional specifics that have an important bearing on which scholarship functions are emphasized. In addition, Boyer appears to view the scholarship of teaching as monolithic. But teaching, like research, can be classified in several ways; ways that are dependent on the institutional setting in which it occurs. For example, Alutto (1993, 38) suggests that business schools can be subdivided into *integrators* and *silo enhancers:* "Integrators are those institutions that truly reflect the integration of discipline-based functional frameworks in *all that they do.* Silo enhancers are institutions that pursue minimal integration while maximizing the focus on individual functional specialties" (emphasis added).

Besides distinguishing between the scholarships of unifunctional discovery and integration, this schema makes two additional points that are of value to our discussion. First, Alutto's schema suggests that institutions tend to support single forms of research. Second, he breaks down Boyer's monolithic concept of teaching by suggesting that there are at least two forms of teaching, and they are determined by the type of research undertaken at an institution (or visa versa).[9] That is, there is silo enhancing teaching (unifunctional teaching) and integration teaching (multifunctional or interfunctional teaching). A point not made by Alutto, but one worth noting nonetheless is that both forms of teaching can be conceptual (for example, generalized abstractions), applied (for example, case analysis, internships) or some combination of these two.

Alutto also asserts that business schools can be classified as teaching-dominant schools, research-dominant schools, and mixed-focused schools (or balanced research-teaching schools). Over time, these three types of schools, in turn, attract faculties with particular sets of skills, interests, and biases that collectively have a direct influence on the sorts of internationalization approaches institutions are capable of adopting and implementing, at least in the short term.

Teaching-Dominant Schools

The primary mission of these schools is teaching, and the most important faculty skill set is the ability to teach. Possibly because of this classroom emphasis, other skills and interests often sought include an ability to work with the business community and as a member of multifunctional teaching teams.

Research-Dominant Schools

Knowledge production is viewed as the primary mission of these schools, and the most important faculty skill set is the ability to conduct significant research. Other skills include an ability to raise research funds and to remain focused (for example, not distracted by teaching, executive education, or consulting activities). It is worthwhile noting that research and teaching are primarily the result of individual effort at many of these schools.

Research-Teaching Balanced Schools

The mission of these schools is to provide a balance between research and teaching. Thus, important faculty skills include an ability to simultaneously undertake significant research while excelling at teaching, to interact effectively with the business community, and, in integrator schools, to remain broadly aware of multifunctional, even multidisciplinary developments.

THE ROLE OF INTERNATIONAL BUSINESS IN BUSINESS EDUCATION AND RESEARCH

What do business schools hope to accomplish as a consequence of internationalizing their business programs? We suspect that the immediate, vocalized goal of many business schools is to make the targeted programs more relevant for today's business challenges. At a minimum, this requires including international material that the school's faculty believe is appropriate; that is, judiciously selected material that focuses on the issues and problems associated with the consequences of the emerging interdependent world of business.

But what is judiciously selected material? A core question not raised in the following papers, but one that needs to be made explicit, deals with the assumptions establishing the relationship between business and international business. That is, which IB paradigm is to be used when selecting the IB material? Another question that also must be dealt with head on concerns the faculty's view of the "contributing value" of IB knowledge to the education/training process.

In the eyes of those whom we seek to convince of the merits of IB scholarship, we suffer from two apparent inadequacies. In the eyes of our university brethren (such as, the humanities, physical sciences, social sciences) we are simply vocational instructors—we train, we do not educate. In the eyes of our immediate colleagues, the business faculty, we provide at best scientific replication, and at worst, interesting, anecdotal, yet spurious examples of business aberrations. According to functional pundits, our research lacks theoretical and methodological rigor (see, for example, Feldman 1997), and—perhaps even worse—most students will never find it necessary to operate in the international arena; the North American Free Trade Agreement (NAFTA), of course, has changed this, but the full educational implications of its message have yet to sink in.

In other words, what can IB scholars add to the already well defined but splintered body of business knowledge and the well entrenched, somewhat impervious business educational process? We believe that IB scholars must convincingly show that the generalized, certified body of business knowledge they are producing has both experiential and theoretical value and thus educational value, and that tomorrow's managers need exposure to (1) international business issues, and (2) the experience that companies and executives have gained from coping with international complexities and peculiarities (for example, foreign exchange, tax law differences, managing envi-

ronmental diversity, ad infinitum). To do this successfully, of course, requires showing how the paradigms that guide IB research and education mesh with those of the business functions, and demonstrating how our "scientific" contributions either confirm what is already known, add to the various bodies of function-splintered business knowledge, or add uniquely to the collective body of business knowledge (see, for example, Toyne 1997).

THE PARADIGMATIC ROOTS OF IB INQUIRY AND EDUCATION

How IB is conceptualized as a field of study and practice has a significant influence on the design and management of educational programs and institutions. Below we discuss the three dominant IB paradigms and their implications for education.[10]

As noted earlier, IB inquiry in the United States sprang from a desire to educate future U.S. international business practitioners. Shortly after World War II, when U.S. business aggressively expanded internationally, a handful of U.S. educators, sensitive to, and knowledgeable about the sociocultural and politico-legal differences existing among nation-states, saw a need to address the issues and problems encountered when crossing national borders in order to conduct business.

To guide them in this educational crusade two paradigms were adopted that still permeate the arguments and thinking of many U.S.-bound business scholars and IB scholars (Vernon 1964). The first paradigm, the extension paradigm, emphasizes the management of functional activities in "foreign economies." The second paradigm, the crossborder management paradigm, focuses attention on the integration and management of operations "within the international environment and across foreign economies." A third, more recent paradigm, the emerging interaction paradigm, attempts to present a more holistic, multilevel view of international business (Toyne 1989; Toyne and Martinez 1988; Toyne and

Nigh 1997) that reflects more recent thinking (see, for example, Boddewyn 1997, Hogner 1997, and Wartick 1997). Table 1.1 lists these three paradigms and some of their implications for "internationalized" business education.

The Extension Paradigm

When seen from this viewpoint, IB practice is modified *domestic* practice. Thus, both IB education and IB research can be, and often are, viewed as mere extensions of domestic business education and research. In fact, judged by U.S.-bound business research standards, much of IB inquiry can be termed "normal science" (Kuhn 1970). It involves, for example, using U.S.-bound business theories, concepts and research methodologies in other business situations, and classifying the output as "international" marketing, "international" management, and so on.

At the core of this paradigm are four assumptions: (1) business is business wherever practiced, only the situation or external circumstances change;[11] (2) business environments are converging; (3) business practices are converging; and (4) since, to many, the U.S. is the most economically advanced country in the world, U.S. business practice leads the world in new styles and new techniques.[12]

The questions raised by this paradigm are essentially concerned with identifying environmental factors that have an influence on a firm's home-country strategies, operations, and managerial practices when venturing overseas. At the same time, the questions concerned with these "foreign situations" are limited to those that can be legitimately raised within the various paradigms accepted by business function disciplines that have been parochially developed. Thus, Vernon (1964, 8) was able to assert:

Table 1.1 Contributions of International Business Inquiry to Generalized Business Education

Prevailing View of International Business	Contributions to Business Knowledge	Contributions to Business Education
Extension of domestic business	IB provides opportunities for replication, and for defining the boundaries of mid-range theories developed by studying business practice in the United States.	The student gains a greater appreciation of the complexities and challenges of managing enterprises subject to environmental diversity.
Cross-border management	In addition to above, focuses attention on the *consequences* of cross-coupling national and regional differences for strategic and operational purposes by enterprises.	In addition to the above, draws attention to the managerial/administrative *consequences* of cross-coupling national and regional differences for strategic and operational purposes by enterprises.
Evolving interactions of socially-embedded business processes	Increased emphasis placed on the embeddedness of business processes within societies and the consequences of their interaction with one another.	Provides a strong argument for a strengthened liberal and liberating form of undergraduate *and* graduate education with an emphasis on the consequences of socio-cultural interaction (i.e., humanities and social sciences).

our existing functional groups—to our production people, our marketing people, our control people, our finance people, and so on. I say this because, as all of you know, we have developed a body of hard conceptions and ideas within the fields of production, marketing, control, and finance. These ideas I assume, can appropriately be extended by observant men who are specialists in their fields. It would seem prudent to me to take the discipline as it exists and to see in what sense these ideas have to be adapted to the peculiar conditions of foreign environments. I think we will learn that, with suitable, sensitive adaptation, many principles we now use can be applied to the circumstances of foreign economies and will continue to be valid.

So what can extension-based IB scholarship add to what is already being done as a result of functional inquiry? The answer, of course, is a great deal. First, the scholarships of discovery, integration, and application are enriched by the opportunities that international business provides for replication, and for defining the boundaries of the mid-range theories developed as a consequence of parochially studying business practice. Second, the teaching of business is enhanced. At the practitioner educational levels (for example, B.B.A. and M.B.A.), the student gains a much greater appreciation of the complexities and challenges of operating successful enterprises; particularly when foreign competitors are involved, and the domestic market becomes increasingly "regionalized" (for example, NAFTA). At the doctoral level, the student gains a broader yet deeper appreciation of the diversity, richness, intricacy and subtlety of human expression and endeavor (albeit as they relate to business).

The Cross-Border Management Paradigm

The second concept that has had a strong and continuing influence on IB inquiry for at least the last 30 years deals with the problems associated with the movement of goods and capital across national borders and the simultaneous monitoring, control

and integration from headquarters of operations existing in two or more countries. Vernon (1964, 9–10) went so far as to suggest that this paradigm supports the argument that IB is distinct from U.S. business for the following four reasons:

1. IB involves both risks and opportunities of a kind not normally encountered within the domestic economy (for example, balance of payment risks and opportunities, import restriction risks and opportunities).
2. IB requires an understanding of the vagaries and intricacies of such things as international taxation, foreign exchange, the international patent system, and the special problems of international oligopoly pricing.
3. IB requires dealing with governments, particularly at the point of entry.
4. IB requires the development of an effective operating discipline for understanding the complexities of moving across borders and operating in many countries.

In Vernon's view, these peculiarities raise questions not addressed by the "functional groups" in their research or teaching. At its core, however, this paradigm is a firm-level paradigm that does not challenge the core assumptions of the extension paradigm (such as, universality of business practice, business practice convergence, and U.S. leadership in new business styles and techniques). Thus, as most U.S.-bound and U.S.-trained business scholars are quick to point out, IB's distinctiveness is not the result of a different worldview, but simply a distinctive opportunity to practice "normal science." The core research/educational question asked is: How does a U.S. firm handle the distinctive peculiarities enumerated by Vernon?

So, again, what can IB scholarship based on a crossborder management paradigm add to what is already being done by

TABLE 7-3. (*Continued*)

SMSA	r_i	Scaled d_F	Scaled s.d.	r_{si}	r_i^*
Indianapolis, IN	22.22	0.289	0.367	0.371	0.368
Houston, TX	26.13	0.338	0.432	0.438	0.435
Cincinnati, OH	27.55	0.355	0.456	0.460	0.456
Buffalo, NY	30.81	0.396	0.509	0.530	0.526
Nashville, TN	34.21	0.438	0.566	0.574	0.570
Toledo, OH	39.23	0.501	0.649	0.655	0.652
Louisville, KY	42.12	0.537	0.696	0.703	0.700
Greensboro, NC	49.02	0.623	0.810	0.826	0.824
Philadelphia, PA	49.50	0.629	0.818	0.842	0.840
Atlanta, GA	50.46	0.641	0.834	0.843	0.841
Albany, NY	52.92	0.672	0.875	0.883	0.881
Cleveland, OH	55.06	0.698	0.910	0.921	0.919
Pittsburgh, PA	55.92	0.709	0.924	0.933	0.932
Chicago, IL	59.02	0.748	0.976	1.005	1.005
Memphis, TN	70.44	0.890	1.164	1.175	1.179
Wilmington, DE	71.37	0.902	1.180	1.192	1.197
Richmond, VA	86.37	1.089	1.428	1.440	1.454
Chattanooga, TN	95.13	1.198	1.573	1.602	1.625
Birmingham, AL	96.28	1.212	1.592	1.607	1.630
Baltimore, MD	101.80	1.281	1.683	1.745	1.777
New Orleans, LA	180.80	2.266	2.989	3.020	3.262

In Chapter 2 we use the fourth-spread, d_F, to define the *outlier cutoffs*:

$$F_U + \tfrac{3}{2}d_F$$

$$F_L - \tfrac{3}{2}d_F.$$

In a symmetric batch F_U and F_L are at $\pm \tfrac{1}{2}d_F$. Therefore, residuals in a symmetric batch scaled by the fourth-spread have values ± 2 at the outlier cutoffs. The resulting numerical rule is to regard a residual scaled by d_F as a possible outlier if its absolute value exceeds 2. For a batch of residuals that follow the Gaussian distribution, the outlier cutoffs are equivalent to roughly ± 2.7 standard deviations. For comparison, the probability that a standard Gaussian variable exceeds 2.6 in absolute value is 1%. Hoaglin, Iglewicz, and Tukey (1981) discuss the (considerably larger) probabilities of points falling outside the outlier cutoffs for small samples.

The largest absolute residual in the regression of mortality on population density is New Orleans, which has a high mortality relative to its population density (3172/square mile). Table 7-3 shows that only this residual would be flagged by each of the criteria for identifying outliers:

1. The outlier cutoffs are -159.83 and 160.97. New Orleans has residual 180.8.
2. When scaled by the fourth-spread after subtraction of the median, the only residual to exceed 2 is New Orleans (2.27).
3. The only residual, when scaled by the standard deviation, to exceed 2.7 is that of New Orleans (2.99).

Displays for the Batch of Residuals

In examining a batch of residuals, we wish to see the skewness of the distribution, the relationship of the extreme values to the central portion, outliers, and notable groupings. Two display techniques that reveal the overall distribution are the *stem-and-leaf display*, introduced in Chapter 1, and the *boxplot*, discussed in Chapter 3.

Figure 7-4 shows a stem-and-leaf display of the raw residuals for the linear regression above, scaled by the fourth-spread (as in the second

```
        (Unit = 0.1)
 -1s │ 6
   f │ 4
   t │
 -1* │ 0 0 0 1 1
 -0· │ 8 9
   s │ 6 7 7
   f │ 4 4 5 5
   t │ 2 3 3 3
 -0* │ 0 0 0 0 0 1 1 1 1 1
  0* │ 0 0 0 1 1 1 1
   t │ 2 2 2 3 3 3
   f │ 4 5 5
   s │ 6 6 6 6 6 7 7
  0· │ 8 9
  1* │ 0 1
   t │ 2 2

  hi │ (22,)
```

Figure 7-4. Stem-and-leaf display of residuals after scaling by the interquartile range.

criterion above). Figure 7-5 is a boxplot of the raw residuals. Both flag the largest positive residual, that belonging to New Orleans. In addition, the displays show the point with the most negative residual, -136.3. This belongs to San Jose, which has unusually low mortality for its population density. The boxplot shows that the batch is very nearly symmetric.

The Quantile–Quantile Plot

We use the quantile–quantile plot to look at the closeness of the distribution of residuals to some ideal distribution. Often we compare the residuals to the Gaussian distribution. The plot is then called a *normal probability plot*. We order the residuals and plot the ith ordered residual from the batch of size n against the corresponding Gaussian quantile. Denoting the Gaussian cumulative distribution function by Φ, the ith quantile is conveniently taken to be

$$\Phi^{-1}\left(\frac{i-\frac{1}{3}}{n+\frac{1}{3}}\right).$$

The shape of the tails of the residual distribution is indicated by the tails of the plot. Figure 7-6 shows, schematically, the normal probability plots for heavy- and light-tailed and right- and left-skewed data. For example, when the distribution of data is skewed to the right, the high observations tend to be far from the center. Similarly, the low observations tend to be close to the center. Thus in Figure 7-6(c), both the highest and lowest observations exceed the expected normal deviates. Other phenomena in the plot are: outliers appear in anomalous positions at the extremes and successive residuals are correlated, producing waves. For a detailed account of probability plotting methods, we recommend Wilk and Gnanadesikan (1968). Figure 7-7 is the normal probability plot of the studentized regression residuals from Table 7-3. The large positive residual of New Orleans (circled) shows up an outlier. Otherwise, the plot is reasonably straight, suggesting that the distribution of residuals is approximately Gaussian.

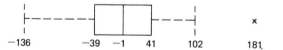

Figure 7-5. Boxplot of the residuals. New Orleans is an outlier (181). Among the remaining values, the most extreme are San Jose (-136) and Baltimore (102).

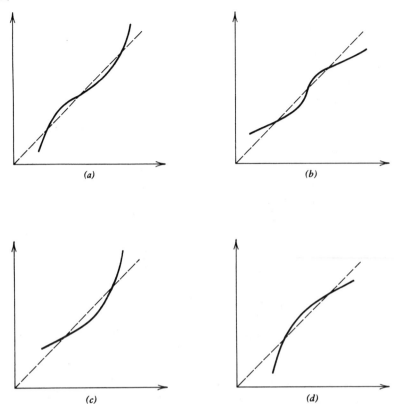

Figure 7-6. Hypothetical patterns in normal probability plots. Data on vertical axis versus Gaussian quantiles on horizontal axis. (*a*) Heavy-tailed. (*b*) Light-tailed. (*c*) Right-skewed. (*d*) Left-skewed.

Distribution of Residuals

When we have a model for the data, we check our assumptions about the error distribution using the distribution of residuals. One method is to use the normal probability plot. Bloomfield (1974) discusses the relationship of the error and residual distributions when fitting a linear model, for example, the multiple regression model, using a particular class of techniques (in fact, generalizations of M-estimators of location, which we present in Chapter 11). He shows that, asymptotically, the distribution functions of the errors and residuals differ by an amount proportional to p/n, where p is the number of carriers in the regression and n is the number of points. The distributions differ in a way that tends to falsely confirm the

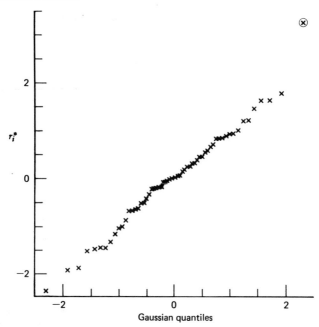

Figure 7-7. Normal probability plot of studentized residuals. The circled point belongs to New Orleans.

choice of fitting technique. Thus residuals of a least-squares fit are closer to Gaussian than the errors. On the other hand, the residuals of a robust fit are heavier-tailed than the errors. Fitting by medians provides a special case. Roughly p residuals will be exactly equal to zero, and the distribution of the remaining residuals will be heavy-tailed.

A distribution of residuals that is heavier-tailed than the Gaussian may be the result of sampling the errors from Gaussian distributions with unequal variances. When we sample from a mixture of two Gaussian distributions with equal means but unequal variances, the distribution of a randomly chosen member of the sample is heavier-tailed than the Gaussian. We suppose that a proportion $(1 - \alpha)$ of the observations is sampled from $\mathrm{Gau}(0, 1)$ and the remaining proportion, α, from $\mathrm{Gau}(0, \sigma^2)$. Then the density of a randomly chosen observation is

$$\frac{1 - \alpha}{\sqrt{2\pi}} e^{-x^2/2} + \frac{\alpha}{\sigma\sqrt{2\pi}} e^{-x^2/2\sigma^2}.$$

For a heavier-tailed distribution, the height of the density decreases more

slowly as we go further out to the tails. We choose to measure distance from the center in standard-deviation units. The variance of the mixture is

$$\tau^2 = (1 - \alpha) + \alpha\sigma^2.$$

When $\alpha \neq 0$ and $\alpha \neq 1$, the mixture is nontrivial and τ^2 lies strictly between 1 and σ^2. The ratio of the mixture and Gaussian densities at y standard deviations is

$$\frac{\left((1 - \alpha)/\sqrt{2\pi}\right)e^{-y^2\tau^2/2} + \left(\alpha/\sigma\sqrt{2\pi}\right)e^{-y^2\tau^2/2\sigma^2}}{\left(1/\sqrt{2\pi}\right)e^{-y^2/2}} = (1 - \alpha)e^{-y^2(\tau^2-1)/2}$$

$$+ \frac{\alpha}{\sigma}e^{-y^2(\tau^2-\sigma^2)/2\sigma^2}$$

Because $\tau^2 - \sigma^2 < 0$ and $\alpha > 0$, the second term increases without bound. We conclude that a nontrivial mixture of Gaussian distributions is heavier-tailed than the Gaussian.

From this result, a heavy-tailed residual distribution may arise when the residuals follow Gaussian distributions with zero mean and unequal variances. This situation may, in particular, be suggested by patterns in the residuals (described in Section 7C together with suggestions for appropriate techniques). Whenever the distribution of residuals is heavy-tailed, a robust fitting technique is appropriate. Good robust techniques are efficient for heavy-tailed error distributions. They lose little efficiency if the errors follow a Gaussian distribution, and they are resistant to outliers.

7C. RESIDUALS AND REGRESSION

We now turn to multiple regression. Our observations consist of a *response variable*, y, and a set of *explanatory variables*, $v_1, v_2, \ldots, v_r$. When the regression is linear, the fit, $\hat{y}$, is a linear combination of prescribed functions of the explanatory variables. Identifying the ith point by subscript i, we have, for example,

$$\hat{y}_i = a_1 + a_2 v_{1i} + a_3 v_{1i}v_{2i} + a_4 v_{3i}^2.$$

When we calculate the fit, we provide values of the *coefficients* a_1, a_2, a_3, and a_4. The *carriers* are the prescribed functions. In the example, the four carriers are

$$1, v_1, v_1 v_2, \quad \text{and} \quad v_3^2.$$

Residual Plots. We can make numerous helpful plots of residuals. Plots of the original data—of the response against functions and combinations of the explanatory variables, and of the explanatory variables against each other—are particularly useful in obtaining a feel for the data set and in constructing an initial model. Residual plots take us a step further and concentrate our attention on the discrepancies between the data and the fit. We describe some of these plots, assuming residuals from a multiple regression.

Plot of Residuals (r) versus a Carrier (x)

The carrier *x* is not necessarily one of those included in the regression. If *x* is not too closely associated with the carriers already fitted, this plot may

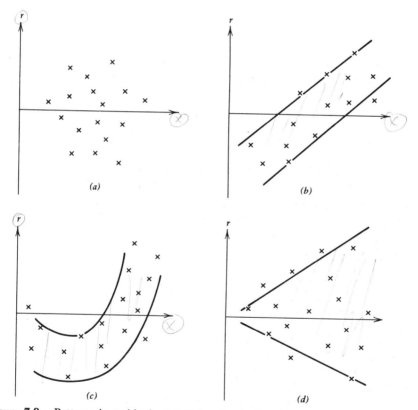

Figure 7-8. Patterns in residuals. (*a*) Point cloud. (*b*) Sloping band. (*c*) Curved band. (*d*) Wedge.

reveal systematic relationships between y and x that have not been accounted for in the fit. Draper and Smith (1966) introduce four patterns that may appear. We discuss each pattern (illustrated in Figure 7-8) in turn.

The *point cloud*, Figure 7-8(a), suggests that there is no simple residual relationship between r and x. The *sloping band*, Figure 7-8(b), indicates that a linear term could be inserted into the model.

When we fit a simple linear regression by least squares, we choose a and b to minimize

$$\sum_{i=1}^{n} r_i^2 = \sum_{i=1}^{n} (y_i - a - bx_i)^2.$$

Differentiation with respect to a and b shows that

$$\sum_{i=1}^{n} r_i = 0, \qquad \sum_{i=1}^{n} r_i x_i = 0.$$

We call these *orthogonality conditions* on the residuals. The slope of the least-squares regression line in the plot of r against x is

$$b_r = \frac{\sum_{i=1}^{n}(r_i - \bar{r})(x_i - \bar{x})}{\sum_{i=1}^{n}(x_i - \bar{x})^2}.$$

If x is one of the carriers in the regression, the orthogonality conditions guarantee that $b_r = 0$. Therefore, when the residuals plotted against such a carrier are a sloping band, either the calculations are erroneous or an extreme outlier has distorted the picture.

When we fit a simple linear regression without the constant, the single orthogonality condition is

$$\sum_{i=1}^{n} r_i x_i = 0.$$

The slope, b_r, of an unrestricted (additive constant included) regression-line fit to the residuals is necessarily 0 only if the residuals fortuitously have 0 mean. Otherwise, we may see a sloping band in the residual plot, one that can be dealt with by also fitting an additive constant.

These consequences of orthogonality conditions apply to multiple regression, with and without the constant carrier, when we take any single carrier x_j from the set $x_1, \ldots, x_p$.

Figure 7-9 plots mortality against household size. The line through the origin has equation

$$\hat{y} = 288 \text{ POP/HSE.}$$

As demonstrated in the figure, the slope of this line (A) is larger than the slope of the regression line with a fitted constant (B). Figure 7-9 also shows that the intercept is far from the data and cannot help us much. Figure 7-10 displays the residuals from the regression through the origin. The plot shows linear dependence of the residuals on household size. We have sketched in the least-squares regression line,

$$r = y - \hat{y} = 404.1 - 123.6 \text{ POP/HSE.}$$

Of course, the composite regression, with slope $288 - 123.6 = 164.4$, is the same as the linear regression with constant term. The equation of a linear regression of mortality on household size is

$$\text{mortality} = 404.1 + 164.4 \text{ POP/HSE}$$

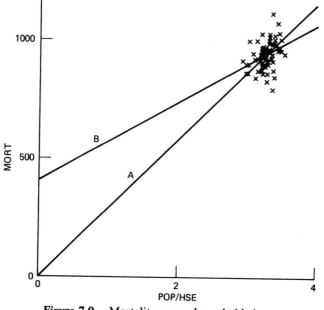

Figure 7-9. Mortality versus household size.

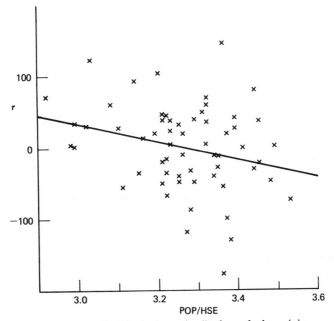

Figure 7-10.   Residuals from the fit through the origin.

or, better, in central value terms

$$\text{mortality} = 940.4 + 164.4(\text{POP/HSE} - 3.263).$$

When we fit by a robust and resistant alternative to least squares, the orthogonality conditions on the residuals do not necessarily hold. Hence the least-squares regression line fitted to such residuals versus x will usually have nonzero slope, although the robust fitted line will have a near-zero slope. This is in accordance with the general notion of residuals; when put back through the same fitting process, they yield zero fit.

The *curved band*, Figure 7-8(c), reveals a nonlinear relationship between the residuals and the carrier x. One choice of a further carrier for the model is a quadratic expression in x; or we might change to exponentials or monomials with a general exponent. Alternatively, we may transform the response variable to give linear dependence on x. Transformations are discussed in Chapters 4 and 8.

The *wedge*, Figure 7-8(d), shows that the spread of the residuals is related to the carrier. This can happen in two ways. When the variability of each of a set of points is identical, the range of a larger number of points is

somewhat greater than that of a smaller number. This is illustrated in Figure 7-11, a plot of the expected value of the range for Gaussian samples of size ranging from 2 to 100. A wedge appearance, therefore, may simply reflect an increasing density of points, and hence an increasing range rather than a change in variance. In a sample of 10 simulations with constant standard deviation but increasing density of points, two or three scatter plots seemed to produce a wedge appearance. When the density of data does not vary across the plot, however, an appearance of changing spread usually does indicate systematic change in variance.

Figure 7-12 displays the residuals against the carrier for a least-squares regression of mortality on household size. The plot hints at a wedge shape, with the width of the wedge increasing as household size increases for about two-thirds of the way across from left to right; this wedge appearance may reflect increasing density of points. Figure 7-13 is a stem-and-leaf display of household size. Comparison of Figures 7-12 and 7-13 shows that the density along the carrier axis does vary with the spread in the residuals, possibly an indication against change in variability. We return in Section 7D for a further look at the possibility of changing variability.

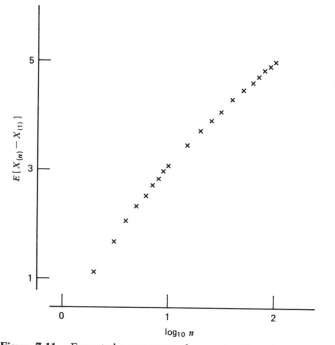

Figure 7-11.   Expected range versus $\log_{10} n$ for Gaussian samples.

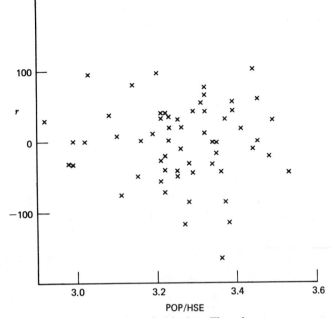

Figure 7-12. Residuals versus household size. The plot may suggest a wedge increasing to the right.

```
            (Unit = 0.01)
29 * | 2
29 • | 8 9 9
30 * | 2 3
30 • | 8
31 * | 0 1 4
31 • | 5 6 9
32 * | 0 1 1 1 1 2 2 2 2 3 3 3
32 • | 5 5 5 6 6 7 8 8 9 9
33 * | 1 2 2 2 2 4 4
33 • | 5 5 6 6 6 7 7 8 9 9
34 * | 1 4 4
34 • | 5 5 8 9
35 * | 3
```

Figure 7-13. Stem-and-leaf display of household size. The batch is skewed to the left, to smaller sizes.

Classical procedures for fitting models often calculate a function of the residuals, such as the sum of squares or sum of absolute residuals, and then minimize the function. Since the function treats each point the same, these procedures are inappropriate when the points have unequal variances. Points with large variance are given improperly large influence on the fit. To improve the fit, we may be able to accommodate unequal variances by transforming either the response or both the response and carrier in such a way that the variability of the new residuals comes quite close to constant.

We may also minimize the sum of squares of weighted residuals. Each point is assigned a weight inversely proportional to our estimate of its variance. A wedge-shaped plot suggests that we choose weights according to the value of the carrier x. We may alternatively calculate the fit from a given set of weights and assign weights according to the fit, as in iteratively reweighted least squares. Transformation and weights are discussed, in the context of least squares, in Chatterjee and Price (1977, Chapter 2).

Sometimes we are able to assign relative values to the error variances for each data point. One possibility arises when the variance of an observation depends on the mean of its sampling distribution. We may then analyze using weighted residuals. As an alternative, we may choose to use ordinary, unweighted, least squares and then standardize.

Suppose that the variance of the ith point is $\tau_i \sigma^2$, where the τ_i are known but σ^2 is unknown. Provided the τ_i are not calculated from the data, we can standardize using the revised expression

$$h_i = 1 - \tau_i \left\{ 1 - \frac{2}{n} - \frac{2(x_i - \bar{x})^2}{\sum_{k=1}^n (x_k - \bar{x})^2} \right\} - \frac{\sum_{j=1}^n \tau_j}{n^2}$$

$$- (x_i - \bar{x})^2 \frac{\sum_{j=1}^n \tau_j (x_j - \bar{x})^2}{\left\{ \sum_{k=1}^n (x_k - \bar{x})^2 \right\}^2} - \frac{2(x_i - \bar{x})}{n} \frac{\sum_{j=1}^n \tau_j (x_j - \bar{x})}{\sum_{k=1}^n (x_k - \bar{x})^2}$$

for

$$h_i = \frac{1}{n} + \frac{(x_i - \bar{x})^2}{\sum_j (x_j - \bar{x})^2}$$

in the formula of Section 7B.

Further Features

If an x is closely related to carriers already fitted, we should use $x_{.rest}$, the residual of x after fitting the earlier carriers to it, in place of x throughout the discussion of the last seven pages.

Other features may arise in residual plots. The residuals may fall into groups. The source of the data, for example, as a number of separate batches, may explain this. The residuals may be rounded to a small number of digits. Rounding may have occurred during the observation, recording, or transcription of the data. The fitting procedure may itself round the residuals.

Both the pattern and magnitude of the residuals should be considered. High-leverage points do not necessarily appear with large residuals but may be apparent in the residual plot. In Figure 7-14 we plot the residuals from the regression of mortality on NO_x pollution potential against the carrier. The two high-leverage points are Los Angeles and San Francisco. These two points disproportionately influence the least-squares regression line; the line

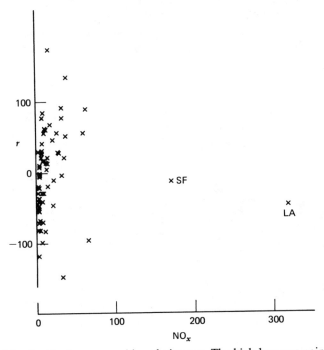

Figure 7-14. Residuals versus oxides of nitrogen. The high-leverage points are Los Angeles and San Francisco.

is almost horizontal (slope $= -0.1$). Without the two points the line is steeply inclined (slope $= 1.1$).

Conversely, points with large residuals may be consistent with a pattern in a residual plot, as illustrated in Figure 7-15. This pattern suggests transforming the response or adding a new carrier such as x^2 or (better) replacing x by a nonlinear expression like e^{cx}.

Plot of Residuals (r) versus Fitted Values ($\hat{y}$)

We look for the same four patterns in this plot as in the plot of residuals against a carrier. The guidance toward improving the fit that each pattern provides is broadly similar for both types of plot. For example, a sloping band suggests that we add a multiple of the fit to the fit. If we use a nonlinear transformation of the fit, in response to the curved band or wedge pattern, say, then the resulting fit will be a nonlinear function of the original carriers.

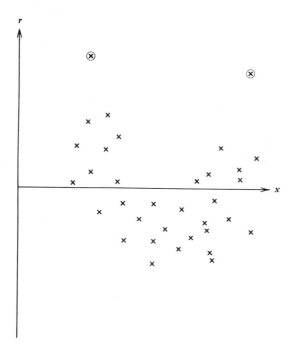

Figure 7-15. A hypothetical residual-versus-carrier plot. The two largest residuals, circled, are extraordinary when the residuals are regarded as a batch but are reasonably consistent with the pattern in the plot.

Plot of Residuals (r) versus Response (y)

This plot behaves in a qualitatively different way from the two residual plots already discussed. Superficially, the difference is that the residual component of the response is represented, in some sense, on both axes of the plot, with only indirect representation of the fit and carrier(s). The most striking phenomenon is that, when the fit is a constant, the points in the plot all fall on a line inclined at 45° to the axes.

In Figure 7-16 we demonstrate how two widely differing linear regression situations give the same suggestive residual plot. The fit of the horizontal line through the data in Figure 7-16(a) is very good. In Figure 7-16(b), the outlier in x influences the fit of the line so that it is again horizontal. Without the outlier the line would be steeply inclined. The residual-versus-response plot, Figure 7-16(c), is the same for both Figures 7-16(a) and 7-16(b).

The message of Figure 7-16 is evident: don't plot the residuals against y, instead of against x or $\hat{y}$, unless you want to be misled!

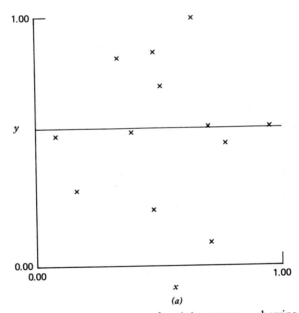

Figure 7-16. The misleading r-versus-y plot. (a) y versus x showing only scatter, with horizontal fitted line. (b) y versus x showing strong relationship and high-leverage outlier which leads to horizontal fitted line. (c) r versus y for both sets of data.

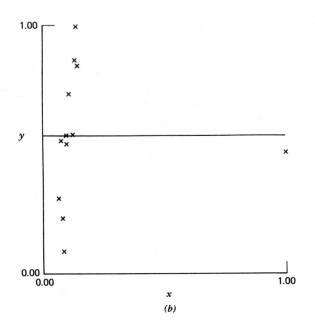

x

(b)

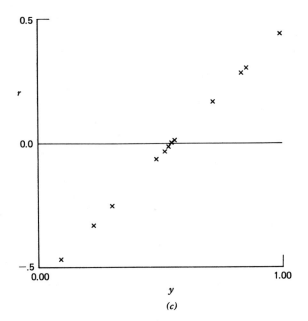

y

(c)

Figure 7-16. (*Continued*).

7D. MORE SOPHISTICATED PLOTS

In Section 7C we discussed three plots of the residuals. Two plots in particular, of the residuals against a carrier and against the fitted values, may exhibit basic phenomena that we find useful for improving the fit. For a more informative look at the data and at the fit, we recommend more types of plots. In this section we indicate a few possibilities for alternative variables against which to plot the residuals.

Alternative Variables

We may plot the residuals against a carrier not already included in the fit. The carrier may be:

1. A transformation of a carrier already in the fit, suggested by nonlinearity in the plot of residuals against the untransformed carrier.
2. The product of two carriers, when we are looking for interaction terms.
3. A new variable to the fit. The new variable may be the time of taking the observation, may be believed a priori to affect the fit, or may be a purely speculative choice.

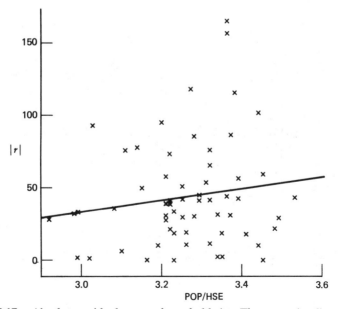

Figure 7-17. Absolute residuals versus household size. The regression line suggests a slight increase of residual spread with household size.

In all these instances, we must be wary of the influence of carriers already included in the fit, often regressing them out of any of the new carriers just mentioned.

To detect change in variance or, more precisely, to detect an increasing or decreasing trend in residual spread with a carrier, we plot absolute or squared residuals against the carrier. First we ensure that either absolute or squared residuals will measure spread by centering the batch of residuals at 0. Whereas a sensible line fitted through a symmetric wedge of residuals has slope 0, when the wedge is folded over (using either the absolute values or the squares of the residuals), the slope of the new fitted line summarizes the monotone trend in residual spread.

Figure 7-17 plots the absolute residuals against the carrier for the simple linear regression of mortality on household size. (This may be compared to Figures 7-12 and 7-13.) The fitted regression line in Figure 7-17 has only very small slope, suggesting that there may well be no dependence of the residual spread on the carrier.

7E. SUMMARY

Residuals arise from the relationship

$$\text{data} = \text{fit} + \text{residual},$$

where the fit is determined by an assumed model and by an algorithm for arriving at a fit. The fit describes the data, and we can often use the residuals to improve upon that description. Strong patterns in the residuals usually indicate that further refinement of the fit will be a worthwhile aid to understanding the structure in the raw data.

The benefits of a careful analysis of residuals are well illustrated in the regression setting. Quantile–quantile plots for residuals (especially the normal probability plot) indicate whether the usual Gaussian errors assumption of regression is justified. Plots of residuals against the fitted values can aid us in elaborating the regression model. However, we can be misled by a plot of the residuals against the response variable.

Patterns that are sometimes evident in residual plots include a

> Point cloud
> Sloping band
> Curved band
> Wedge

A point cloud indicates no residual relationship between r and x. A sloping

band argues for adding a linear term, whereas a curved band suggests using a more flexible dependence, possibly by adding a quadratic expression in x. A wedge shape occurs either when the density of points changes with x, or when variability systematically increases or decreases with increasing values of x.

Analysis of residuals is also an essential part of exploratory data analysis in other structures of data—for example, in the two-way table. In general, an analysis of residuals provides a magnifying glass that permits patterns and underlying structure to be readily viewed. Our awareness of this structure can then guide us to the next step in an analysis.

REFERENCES

Beale, E. M. L. (1969). "Euclidean cluster analysis." Contributed paper to the 37th session of the International Statistical Institute.

Behnken, D. W. and Draper, N. R. (1972). "Residuals and their variance patterns," *Technometrics*, **14**, 101–111.

Belsley, D. A., Kuh, E., and Welsch, R. E. (1980). *Regression Diagnostics*, New York: Wiley.

Bloomfield, P. (1974). "On the distribution of the residuals from a fitted linear model." Technical Report 56, Series 2, Department of Statistics, Princeton University.

Box, G. E. P. (1980). "Sampling and Bayes' inference in scientific modeling and robustness," with Discussion, *Journal of the Royal Statistical Society, Series A*, **143**, 383–430.

Chatterjee, S. and Price, B. (1977). *Regression Analysis by Example*. New York: Wiley.

Chernoff, H. (1973), "The use of faces to represent points in k-dimensional space graphically," *Journal of the American Statistical Association*, **68**, 361–368.

Daniel, C. and Wood, F. S. (1980). *Fitting Equations to Data*, 2nd edition. New York: Wiley.

Draper, N. R. and Smith, H. (1966). *Applied Regression Analysis*. New York: Wiley.

Fisher, R. A. (1973). *Statistical Methods and Scientific Inference*, 3rd edition. New York: Hafner Press.

Harter, H. L. (1969). *Order Statistics and Their Use in Testing and Estimation*, Vol. 1. Aerospace Research Laboratories. Washington, DC: U.S. Government Printing Office.

Henderson, H. V. and Velleman, P. F. (1981). "Building multiple regression models interactively," *Biometrics*, **37**, 391–411.

Hoaglin, D. C., Iglewicz, B., and Tukey, J. W. (1981). "Small-sample performance of a resistant rule for outlier detection." *1980 Proceedings of the Statistical Computing Section*. Washington, DC: American Statistical Association, pp. 148–152.

Hocking, R. R. (1976). "The analysis and selection of variables in linear regression," *Biometrics*, **32**, 1–44.

Hoerl, A. E. and Kennard, R. W. (1970). "Ridge regression: application to nonorthogonal problems," *Technometrics*, **12**, 55–67.

McDonald, G. C. and Ayers, J. A. (1978). "Some applications of the 'Chernoff faces': a technique for graphically representing multivariate data." In P. C. C. Wang (Ed.), *Graphical Representation of Multivariate Data*. New York: Academic, pp. 183–197.

McDonald, G. C. and Schwing, R. C. (1973). "Instabilities of regression estimates relating air pollution to mortality,' *Technometrics*, **15**, 463–481.

Mosteller, F. and Tukey, J. W. (1977). *Data Analysis and Regression.* Reading, MA: Addison–Wesley.

Ryan, T. A., Joiner, B. L., and Ryan, B. F. (1981). *Minitab Reference Manual.* University Park, PA: Minitab Project, The Pennsylvania State University.

Tukey, J. W. (1977). *Exploratory Data Analysis.* Reading, MA: Addison–Wesley.

Velleman, P. F. and Hoaglin, D. C. (1981). *Applications, Basics, and Computing of Exploratory Data Analysis.* Boston: Duxbury Press.

Wilk, M. B. and Gnanadesikan, R. (1968), "Probability plotting methods for the analysis of data," *Biometrika*, **55**, 1–17.

Additional Literature

Andrews, D. F. (1979). "The robustness of residual displays." In R. L. Launer and G. N. Wilkinson (Eds.), *Robustness in Statistics.* New York: Academic, pp. 19–32.

Brown, B. M. and Kildea, D. G. (1979). "Outlier-detection tests and robust estimators based on signs of residuals," *Communications in Statistics*, **A8**, 257–269.

Dempster, A. P. and Gasko-Green, M. (1981). "New tools for residual analysis," *Annals of Statistics*, **9**, 945–959.

Hickman, E. P. and Long, C. S. (1980). "A note on Glejser's test for heteroscedasticity," *Communications in Statistics*, **A9**, 1209–1220.

Lund, R. (1975). "Tables for an approximate test for outliers in linear models," *Technometrics*, **17**, 473–476.

Prescott, P. (1975). "An approximate test for outliers in linear models," *Technometrics*, **17**, 129–132.

EXERCISES

1. Section 7A discusses the relationship

$$\text{data} = \text{model} + \text{error}.$$

Identify a possible meaning of the word "model," giving an algebraic expression where appropriate in each of the following settings:
- (a) a single symmetric batch,
- (b) k batches at k different levels,
- (c) simple linear regression of y on x,
- (d) a two-way table of amounts or counts.

2. For each of the four models you described in Exercise 1, describe one way in which the residuals from a fit could display systematic behavior. Explain the meaning of this behavior and indicate a way in which

a model might be further elaborated to remove additional structure from the residuals.

Exercises 3 through 6 refer to socioeconomic data from Table 7-2. We focus on the following variables: GDHSE—percentage of housing units that are sound with all facilities, POOR—percentage of families with income under \$3000 in 1960 urbanized area, and MORT—total age-adjusted mortality rate, expressed as deaths per 100,000 population.

3. Consider the simple linear regression of mortality (y) on the percentage of poor families (x).

   (a) Plot the residuals from this regression against the percentage of poor families.

   (b) Plot leverage against the percentage of poor families and discuss the reason for the systematic behavior in your plot.

   (c) Plot the standardized residuals against the percentage of poor families. Can you see any qualitative differences between this plot and that of part (a)?

4. Fit a resistant line to the scatter plot of mortality against the percentage of poor families and find the residuals from this fit.

   (a) Compare these residuals to those for least-squares regression in Exercise 3(a) by
      (i)   Use of parallel stem-and-leaf displays, and
      (ii) A plot of one set of residuals against the other.
      Discuss your findings.

   (b) For each of the two sets of residuals you compared in part (a), find the outlier cutoffs. Do the outliers for the two batches of residuals come from the same points in the original scatter plot?

5. Construct the normal probability plot for the standardized residuals found in Exercise 3(c).

   (a) By referring to Figure 7-6, discuss the meaning of this plot. Are there any unusual points?

   (b) Explain why a normal probability plot for the residuals from the resistant fit of Exercise 4 may be of less interest and importance than those you plotted in this problem.

6. Perform the regression of mortality (y) on the variable GDHSE.

   (a) Plot the residuals from this regression against GDHSE and compare to the results of Exercise 3(a).

   (b) Are there systematic patterns in these residuals? If so, what might they suggest as a next step in the analysis?

* (c) Suppose that you performed a multiple regression of mortality on POOR (v_1) and GDHSE (v_2). Explain why the magnitudes of the residuals may not be substantially reduced from those produced by the simple linear regression of parts 3(a) and 6(a). How might a plot of POOR against GDHSE provide additional insight?

Exercises 7 through 10 deal with the following data on lithogenic bile concentrations in Pima Indians. For 29 females, the data give age and percent saturation of bile cholesterol.

Bile cholesterol concentration in Pima Indians (age is in years; concentration in percent).

Age	Conc.	Age	Conc.
10.0	98	14.6	122
10.3	120	15.4	122
10.6	111	16.8	122
10.6	93	17.0	177
11.0	159	17.7	93
11.4	120	18.2	111
11.0	101	18.7	148
12.4	130	19.8	143
12.8	65	19.9	122
13.2	165	20.1	101
13.2	106	20.2	150
13.2	101	20.7	165
13.6	152	20.7	250
13.9	169	21.0	187
14.2	120		

Source: Lynn J. Bennion et al. (1979). "Development of lithogenic bile during puberty in Pima Indians," *New England Journal of Medicine*, **300**, 873–876 (data read from Figure 1, p. 874).

7. (a) Plot the Pima Indian data, percent concentration (y) versus age (x).

(b) Eye-fit a line to the data and record the slope and the level (at age 14).

(c) Do any points in the data strike you as outliers? If so, remove them and refit (by eye) the slope and the level (at age 14). How resistant was your eye-fitted line to the outliers?

8. **(a)** Fit a least-squares regression line to the Pima Indian data and calculate the residuals.

   (b) Plot and examine the residuals (r versus x or r versus $\hat{y}$). Do any residuals appear to be outliers? Compare the corresponding (x, y) values for these points to the points you detected in Exercise 7(c).

   (c) Use the residual standard deviation to standardize the residuals. Are there any outliers?

   (d) Calculate the leverage for the outliers you detected.

9. **(a)** Refit a least-squares regression line to the Pima Indian data after removing the outliers you detected in Exercises 8(b) and 8(c).

   (b) Compare the old and new regression fits.

   (c) Plot the raw and standardized residuals from the new data set (r versus $\hat{y}$ or r versus x). Do any residuals appear to be outliers now? If so, remove them and repeat the refitting process on the new data set.

10. This problem refers to fitting methods described in Chapter 5. Some parts of this problem require specialized computer programs that may not be available in many computer installations.

   (a) Calculate the resistant line fit to the data.

   (b) Calculate the repeated-median fit to the data.

   (c) Calculate the LAR fit to the data.

   (d) Compare the fits in (a), (b), (c) to your original and final least-squares regression fits from Exercises 8 and 9, and to your eye-fits from Exercise 7. How successful were the resistant, LAR, and repeated-median fits in avoiding undue influences from outliers?

CHAPTER 8

Mathematical Aspects
of Transformation

John D. Emerson
Middlebury College

Power transformations often simplify the task of describing data that consist of positive amounts or counts. We have illustrated and discussed transformations in several earlier chapters, especially Chapters 3, 4, and 6. In particular, Chapter 4 examined the objectives of transformations. The present chapter provides a variety of justifications for the assertions and techniques already introduced.

We use transformations in diverse data structures:

Single batches,

Several batches at different levels,

y versus x, and

Two-way tables,

as well as in other settings that we do not discuss in this volume. Our objectives in transforming depend on our own interests and on the type of data structure with which we are working. Four desirable features for a data set, corresponding to the structures listed above, are

Symmetry,

Equal spread,

Straightness, and

Additive structure.

Each of these properties is a primary objective of transforming data in the corresponding structure. For each of the four kinds of data, we introduce a

special plot to aid in finding a suitable power transformation. These plots share several properties.

1. They are two-variable plots.
2. They indicate by their straightness or lack of straightness whether a power transformation is likely to achieve its objective.
3. When they are nearly straight, they indicate the approximate power of a transformation aimed toward the particular objective. A "transformation plot" with slope m suggests a power transformation whose exponent is $p \approx 1 - m$.

The next section briefly summarizes four transformation plots, three of which were illustrated in Chapters 3, 4, and 6. Then we explore relationships among the power transformations; in particular, we explore why they are considered as a family. The next four sections provide mathematical justifications for the four transformation plots. Each plot arises from series approximations to certain functions that reflect the objective of transformation. Thus we provide insight into the techniques for choosing transformations, and we show why the techniques work. We will see why each transformation plot gives power p through

$$p \approx 1 - m,$$

where m is the slope of an approximately linear plot.

The main mathematical prerequisites for this chapter come from calculus:

Derivatives of elementary functions,
The geometry of first and second derivatives, and
Series expansions of differentiable functions.

We make no attempt at mathematical rigor. Instead, we emphasize the geometric content of much of our development in order to promote a feel for the techniques.

We conclude the chapter with some historical remarks and references for readers who want to learn more of the origins, development, and characteristics of power transformations in data analysis.

8A. SUMMARY OF FOUR TRANSFORMATION PLOTS

Four transformation plots can be used, each in its own context. Table 8-1 summarizes these as to structure of data, objective of transformation, notation, and plotting coordinates.

TABLE 8-1. Summary of transformation plots.

Structure	Objective	Notation	Plotting Coordinates[a]	
			Horizontal	Vertical
Single batch[b]	Symmetry	M = median y_q = lower qth quantile[f] y_{1-q} = upper qth quantile	$\dfrac{(y_{1-q} - M)^2 + (M - y_q)^2}{4M}$	$\dfrac{y_{1-q} + y_q}{2} - M$
Several batches[c]	Equal spread	M_i = median for ith batch Q_i = interquartile range for ith batch	$\log M_i$ (measure of location)	$\log Q_i$ (measure of spread)
y versus[d] x	Straight line	M_x = median x M_y = median y C = estimated slope of y versus x through (M_x, M_y)	$\dfrac{C^2(x - M_x)^2}{2M_y}$	$y - M_y - C(x - M_x)$
Two-way[e] table	Additivity	$y_{ij} = m + a_i + b_j + r_{ij}$	$\dfrac{a_i b_j}{m}$ (comparison values)	$r_{ij} = y_{ij} - (m + a_i + b_j)$ (residuals from additive fit)

Source: Emerson and Stoto (1982).

[a]The indicated transformation has power $p = 1 - $ slope, for each plot. When $p = 0$, a log transformation is indicated.

[b]One point is plotted for each quantile pair.

[c]This plot has been called the *spread-versus-level* plot; one point is plotted for each batch.

[d]One point is plotted for each (x, y) pair.

[e]This plot is known as the *diagnostic* plot; one point is plotted for each entry in the table.

[f]Quantiles corresponding to powers of $\frac{1}{2}$ and sometimes called *letter values* may be used; see text.

8B. THE POWER TRANSFORMATIONS AS A FAMILY

We treat the power transformations, including the logarithmic transformation, as a *family* of transformations. This language suggests unity and coherence among these transformations. Chapter 4 showed some of this unity through a sketch of members of the family in the same coordinate system; we repeat that sketch here as Figure 8-1. Taking a more analytic approach, we show that the family is continuously parametrized by the power p. We also provide a basis for comparing the strengths of transformations, an idea related to curvature.

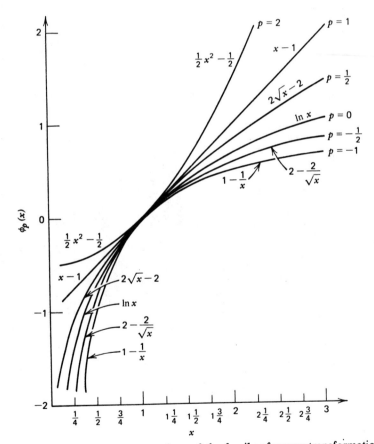

Figure 8-1. Graphs of some members of the family of power transformations.

Analytical Properties

The family of power transformations is sometimes defined as

$$
\phi_p(x) = \begin{cases} \dfrac{x^p - 1}{p} & p \neq 0 \\ \ln x & p = 0, \end{cases}
\tag{1}
$$

where x is a positive variable and p is any real number. (We use $\ln x$ for the logarithm of x to the base e throughout.) This form of the definition offers three advantages:

1. The curves are monotone increasing so that, for each p, ϕ_p preserves the order of the data being transformed.
2. The curves share a common point, $(1, 0)$, for all p.
3. The curves nearly coincide at points very close to $(1, 0)$; that is, they share a common tangent line at that point.

Each of these geometric properties was evident in Chapter 4, and each property is displayed in Figure 8-1, where we have sketched some of the curves defined in equations (1). Properties 2 and 3 give us the matching of the transformations at the point $(1, 0)$.

We now provide analytical justification for these properties. For each p, including $p = 0$, note that $\phi_p(1) = 0$, so that property 2 holds.

The derivative of $\phi_p(x)$ is $\phi_p'(x) = x^{p-1}$ for all values of p, including 0. Because ϕ_p' exists and is positive for all positive x, ϕ_p is a monotone increasing continuous function of x for every p. Thus property 1 holds.

Finally, $\phi_p'(1) = 1$, so that the slope of the tangent line to each curve at $x = 1$ is 1. Thus the curves share a common tangent line. The derivatives ϕ_p' are also continuous at all positive x and, in particular, for values of x close to 1. Because $\phi_p'(x)$ is near 1 when x is near 1, the curves have almost the same slope at values of x close to 1. Thus they nearly coincide as property 3 requires.

A Continuous-Parameter Family

A fourth, and possibly the most fundamental, reason for the unity of the family of power transformations is more subtle. As p changes in value, the resulting change from one member of the family to another occurs in a smooth and continuous way. This concept is captured mathematically by

showing that for each fixed x, $y(p, x) = \phi_p(x)$ is a continuous function of p, as are its first, second,... derivatives.

This result is easily demonstrated for $p \neq 0$. Since $x^p - 1$ and p are continuous functions of p, their quotient is also continuous for $p \neq 0$. When p is 0, the quotient is an indeterminate form, but we can handle it with a standard method. We rewrite x^p as $e^{p \ln x}$, and we note that the derivative of this expression with respect to p is $e^{p \ln x} \cdot \ln x$. Then we consider the limit

$$\lim_{p \to 0} y(p, x) = \lim_{p \to 0} \frac{e^{p \ln x} - 1}{p}.$$

Because both the numerator and denominator of this expression go to 0 as $p \to 0$, l'Hospital's rule allows us to differentiate the numerator and denominator separately and then take the limit of the derivatives:

$$\lim_{p \to 0} y(p, x) = \lim_{p \to 0} \frac{e^{p \ln x} \cdot \ln x}{1}$$

$$= \ln x.$$

Since this result shows that

$$\lim_{p \to 0} y(p, x) = y(0, x),$$

it follows by definition that y is continuous at $p = 0$ for each positive x. We summarize by saying that $\{\phi_p(x)\}$ is *a family of functions that is indexed continuously by the parameter* p.

A similar argument shows that the first, second,... derivatives $\{\phi_p'(x)\}$, $\{\phi_p''(x)\}$,... are also indexed continuously by the parameter p.

Strength and Curvature

Chapter 4 discusses a hierarchy for the power transformations by introducing the ladder of powers. Transformations with power greater than 1 are curved upward, and those with power less than 1 are curved downward; we use the latter transformations more frequently when transforming amounts or counts. We think of the transformations that are far away from $y = x$ on the ladder as being stronger than transformations that are closer to $y = x$. Thus we speak of the log transformation ($p = 0$) as being stronger than the square-root transformation ($p = \frac{1}{2}$), but weaker than the reciprocal transformation ($p = -1$). The stronger transformations are those with p farther

from 1. It is evident that the stronger transformations may help to improve:

Batches that are highly asymmetric,
Multiple batches where spread increases rapidly with level,
y versus x where deviation from linearity is large, and
Two-way tables where nonadditivity results from a strong and systematic row-and-column interaction.

A notion of curvature can aid our study of transformations. To motivate this notion, we consider the curvature of a circle of radius R. Intuitively, a larger value of R should correspond to less curvature, whereas the curvature of a small circle should be relatively large. In particular, a circle of radius $2R$ will have less curvature than one of radius R.

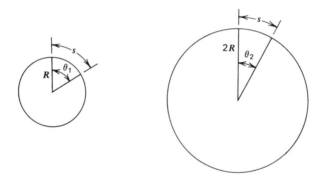

For the two circles pictured, suppose that we wish to move a fixed distance s on the circle. The angles required to define this arclength are denoted by θ_1 and θ_2; we give the angles in radians, so that the relationship

$$\text{angle} = \frac{\text{arclength}}{\text{radius}}$$

holds. The larger the angle needed to cut off a fixed arclength, the greater the amount of curvature; thus the smaller of the two circles has greater curvature. We now formally define the curvature of a circle.

DEFINITION: The *curvature of a circle* is the angle (in radians) required to cut off an arc of unit length; thus curvature is the ratio of angle to

arclength. For a circle of radius R,

$$\text{curvature} = \frac{\theta}{s} = \frac{1}{R},\tag{2}$$

where θ is the central angle corresponding to an arc of length s.

From the definition, it is easy to see that a circle of radius $2R$ has half as much curvature as a circle of radius R. The definition can be given in slightly different language: the curvature of a circle is the rate of change of the central angle θ with respect to arclength. We will see that this definition generalizes to other curves and, in particular, to the curves defined by the power transformations.

For other curves, such as an ellipse or the curve defined by $y = \sqrt{x}$, the definition of curvature is necessarily more complex: it must depend on where we look on the curve. For example, the curvature of $y = \sqrt{x}$ is greater at $x = 1$ than it is at $x = 10$. Mathematicians would say that curvature is a *local* property of a curve, and they speak of the curvature K at a point P on a curve. *Just as the tangent line to a curve at a point is the line that best approximates the curve at that point, the curvature at a point on a curve is the curvature of the circle that best approximates the curve at the chosen point.*

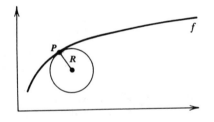

Thus the curvature of f at P is the same as the curvature of a circle that best approximates f at P. This concept is precisely captured in the following definition.

DEFINITION: The *curvature* of a function (or relation) f at a point P is defined as

$$K(P) = \left| \frac{d\theta}{ds}(P) \right|,\tag{3}$$

where s is arclength (measured from any other point on f) and θ is the angle

that the perpendicular (or normal) line to f at P makes with the x-axis. The right-hand side of equation (3) is the absolute value of the derivative of θ with respect to s, evaluated at the point P.

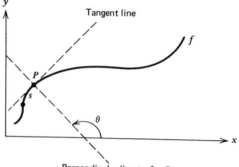

This definition provides a measure of the rapidity with which a curve or its normal line is turning at a particular point on the curve. The definition could just as well use the tangent line, and the angle could be measured from any fixed reference line. We have stated the definition in a way that is easily related to the simpler definition used for the circle.

Consider a function f that is twice-differentiable. The curvature of f at x can be given in terms of the first two derivatives of f. The curvature of f at x is

$$K(x) = \frac{|f''(x)|}{\{1 + [f'(x)]^2\}^{3/2}} \tag{4}$$

This result can be shown by applying techniques of calculus to the definition of curvature (see Taylor, 1955, pp. 357–360). With it, we can verify that the curvature at any point on a line is zero, and that the curvature at any point on a circle of radius R is $1/R$.

We now apply the notion of curvature to the members of the family of power transformations. We have already compared the properties of these curves at $x = 1$, where they share a common point and a common tangent line at that point. We now compare the curvatures at $x = 1$. We have seen that

$$\phi_p'(x) = x^{p-1}$$

holds for all $x > 0$ and for all values of p. Then

$$\phi_p''(x) = (p - 1)x^{p-2}$$

is the second derivative. For positive x, we may write

$$|\phi_p''(x)| = |p - 1| x^{p-2}.$$

Then the curvature at x is

$$K(x) = \frac{|p - 1| x^{p-2}}{(1 + x^{2p-2})^{3/2}},$$

and for $x = 1$ this gives

$$K(1) = \frac{|p - 1|}{2^{3/2}}. \tag{5}$$

Equation (5) shows that for $p < 1$, the curvature of ϕ_p at $x = 1$ is proportional to $1 - p$, an expression we encountered earlier as the slope of each of our transformation plots. Notice that the power transformations with exponents -2, $-\frac{3}{2}$, -1, $-\frac{1}{2}$, 0, $\frac{1}{2}$, 1, members of the ladder of powers, are equally spaced in curvature at $x = 1$. This fact offers some support to our choice of these members of the family of power transformations, instead of some other members, when we want to consider only a few transformations.

The discussion in this section pertains to analytical properties of our curves *at* $x = 1$. Since we almost always want to transform batches of amounts or counts that range well beyond 1, we may wonder whether the present discussion applies to transformations we use in practice. The concepts discussed above do generalize, as we now indicate.

First, we review an important concept from Chapter 4.

Transformations which *share a common point* and *have a common slope at that point* are said to be *matched* at that point.

Thus members of the family (1) are matched at $x = 1$. As discussed in Chapter 4, we may decide to match the transformation at some other point. We may, for example, define functions g_p that are matched at x_0 in that for each p the function passes through the point $(x_0, 0)$ and has slope 1 at that

point. Power transformations with these properties may be given as

$$g_p(x) = \begin{cases} \dfrac{x^p - x_0^p}{px_0^{p-1}} & \text{for } p \neq 0 \\ x_0(\ln x - \ln x_0) & \text{for } p = 0. \end{cases} \tag{6}$$

It is easy to verify that these curves are matched at x_0.

Let us next consider the curvature of g_p at x_0. Since $g_p'(x_0) = 1$ and $g_p''(x_0) = (p - 1)/x_0$, the curvature at x_0 is

$$K(x_0) = \frac{1 - p}{2^{3/2}x_0}, \tag{7}$$

when p is less than one. Once again, we see that the curvature at x_0 satisfies two key properties:

1. Curvature is proportional to $1 - p$, the slope of our four transformation plots when they are linear.
2. Equal spacings in curvature correspond to equal differences between powers in the ladder of powers.

Because the constant of proportionality in equation (7) is known, the value of curvature and the power p uniquely determine each other when $p < 1$.

Let us assemble the results of our study of curvature. We know that, for the power transformations, curvature increases as p decreases from one. If we identify curvature with the strength of a transformation, we can say that, for p less than one, smaller values of p correspond to stronger transformations. In the next four sections of this chapter, we show why the slopes of each of four transformation plots are proportional to the curvature of a power transformation that can improve the data with respect to a desired characteristic.

8C. A TRANSFORMATION PLOT FOR SYMMETRY

Chapter 4 discusses several reasons for seeking symmetry in a batch. The basic argument for symmetry is the ease and clarity of summarization and comparison that it brings. At the same time, although it is useful, symmetry may not be either a critical issue or an important one.

Construction of a Transformation Plot for Symmetry

Let M be the median of a batch, and let x_L and x_U represent lower and upper letter values for a fixed depth. The transformation plot for symmetry

considers, for various pairs of letter values,

$$\frac{(x_U - M)^2 + (M - x_L)^2}{4M}$$

as the horizontal coordinate and

$$\frac{x_U + x_L}{2} - M$$

as the vertical coordinate. If the resulting graph is roughly linear, then one-minus-slope is the indicated power of a transformation for symmetry.

Development

We restrict ourselves to nonnegative xs. Amounts or counts will provide this automatically. (Other sorts of data may have to be modified by adding a constant.)

Let $x_1, x_2, \ldots, x_n$ represent the data in a single batch. We seek a power, p, for which the transformed batch $x_1^p, x_2^p, \ldots, x_n^p$ is approximately symmetric. Let x_L and x_U be lower and upper letter values for any fixed depth; thus they can represent the fourths, eighths, sixteenths, and so on (as in Section 2B). We use M for the median of the batch.

Essentially, x_L^p, M^p, and x_U^p are approximate quantiles for the transformed batch, corresponding to those of the original batch. (Here the power transformations are defined to be monotone increasing; we use $-x^p$ when p is negative to satisfy this requirement.)

If the transformed batch is symmetric, then for all letter values we have

$$x_U^p - M^p = M^p - x_L^p. \tag{8}$$

This may be rewritten

$$\frac{x_U^p + x_L^p}{2} = M^p. \tag{9}$$

The expressions on the left in equation (9) are called *midsummaries*; each quantile selected has a midsummary.

For p not zero, a second-order Taylor series expansion of x_U^p and x_L^p about M gives (except for a minus sign before each term on both sides of

the equation when $p < 0$):

$$x_U^p \approx M^p + pM^{p-1}(x_U - M) + \frac{p(p-1)}{2} M^{p-2}(x_U - M)^2$$

and

$$x_L^p \approx M^p + pM^{p-1}(x_L - M) + \frac{p(p-1)}{2} M^{p-2}(x_L - M)^2.$$

By substituting these approximations into equation (9) we obtain

$$\frac{1}{2}\left\{ 2M^p + pM^{p-1}(x_U + x_L - 2M) \right.$$

$$\left. + \frac{p(p-1)}{2} M^{p-2}\left[(x_U - M)^2 + (x_L - M)^2\right] \right\} \approx M^p.$$

Algebraic simplification and rearrangement give

$$M(x_U + x_L - 2M) + \frac{p-1}{2}\left[(x_U - M)^2 + (x_L - M)^2\right] \approx 0$$

or

$$\frac{x_U + x_L}{2} - M \approx (1 - p)\frac{\left[(x_U - M)^2 + (M - x_L)^2\right]}{4M}. \qquad (10)$$

Note that, because we are dealing with nonnegative amounts or counts, M must be positive.

Approximation (10) suggests a transformation that aims toward symmetry in a batch. The left side of approximation (10) represents the distance between the midsummary and the median, for various quantiles. In a symmetric batch, the difference is 0, and a horizontal line results. Then the slope is 0, p is 1, and no transformation is needed or implied by the plot.

The expression

$$\frac{(x_U - M)^2 + (M - x_L)^2}{4M}$$

is nondecreasing as the pair of letter values moves outward from the median toward the extremes. Thus if the mids increase, as they will when the batch is skewed to the right, $1 - p$ will be positive and so p will be less than 1.

Such a transformation pulls in the right tail, and the transformed batch becomes more nearly symmetric. We will transform to lower powers precisely when the midsummaries increase from the median outward.

8D. TRANSFORMATION PLOT FOR EQUAL SPREAD: THE SPREAD-VERSUS-LEVEL PLOT

In Chapter 3 we used the spread-versus-level plot to suggest a power transformation. The transformation was aimed at equalizing the spreads of several batches of data having different levels; we illustrated the technique in the largest-cities example. We now turn to the justification of the spread-versus-level plot.

For mathematical convenience, our random variables are assumed to have continuous distributions. We use the results derived here as an approximation for discrete variables. We continue to assume that these random variables have nonnegative values only.

When using exploratory techniques for location and scale, we prefer the median and fourth-spread to the mean and standard deviation because of the resistance of the former pair to outliers. In this section, we work with the population median, ν, and the population fourth-spread, τ. For a continuous distribution, the population fourth-spread is the interquartile range. Note that our notation distinguishes the population parameters from the corresponding statistics of the sample, M and d_F. Finally, we mention that the ideas used parallel those of classical "variance stabilization," a subject discussed in Section 8G.

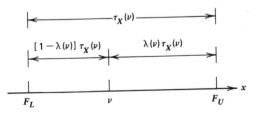

Figure 8-2. Relationships among the population median, fourth-spread, upper fourth, and lower fourth.

Construction of the Spread-versus-Level Plot

Consider several batches, indexed by i, and let M_i and Q_i denote the median and the interquartile range for the ith batch. The spread-versus-level plot uses $\log M_i$ as the horizontal coordinate and $\log Q_i$ as the vertical coordinate. When the pattern is roughly linear, one-minus-slope is the indicated power of a transformation for stable spread.

Development

Let X be a real random variable with median ν, lower fourth F_L, upper fourth F_U, and fourth-spread $\tau_X(\nu)$. We seek a transformation $y = \phi(x)$ for which the fourth-spread of Y, τ_Y, is constant. Under reasonable restrictions,* ϕ will have a Taylor series expansion around the value ν:

$$\phi(x) = \phi(\nu) + \phi'(\nu)(x - \nu) + \phi''(\nu)\frac{(x - \nu)^2}{2!} + \cdots . \quad (11)$$

Let $\lambda(\nu)$ be the distance from ν to F_U as a fraction of $\tau_X(\nu)$. Thus

$$\text{upper-fourth minus median} = F_U - \nu$$

$$= \lambda(\nu)\tau_X(\nu)$$

$$\text{median minus lower-fourth} = \nu - F_L$$

$$= [1 - \lambda(\nu)]\tau_X(\nu).$$

The existence of such a $\lambda(\nu)$ is easy to demonstrate algebraically, but the diagram in Figure 8-2 may help to clarify ideas. In particular, notice that $0 \leqslant \lambda(\nu) \leqslant 1$.

After transforming with ϕ, we will have the following parameter values for $Y = \phi(X)$:

$$\nu_Y = \phi(\nu)$$

$$(F_U)_Y = \phi(F_U) = \phi[\nu + \lambda(\nu)\tau_X(\nu)]$$

$$(F_L)_Y = \phi(F_L) = \phi\{\nu - [1 - \lambda(\nu)]\tau_X(\nu)\}.$$

*In this context, "reasonable restrictions" and "nice function" refer to the requirement that the function ϕ have derivatives of all orders and a Taylor series that converges for all x. To use a linear approximation, one needs the existence (though not necessarily the continuity) of ϕ'' for all x. In general, convergence is assured only if the remainder term converges to 0 as the order of the term increases. (Actually, if we use Taylor series with a remainder term, here and in the rest of this chapter, it suffices to have a continuous third derivative.)

If we use the Taylor series expansion of ϕ around the point ν to get $(F_U)_Y = \phi(F_U)$ and $(F_L)_Y = \phi(F_L)$, we obtain

$$(F_U)_Y = \phi(\nu) + \lambda(\nu)\tau_X(\nu)\phi'(\nu) + \frac{\lambda(\nu)^2 \tau_X(\nu)^2}{2!}\phi''(\nu) + \cdots$$

and

$$(F_L)_Y = \phi(\nu) - [1 - \lambda(\nu)]\tau_X(\nu)\phi'(\nu) + \frac{[1 - \lambda(\nu)]^2 \tau_X(\nu)^2}{2!}\phi''(\nu) + \cdots .$$

Now the fourth-spread of the random variable Y, τ_Y, is just $(F_U)_Y - (F_L)_Y$. After algebraic simplification, we obtain

$$\tau_Y = \tau_X(\nu)\phi'(\nu) + \frac{[2\lambda(\nu) - 1]\tau_X(\nu)^2}{2!}\phi''(\nu) + \cdots . \qquad (12)$$

To this point in the argument, we have not used an approximation for the series expansion; we now examine the higher-order terms.

Consider first the second-order term of equation (12). The factor $2\lambda(\nu) - 1$ is at most 1 in magnitude. If X were symmetric, this factor would be 0. More realistically, if the upper fourth were twice as far from the median as the lower fourth, then $\lambda(\nu) = \frac{2}{3}$ and the factor becomes $\frac{1}{3}$. The factor $\phi''(\nu)$ measures the concavity of ϕ at the median ν, in that it tells the rate at which the slopes of tangents to ϕ near ν are changing. If ν is not close to 0 and if ϕ is reasonably linear near ν, then $\phi''(\nu)$ is relatively small. [Readers unaccustomed to interpreting second derivatives may wish a small numerical example. Consider the transformation $\phi(x) = \ln x$ and assume that $\nu = 10$. Then $\phi'(10) = 0.1$ and $\phi''(10) = -0.01$.] Finally, we note that the fourth-spread $\tau_X(\nu)$ is likely to be of the same order of magnitude as the standard deviation. Altogether, the quadratic term in expression (12) is typically much smaller than the leading term. Since subsequent terms involve higher-order derivatives and larger denominators, we make the approximation

$$\tau_Y \approx \tau_X(\nu)\phi'(\nu). \qquad (13)$$

With this approximation, the stabilization of spread corresponds to

$$\tau_X(\nu)\phi'(\nu) = c,$$

where c is a constant; this leads to

$$\phi(x) = c \int \frac{1}{\tau_X(x)} dx, \qquad (14)$$

which constructs the transformation ϕ for the median, ν, and ultimately for the data, x, from the relationship between the spread $\tau_X(\nu)$ and the level ν.

We now return to the spread-versus-level plot. Suppose that the dependence of τ_X on ν has the form

$$\tau_X(\nu) = k\nu^b,$$

where k and b are arbitrary constants. (This assumption offers considerable flexibility.) We can then show

1. The function $\phi(x) = x^{1-b}$ is a transformation that stabilizes the fourth-spread.
2. The slope of the spread-versus-level plot is b. Thus the suggested power transformation is $x^p = x^{1-b}$, indicating agreement with the first statement.

Let $\phi(x)$ denote the transformation under consideration. Because $\tau_X(\nu) = k\nu^b$, it follows that

$$\phi(x) = \frac{1}{k}\int x^{-b}\,dx = \begin{cases} c_1 x^{1-b} + c_2 & \text{for } b \neq 1 \\ c_3 \ln x + c_4 & \text{for } b = 1, \end{cases}$$

where c_1, c_2, c_3, and c_4 are constants. Since a transformation need only be determined up to multiplicative and additive constants, property 1 follows.* Notice the emergence of $\phi(x) = \ln(x)$ for the case $b = 1$. This special case helps explain why we have included $\ln x$ among the power transformations.

Consider next the spread-versus-level plot. For the spread part—the vertical coordinate—we have

$$\ln[\tau_X(\nu)] = \ln k\nu^b$$

$$= \ln k + b \ln \nu.$$

The level part of the plot—the horizontal coordinate—is $\ln \nu$. The plot involves graphing $\ln k + b \ln \nu$ against $\ln \nu$, so that the slope is b. Statement 2 follows, with the understanding that x^0 is replaced by $\ln x$.

The argument given here offers persuasive, though not conclusive, evidence in favor of trying $\phi(x) = x^{1-b}$ as a probable improvement and

---

*To say that a transformation need only be determined up to multiplicative and additive constants is equivalent to saying that a change of scale and translation of the origin will not alter subsequent analysis. The question of how the constants can be determined so as to facilitate further analysis is addressed in detail in Chapter 4.

possible success in stabilizing the spread. The argument is safer than the corresponding classical argument for stabilization of variance (see Section 8G). Whereas the classical Taylor series expansion based on mean and variance involves all x values, including those far out in the tails, the expansion used here involves only values of x as far out as the fourths.

The development in terms of median and fourth-spread has the following potential advantages over the more classical approach:

1. The present development does not require the existence of a finite mean or variance.
2. The truncation of a Taylor series is more easily justified because one needs to consider the series only for values between the fourths.
3. Because $\tau_X(\nu)$ does not depend on values beyond the fourths, the determination of a transformation will not be unduly influenced by outliers, an advantage if we want the choice of a transformation to be insensitive to values in the tails of a batch. Only the middle 50% of each batch contributes to the selection of a transformation. The property follows from the defining relationship

$$\phi(x) = c \int \frac{1}{\tau_X(x)} dx,$$

for ϕ, since τ_X does not reflect data beyond the fourths.
4. The calculations for the fourth-spread involve less arithmetic than the standard deviation and thus are less affected by accumulated rounding error in a computer.

The present development can be easily carried out with the "eighth-spread," the "sixteenth-spread," or even the range as a replacement for the fourth-spread. One can thus try at least two of these approaches, obtaining a spread-versus-level plot for each, to aid in choosing a transformation. Of course, as we move further into the tails, we lose some of the protection that the fourth-spread offers against outliers. We also weaken some of the other advantages mentioned above.

8E. A TRANSFORMATION PLOT FOR STRAIGHTNESS

We gain some advantages when dealing with relationships between two variables, x and y, if we can express the relationship linearly. In particular, departures from fit are more easily detected, and interpretation is easier.

Transformations of one or both variables sometimes enable us to straighten relations that are curved. In this section, we describe a graphical technique for choosing among the power transformations for one of the variables so as to move toward straightening the relationship.

Construction of a Transformation Plot for Straightness

Let x and y represent paired observations on two variables with medians M_x and M_y, respectively. Let C be the slope of a resistantly fitted line for y in terms of x. The transformation plot for straightness uses

$$\frac{C^2(x - M_x)^2}{2M_y}$$

as the horizontal coordinate and

$$y - M_y - C(x - M_x)$$

as the vertical coordinate. If the resulting graph is nearly linear, then one-minus-slope is the indicated power of a transformation for y to promote straightness.

Development

Let $(x_1, y_1), (x_2, y_2), \ldots, (x_n, y_n)$ represent n paired observations on the variables x and y. We consider first the problem of choosing a transformation for y. We seek a power transformation $\phi(y)$ such that the points $[x_1, \phi(y_1)], [x_2, \phi(y_2)], \ldots, [x_n, \phi(y_n)]$ fall approximately on a straight line.

Let M_x and M_y denote the medians for x and y. Suppose that the true model for the data takes the form

$$y^p - M_y^p = K(x - M_x). \tag{15}$$

(As before, $p = 0$ corresponds to the logarithm.) The simplest form for this fit is

$$y - M_y = C(x - M_x), \tag{16}$$

and we find this fit as a first step, thus obtaining a value for C. When the residuals (or a plot of y against x) indicate a systematic departure from this linear fit, we consider transforming y. We cannot use a power transformation on $y - M_y$ because it has both positive and negative values. For ys that

are positive measurements or counts, we can use a power transformation on y itself. The model indicated in equation (15), although general, permits expansion around a central y value and is appropriate for the positive y values.

Define $z = y^p$ (so $y = z^{1/p}$). If p is nonzero, then $M_y \approx M_z^{1/p}$, with exact equality when n is odd. By expanding $z^{1/p}$ in a Taylor series around M_z, we obtain

$$y = z^{1/p} \approx M_z^{1/p} + \frac{1}{p} M_z^{(1/p)-1}(z - M_z) + \frac{1-p}{2p^2} M_z^{(1/p)-2}(z - M_z)^2$$

as a second-order approximation. Expression (15) gives, in terms of x and y:

$$y \approx M_y + \frac{KM_y}{pM_z}(x - M_x) + \frac{1-p}{2p^2}\left(\frac{KM_y}{pM_z}\right)^2 (x - M_x)^2.$$

We thus obtain

$$y \approx M_y + C(x - M_x) + \frac{1-p}{2M_y} C^2(x - M_x)^2,$$

where C has replaced KM_y/pM_z. The numerical estimate for C is obtained by first fitting equation (16) to the raw data. This estimate is then used to write

$$y - M_y - C(x - M_x) \approx (1 - p)\frac{C^2(x - M_x)^2}{2M_y}, \tag{17}$$

where only $1 - p$ is unknown.

Approximation (17) suggests plotting $[C^2(x - M_x)^2]/2M_y$ on the horizontal axis and $y - M_y - C(x - M_x)$ on the vertical axis. If the plot is nearly linear and if the slope of a line fitted to this plot is subtracted from 1, we obtain the power for the suggested transformation.

One may ask whether it is appropriate to use equation (16) to produce the value for C in approximation (17) and, if so, how this is to be done. Calculus shows us that the slope of the tangent line to the quadratic in approximation (17) at the median M_x is also C. Thus the quadratic is constructed so that its tangent line at M_x has slope equal to that of a line fitted to the data and constrained to go through (M_x, M_y). [In practice we fit a line without this constraint, and this suffices because only a slope is required. A well-fitted line for a batch with curvature need not pass through (M_x, M_y).]

The development given here does not handle the case with $p = 0$ in equation (15). We saw geometric reasons (in Chapter 4) and analytical reasons (in Section 8B) for using the log transformation in place of x^0. The development of this section is valid for transformations x^λ and $x^{-\lambda}$ with arbitrarily small positive λ; the continuous parameter property of the transformations (see Section 8B) permits extension to the logarithmic transformation.

By interchanging the roles of x and y, we can use the same plotting technique for transforming x with an aim toward straightening. We must remember, however, that regression of y on x is not the same as regression of x on y, even when x and y are both random variables (instead of, say, x being fixed). Still, it may be useful to transform x instead of y and to compare the result with that achieved when y is transformed. It may sometimes be useful to allow the simultaneous transformation of both variables. For a multiple regression problem, transformation of the factors is often more useful than transformation of a single response variable; transforming y to straighten its relationship with one variable may lead to a more curved relationship with another variable. This is especially illustrated when we fit a quadratic ($y = b_0 + b_1 x + b_2 x^2$) in which the carriers are 1, x, and x^2.

8F. TRANSFORMATION PLOT FOR THE TWO-WAY TABLE: THE DIAGNOSTIC PLOT

We turn next to two-way tables. We saw in Chapter 6 that the diagnostic plot can indicate a useful power transformation to promote additivity of effects in the data. As we discuss below, it may also suggest an appropriate model (one degree of freedom for nonadditivity) for the data of the two-way table. In this section, we explore the mathematical basis for the diagnostic plot; again we use arguments based on series expansions.

Construction of the Diagnostic Plot

Let y_{ij} be the response for row i and column j of a two-way table. Decompose the data according to $y_{ij} = m + a_i + b_j + r_{ij}$, where m, a_i, and b_j are resistantly determined estimates for the common value, row effects, and column effects, respectively. The diagnostic plot has the *comparison values*,

$$\frac{a_i b_j}{m},$$

on its horizontal axis and the residuals from the additive fit,

$$r_{ij} = y_{ij} - (m + a_i + b_j),$$

on its vertical axis. When the pattern is roughly linear, one-minus-slope is the indicated power of a transformation for the y_{ij} to promote additive structure.

Background and Review

In Chapter 6, we learned that an especially convenient way to model the data in a two-way table provides for a common value, a row effect, a column effect, and a fluctuation:

$$y_{ij} = \mu + \alpha_i + \beta_j + \varepsilon_{ij}. \tag{18}$$

Under such a model, the fitted values can be provided by median polish of the table. It often happens, however, that this simple additive model does not adequately reflect the relationship between the response and the two factors. We would suspect this if we were able to detect structure in the residuals.

When the additive model does not adequately represent the data, we may want to improve the fit by adding another term to the model. One such term, discussed by Tukey (1949), yields the model

$$y_{ij} = \mu + \alpha_i + \beta_j + \frac{K\alpha_i\beta_j}{\mu} + \varepsilon_{ij}, \tag{19}$$

where K is a constant to be determined. The selection of K is facilitated by the *diagnostic plot*, a plot of the residuals from model (18) against the *comparison values* $\alpha_i\beta_j/\mu$ calculated from the effects found for the model. An alternative approach when the simple additive model is inadequate is to transform the data and hope that such a model will work in the transformed scale. Again, the diagnostic plot is useful, this time in suggesting a power transformation that may achieve this goal. When the technique is successful, the resulting fit will have the form

$$y_{ij}^p = m + a_i + b_j + r_{ij}, \tag{20}$$

where y_{ij}^0 is replaced by $\ln y_{ij}$ when $p = 0$.

If the diagnostic plot is reasonably linear, its slope indicates a value for K in the extended model (19). We have also seen that $p =$ one-minus-slope is

the power of a transformation suggested by the diagnostic plot when model (20) is adopted. This chapter is about transformations, so our primary interest is in the latter approach; our development provides insight into the workings of both techniques, with little additional effort needed to discuss the extended model.

Development

We ask: can we find a power transformation of the data so that model (18) will adequately summarize the transformed data? If so, equation (20) will hold for some value of p. If the fit were exact, then

$$y_{ij}^p = m + a_i + b_j,$$

so

$$y_{ij} = \left(m + a_i + b_j \right)^{1/p}. \tag{21}$$

Note that the a_i and the b_j do not have the same values as in the simple additive model. Because we are working with data that are amounts or counts, y_{ij} and $m + a_i + b_j$ are positive quantities, and so power transformations are at least reasonable.

A Series Approximation

To compare the fit given in equation (21) to that of the simple additive model, we use a second-order approximation to equation (21). When model (20) is a suitable model for the data, we would like to see what structure we should expect in the y_{ij} or, more informatively, in the residuals from the additive model. To begin to do this, we rewrite equation (21) as

$$y_{ij} = m^{1/p} \left(1 + \frac{a_i}{m} + \frac{b_j}{m} \right)^{1/p}.$$

After expanding the second factor through the quadratic term in a Taylor series expansion for $(1 + t)^{1/p}$, we obtain

$$y_{ij} \approx m^{1/p} \left[1 + \frac{1}{p} \left(\frac{a_i}{m} + \frac{b_j}{m} \right) + \frac{1-p}{2p^2} \left(\frac{a_i}{m} + \frac{b_j}{m} \right)^2 \right]. \tag{22}$$

We now arrange the terms in this expansion into four groups: terms that

depend on neither i nor j, terms that depend only on i, terms that depend only on j, and terms that depend on both i and j. Then

$$
y_{ij} \approx m^{1/p} \left[1 + \left(\frac{1}{p} \frac{a_i}{m} + \frac{1-p}{2p^2} \frac{a_i^2}{m^2} \right) \right.
$$

$$
\left. + \left(\frac{1}{p} \frac{b_j}{m} + \frac{1-p}{2p^2} \frac{b_j^2}{m^2} \right) + \left(\frac{1-p}{2p^2} \cdot \frac{2a_i b_j}{m^2} \right) \right]. \tag{23}
$$

To simplify the notation, we let

$$
D = m^{1/p}, \tag{24a}
$$

$$
\frac{A_i}{D} = \frac{1}{p} \frac{a_i}{m} + \frac{1-p}{2p^2} \frac{a_i^2}{m^2}, \tag{24b}
$$

$$
\frac{B_j}{D} = \frac{1}{p} \frac{b_j}{m} + \frac{1-p}{2p^2} \frac{b_j^2}{m^2}, \tag{24c}
$$

and

$$
\frac{C_{ij}}{D} = \frac{1-p}{2p^2} \frac{2a_i b_j}{m^2} = \frac{1-p}{p^2} \frac{a_i}{m} \frac{b_j}{m}. \tag{24d}
$$

Then we can write

$$
y_{ij} \approx D \left(1 + \frac{A_i}{D} + \frac{B_j}{D} + \frac{C_{ij}}{D} \right) \tag{25a}
$$

or

$$
y_{ij} \approx D + A_i + B_j + C_{ij}, \tag{25b}
$$

where "$\approx$" indicates that terms higher than second-order have been discarded.

A Simpler Approximation

We have worked through some tedious algebra, and more is yet to come. Let us take stock of what has been accomplished and what we will tackle next.

We began with an additive model for some power of the data, y_{ij}^p. Using series approximations, we have shown that y_{ij} can be approximated by expression (25b), an additive representation for y_{ij} that parallels the structure of model (18).

The C_{ij} in expression (25b), however, may bear no resemblance to structureless residuals. Our next task is to look carefully at the C_{ij} and attempt to discover and accommodate any structure in them. This effort will lead to an extension of the simple additive model and ultimately to the diagnostic plot.

The series expansion for y_{ij}, whose first terms are given in approximation (22), converges whenever $a_i/m + b_j/m$ is less than 1 in absolute value. We examine the behavior of the terms in equations (24) when a_i/m and b_j/m are close to 0, or, equivalently, when the row and column effects in the additive model for y_{ij}^p are much smaller than the common value. With this assumption, expressions such as a_i^2/m^2, b_j^2/m^2, and $a_i b_j/m^2$ might be considered negligible when compared with a_i/m and b_j/m. If so, approximation (25b) reduces to a simple additive model:

$$y_{ij} \approx D + A_i + B_j.$$

We refer to this as giving a first-order approximation. A more generous assumption would keep the terms such as a_i^2/m^2, b_j^2/m^2, and $a_i b_j/m^2$ and ignore only terms that involve three or more factors of the form a_i/m or b_j/m. [This is what we did in approximation (22).]

When the additive model for the table of y_{ij} does not adequately describe the data, it is reasonable to retain all the second-order terms: a_i^2/m^2, b_j^2/m^2, and $a_i b_j/m^2$. For convenience, we think of this as providing a second-order approximation to the data.

In a second-order approximation, we see from terms (24b, c) that

$$\frac{A_i}{D} \frac{B_j}{D} \approx \frac{1}{p^2} \frac{a_i}{m} \frac{b_j}{m}.$$

Using this in term (24d), we see that

$$\frac{C_{ij}}{D} \approx (1 - p) \frac{A_i}{D} \frac{B_j}{D}.$$

Using the result in approximation (25) gives

$$y_{ij} \approx D\left[1 + \frac{A_i}{D} + \frac{B_j}{D} + (1 - p)\frac{A_i}{D} \frac{B_j}{D}\right]$$

or

$$y_{ij} \approx D + A_i + B_j + (1 - p)\frac{A_i B_j}{D}. \tag{26}$$

We conclude that if y_{ij}^p is approximated by an additive model, then, to a second-order approximation, y_{ij} is given by approximation (26). Conversely, if y_{ij} is given approximately by approximation (26), then

$$y_{ij}^p \approx m + a_i + b_j$$

will hold.

The Diagnostic Plot

Approximation (26) provides an extension of the simple additive fit for a two-way table given in model (18). It also leads directly to the diagnostic plot. This approximation gives

$$y_{ij} - D - A_i - B_j \approx (1 - p)\frac{A_i B_j}{D}.$$

If $R_{ij} = y_{ij} - D - A_i - B_j$, then the R_{ij} are the residuals obtained when we fit an additive model to the data. To the extent that the model (26) is good,

$$R_{ij} \approx (1 - p)\frac{A_i B_j}{D}, \tag{27}$$

and plotting R_{ij} against $A_i B_j/D$ provides the diagnostic plot. If approximation (27) is reasonably good, the diagnostic plot will approximate a line having slope $1 - p$. In practice, we turn the argument around and say that if the diagnostic plot shows a roughly linear trend with slope $1 - p$, then transformation of the data using the pth power will approach an additive fit.

As a corollary to our exploration of the diagnostic plot, we can see directly the relationship between the diagnostic plot and the extended fit. If the diagnostic plot displays a linear trend with slope K, then

$$R_{ij} \approx \frac{K A_i B_j}{D}.$$

Thus

$$y_{ij} \approx D + A_i + B_j + \frac{K A_i B_j}{D} \tag{28}$$

holds, up to a second-order approximation. Instead of transforming the data, we may choose to fit an extended model of the form given by approximation (28). The diagnostic plot then provides the value of K.

Special Case: A Multiplicative Fit

Special consideration is again needed when the slope of the diagnostic plot is 1, so that p is 0. In this case, approximation (26) gives us

$$y_{ij} \approx D + A_i + B_j + \frac{A_i B_j}{D}$$

$$\approx D\left(1 + \frac{A_i}{D} + \frac{B_j}{D} + \frac{A_i B_j}{D^2}\right)$$

$$\approx D\left(1 + \frac{A_i}{D}\right)\left(1 + \frac{B_j}{D}\right),$$

a multiplicative fit. Taking logarithms now gives us an additive fit in the log scale:

$$\log y_{ij} \approx \log D + \log\left(1 + \frac{A_i}{D}\right) + \log\left(1 + \frac{B_j}{D}\right).$$

We see once again why a slope of 1 leads us to the logarithm; thus y_{ij}^0 is replaced by $\log y_{ij}$.

8G. HISTORICAL NOTES AND REFERENCES

General Background

Transformations have long been used in data analysis. Early work centered around analysis of variance and was reviewed and extended in papers by Cochran (1940), Curtiss (1943), and Bartlett (1947). Tukey (1957) recognized the value of studying the power transformations as a family, and he gave a more general definition of strength of a transformation than is used here. Box and Cox (1964) applied likelihood and Bayesian methods to the problem of identifying power transformations to achieve any of several

objectives. Their work has led to a series of articles, including those of Draper and Hunter (1969), Schlesselman (1973), and Fuchs (1979). Bartlett (1947), J. B. Kruskal (1968), and Hoyle (1973) provide valuable survey articles; the article by Hoyle also contains an extensive bibliography. Tukey (1977) and Mosteller and Tukey (1977) treat power transformations and their applications in exploratory data analysis. Leinhardt and Wasserman (1979) discuss reasons for using power transformations and derive methods for selecting an appropriate power.

Background for Mathematical Unity

The consideration of the power transformations as a family was advanced by Tukey and his collaborators over twenty years ago [Moore and Tukey (1954), Anscombe and Tukey (1955), Tukey (1957)]. All of the more recent references given above have continued to view the power transformations as a coherent family.

Background for Symmetry Plot

Many authors [e.g., Moore (1957), Box and Cox (1964), Draper and Cox (1969), and Atkinson (1973)] have considered the use of transformations to achieve near-normality. Hinkley (1975, 1977) studies both theoretical and practical aspects of choosing power transformations to symmetry. Leinhardt and Wasserman (1979) also propose a way to select a transformation for symmetry. Their method resembles the one presented here in that it uses a series approximation; but their approximation is first-order, and they do not use information from the data beyond the fourths. The discussion of the symmetry plot in Section 8C is expanded by Emerson and Stoto (1982).

Background for Spread-versus-Level Plot

The origins of the spread-versus-level plot lie in the classical notion of a variance-stabilizing transformation and have a rich and fascinating history. Variance stabilization was applied in an analysis-of-variance context even when the theory of analysis of variance was in its infancy [see Bartlett (1936), Cochran (1940), and Fisher (1930)]. The selection of a variance-stabilizing transformation was often "justified" in a way that is largely heuristic. We state the result with its assumptions. Then we review the classical argument that has been used by many authors [Bartlett (1936, 1947), Kenney and Keeping (1951), Snedecor and Cochran (1967)].

For this discussion, it is useful to use upper-case letters (X and Y) for random variables and lower-case letters (x and y) for algebraic variables.

Let X be a continuous random variable with mean μ and variance $\sigma_X^2(\mu)$. Strictly, X will represent more than one random variable, each with its own mean. (Think of these as being the variables $X_1, X_2, \ldots, X_K$ with means $\mu_1, \mu_2, \ldots, \mu_K$. These variables underlie K batches of data at the K different levels.) When the need arises, we indicate the variable for which μ is the mean by placing a subscript on μ. The notation for variance reminds us that the variance depends functionally on the mean μ. (With several batches, the variance is often an increasing function of the mean.) We emphasize that $\sigma_X^2(\mu)$ denotes the variance of the random variable X; the parameter μ is an algebraic variable in this context. The function

$$\phi(\mu) = c \int \frac{1}{\sigma_X(\mu)} d\mu, \tag{29}$$

for any constant c, is used to suggest a transformation:

$$\phi(x) = c \int \frac{1}{\sigma_X(x)} dx. \tag{30}$$

It is natural that we use the same transformation, ϕ, for the raw data, x, that (nearly) removes the dependence of the variance on the mean, μ. We denote this transformation by $Y = \phi(X)$.

Principle of Variance Stabilization. The random variable $Y = \phi(X)$ has variance σ_Y^2 which is (approximately) independent of μ_Y, and the transformed variable Y is said to have *stable variance.*

Heuristic Discussion

We seek a transformation $Y = \phi(X)$ for which σ_Y^2 is constant. If ϕ is a "sufficiently nice" function* of x, it will have a Taylor series expansion at μ:

$$\phi(x) = \phi(\mu) + (x - \mu)\phi'(\mu) + \frac{(x-\mu)^2}{2!}\phi''(\mu) + \cdots. \tag{31}$$

If the expansion is valid at each positive value x of X, then we may write:

$$\phi(X) = \phi(\mu) + (X - \mu)\phi'(\mu) + \frac{(X-\mu)^2}{2!}\phi''(\mu) + \cdots. \tag{32}$$

*See footnote to *Development*, Section 8D.

The series gives the following first-order approximation:

$$\phi(X) \doteq \phi(\mu) + (X - \mu)\phi'(\mu). \tag{33}$$

Under the approximation, since $E(X - \mu) = 0$, we have

$$E\phi(X) = \phi(\mu)$$

and

$$\operatorname{var} \phi(X) = E[\phi'(\mu)(X - \mu)]^2 = [\phi'(\mu)]^2 \sigma_X^2(\mu).$$

To pursue constant variance, we set

$$\operatorname{var} \phi(X) = c^2,$$

where c is a positive constant. Then

$$[\phi'(\mu)]^2 \sigma_X^2(\mu) = c^2,$$

or

$$\phi'(\mu) = \frac{c}{\sigma_X(\mu)},$$

from which

$$\phi(\mu) = c \int \frac{1}{\sigma_X(\mu)} d\mu.$$

In terms of x we have

$$\phi(x) = c \int \frac{1}{\sigma_X(x)} dx.$$

EXAMPLE:

Let X_1 and X_2 be random variables with a bivariate Gaussian distribution. Let $\hat{\rho}_n$ denote the sample correlation coefficient:

$$\hat{\rho}_n = \frac{\sum_{i=1}^n (x_{i1} - \bar{x}_1)(x_{i2} - \bar{x}_2)}{\left[\sum_{i=1}^n (x_{i1} - \bar{x}_1)^2 \sum_{i=1}^n (x_{i2} - \bar{x}_2)^2\right]^{1/2}},$$

and let ρ denote the population correlation coefficient. It is well known that the asymptotic distribution of $\hat{\rho}_n$ is Gaussian, $\text{Gau}[\rho, (1 - \rho^2)^2/n]$. The variance is a function of the mean ρ, where $-1 \leq \rho \leq 1$. Application of variance stabilization suggests

$$\phi(\rho) = \int \frac{c\sqrt{n}}{1 - \rho^2} d\rho$$

$$= \frac{c\sqrt{n}}{2} \int \left(\frac{1}{1 - \rho} + \frac{1}{1 + \rho} \right) d\rho$$

$$= \frac{c\sqrt{n}}{2} \ln\left(\frac{1 + \rho}{1 - \rho} \right) + k,$$

where c and k are constants. The function $\ln[(1 + \rho)/(1 - \rho)]$ is known as *Fisher's z-transformation* for the correlation coefficient.

The general argument we have presented and illustrated above may be regarded with skepticism. Some authors who have used it mention its shortcomings. In 1944 Tippett remarked, "This derivation is not mathematically sound, and the result is only justified if on application it is found to be satisfactory." Curtiss (1943, p. 108) commented on the approximation in a more explicit way. He notes that for X normally distributed, the variance of $\phi(X) = X^2$ is given by the approximation as $4\sigma^2\mu^2$, whereas the actual variance of X^2 is $4\sigma^2\mu^2 + 2\sigma^4$. This result warns that we must be cautious when using the first terms of a Taylor series for an approximation. The approximation would be helpful only when μ is large compared with σ. This does often happen in problems of physical interest.

Curtiss discusses another potential problem with the stabilization of variance. He shows that if X is a Poisson variable, the problem of stabilization has only the trivial solution in which ϕ is identically constant. [See also Bartlett (1947) and Cochran (1940).] We present Curtiss' argument in the next example.

EXAMPLE:

Let X be a discrete Poisson variable with probability function

$$f_X(k) = \frac{e^{-\mu}\mu^k}{k!} \qquad \text{for } k = 0, 1, 2, \ldots$$

and $\mu > 0$. The mean and variance of X are both μ. To stabilize variance, we would seek $\phi(X)$ for which $E[\phi(X) - E\phi(X)]^2$ equals a constant, c^2. This requirement gives

$$E[\phi(X)]^2 = c^2 + [E\phi(X)]^2,$$

or

$$\sum_{k=0}^{\infty} \phi(k)^2 \frac{e^{-\mu}\mu^k}{k!} = c^2 + \left[\sum_{k=0}^{\infty} \phi(k) \frac{e^{-\mu}\mu^k}{k!} \right]^2.$$

Since

$$e^{-\mu} = \sum_{j=0}^{\infty} \frac{(-\mu)^j}{j!},$$

we can expand both sides of the previous equation in powers of μ. For our purposes, we only need to examine the first (constant) terms. We have

$$\phi(0)^2 = c^2 + \phi(0)^2.$$

Thus $c^2 = 0$ and so var $\phi(X) = 0$. Of course, this condition makes $\phi(X)$ a constant. We conclude that the only transformation of X that exactly stabilizes variance is the trivial one for which $\phi(X)$ is identically constant. Even so, if one uses the fact that $\sigma(\mu) = \mu^{1/2}$ and thus derives

$$\phi(x) = c \int \frac{1}{x^{1/2}} dx = c_1 x^{1/2} + c_2,$$

a useful transformation for the Poisson variate results. The apparent inconsistency here arises because Curtiss' analysis is exact, whereas the square-root transformation follows from a truncated Taylor series as an approximation.

Curtiss (1943, p. 108) asserts that a situation similar to that discussed for the Poisson arises when variance stabilization is applied to a binomial variate. Cochran (1940) also discusses transformation of Poisson and binomial variables; Freeman and Tukey (1950) give improved variance-stabilizing transformations for the Poisson and binomial, and Mosteller and Youtz (1961) give tables for these transformations.

The spread-versus-level plot, as presented in Section 8D, had its origins in variance stabilization. It has been popularized by Tukey (1977, Chapter 4). A derivation somewhat like that of Section 8D appears in Leinhardt and Wasserman (1979).

Background for Straightness Plot

Transformations have long been used in a regression context, although the literature may not be as rich as it is for variance stabilization and for two-way tables. Box and Tidwell (1962) and Box and Cox (1964) consider transformations of variables to promote linearity. Tukey (1977, Chapter 6) and Mosteller and Tukey (1977, Chapter 4) consider transformations for straightening in an exploratory setting.

The development in Section 8E is given by Emerson and Stoto (1982). Leinhardt and Wasserman (1979) present a somewhat analogous development for transforming the explanatory variable as well as the dependent variable.

Background for the Diagnostic Plot

Many authors consider transformations in the context of analysis of variance; see, for example, papers by Bartlett (1936, 1947), Cochran (1940), Curtiss (1943), Box and Cox (1964), Draper and Hunter (1969), Schlesselman (1973), and Fuchs (1979).

Tukey writes about the one-degree-of-freedom-for-nonadditivity model (1949), and this work contains the ideas that led to the diagnostic plot (see Tukey, 1977).

Additional Remarks about Background

In this section we have attempted to cite a few key papers that relate to the evolution of the concepts discussed earlier in this chapter and in Chapter 4. Our discussion does not begin to be comprehensive, but it should provide an adequate introduction to the literature. Many additional references may be traced by using the references cited here; see especially the article by Hoyle (1973).

REFERENCES

Anscombe, F. J. and Tukey, J. W. (1955). "The criticism of transformations," *Journal of the American Statistical Association*, **50**, 566 (abstract of a paper presented before the American Statistical Association and the Biometric Society, Montreal, September 12, 1954).

Atkinson, A. C. (1973). "Testing transformations to normality," *Journal of the Royal Statistical Society, Series B*, **35**, 473–479.

Bartlett, M. S. (1936). "Square-root transformation in analysis of variance," *Journal of the Royal Statistical Society, Supplement*, **3**, 68–78.

Bartlett, M. S. (1947). "The use of transformations," *Biometrics*, **3**, 39–52.

Box, G. E. P. and Cox, D. R. (1964). "An analysis of transformations," *Journal of the Royal Statistical Society, Series B*, **26**, 211–252.

Box, G. E. P. and Tidwell, P. W. (1962). "Transformations of the independent variables," *Technometrics*, **4**, 531–550.

Cochran, W. G. (1940). "Analysis of variance when experimental errors follow Poisson or binomial laws," *Annals of Mathematical Statistics*, **11**, 335–347.

Curtiss, J. H. (1943). "On transformations used in the analysis of variance," *Annals of Mathematical Statistics*, **14**, 107–132.

Draper, N. R. and Cox, D. R. (1969). "On distributions and their transformations to normality," *Journal of the Royal Statistical Society, Series B*, **31**, 472–476.

Draper, N. R. and Hunter, W. G. (1969). "Transformations: some examples revisited," *Technometrics*, **11**, 23–40.

Emerson, J. D. and Stoto, M. A. (1982). "Exploratory methods for choosing power transformations," *Journal of the American Statistical Association*, **77**, 103–108.

Fisher, A. (1930). *The Mathematical Theory of Probabilities*, Second Edition. New York: Macmillan.

Freeman, M. F. and Tukey, J. W. (1950). "Transformations related to the angular and the square root," *Annals of Mathematical Statistics*, **21**, 607–611.

Fuchs, C. (1979). "Comments on a criterion of transformation proposed by Schlesselman," *Journal of the American Statistical Association*, **74**, 238–239.

Hinkley, D. V. (1975). "On power transformations to symmetry," *Biometrika*, **62**, 101–111.

——— (1977), "On quick choice of power transformation," *Applied Statistics*, **26**, 67–69.

Hoyle, M. H. (1973). "Transformations—an introduction and bibliography," *International Statistical Review*, **41**, 203–223.

Kenney, J. F. and Keeping, E. S. (1951). *Mathematics of Statistics, Part Two*, Second Edition. New York: Van Nostrand.

Kruskal, J. B. (1968). "Statistical analysis: transformations of data." In D. L. Sills (Ed.), *International Encyclopedia of the Social Sciences*. Chicago: Macmillan and the Free Press.

Leinhardt, S. and Wasserman, S. S. (1979). "Exploratory data analysis: an introduction to selected methods," In K. F. Schuessler (Ed.), *Sociological Methodology 1979*. San Francisco: Jossey-Bass.

Moore, P. G. and Tukey, J. W. (1954). "Answer to query 112," *Biometrics*, **10**, 562–568.

Moore, P. G. (1957). "Transformation to normality using fractional powers of the variables," *Journal of the American Statistical Association*, **52**, 237–246.

Mosteller, F. and Tukey, J. W. (1977). *Data Analysis and Regression*. Reading, MA: Addison–Wesley.

Mosteller, F. and Youtz, C. (1961). "Tables of the Freeman–Tukey transformations for the binomial and Poisson distributions," *Biometrika*, **48**, 433–440.

Schlesselman, J. J. (1973). "Data transformation in two-way analysis of variance," *Journal of the American Statistical Association*, **68**, 369–378.

Snedecor, G. W. and Cochran, W. G. (1967). *Statistical Methods*, Sixth Edition. Ames, IA: The Iowa State University Press.

Taylor, A. E. (1955). *Advanced Calculus*. Waltham, MA: Blaisdell Publishing Company.

Tippett, L. H. C. (1934). "Statistical methods in textile research. Part 2, uses of the binomial and Poisson distributions," *Shirley Institute Memoirs*, **13**, 35–72. [Cited by Curtiss (1943).]

Tukey, J. W. (1949). "One degree of freedom for non-additivity," *Biometrics*, **5**, 232–242.

———— (1957). "On the comparative anatomy of transformations," *Annals of Mathematical Statistics*, **28**, 602–632.

———— (1977). *Exploratory Data Analysis*. Reading, MA: Addison–Wesley.

Additional Literature

Bickel, P. J. and Doksum, K. A. (1981). "An analysis of transformations revisited," *Journal of the American Statistical Association*, **76**, 296–311.

Carroll, R. J. (1980). "A robust method for testing transformations to achieve approximate normality," *Journal of the Royal Statistical Society, Series B*, **42**, 71–78.

John, J. A. and Draper, N. R. (1980). "An alternative family of transformations," *Applied Statistics*, **29**, 190–197.

EXERCISES

1. A family of power transformations is defined in equations (1); it includes the natural logarithm function in a simple way. If $\ln x$ were replaced by $\log x$ (base 10), what definition of a family of power transformations would be consistent with this change? (Hint: $\log x = \ln x / \ln 10$. It may be useful to review the ideas of matching discussed in Chapter 4.)

2. Verify that the functions given in equations (6) are matched at x_0.

3. Suppose that we wished to have a family of power transformations analogous to those defined in expressions (1) but with the following properties:

   (a) The curves are monotone increasing so that the order of the data is preserved.

   (b) The curves share a common point, $(2, 0)$, for each p.

   (c) The curves share a common tangent line having slope 1 at $(2, 0)$.

   Give explicitly the family of power transformations that is implied by these properties.

4. Show that the family of functions you derived in Exercise 3 is continuous in the parameter p at $p = 0$. Explain why this result implies that this family of functions is indexed continuously by the parameter p.

5. Consider the transformation $f(x) = 3x^{1/3} + 2$ for $x \geq 0$. At what value of x is the curvature of f largest?

6. Let $g(x) = C \ln x$. For what value of C will $g(x)$ have the same curvature that $f(x) = x^2$ has at the point $x = 2$?

7. Verify that approximation (10) and the transformation plot for symmetry follow from equation (9) and the second-order Taylor series expansions for x_L^p and x_U^p by filling in the algebraic details.

8. Fill in the algebraic details that give equation (12) from equation (11).

9. Near the end of Section 8D, we suggest that the spread-versus-level plot could have been developed using "sixteenth-spread" instead of fourth-spread. In many situations, such a change might be quite undesirable. Discuss.

10. Verify that the slope of the tangent line to the quadratic at the median, M_x, in expression (17) is C.

11. A multiplicative fit for a two-way table is discussed in Section 8F. Explain what a multiplicative model would say about the structure of a two-way table. Describe a physical context in which such a model might be plausible.

*12. Let X be a random variable and suppose that $Y = \ln X$ has a Gaussian distribution with mean μ and variance σ^2. Find the density function for X and sketch its graph for a few values of μ and σ. (The variable X is said to have a log-normal distribution.)

13. Verify that if X is a Gaussian random variable with mean μ and variance σ^2, the variance of X^2 is $4\sigma^2\mu^2 + 2\sigma^4$.

*14. For selected values of μ, the parameter of the Poisson random variable X, calculate (numerically) the mean and variance of $\sqrt{X}$. Use these results to assess the effectiveness of the square-root transformation in stabilizing the variance of Poisson data.

CHAPTER 9

Introduction to
More Refined
Estimators

David C. Hoaglin
Harvard University and Abt Associates Inc.

Frederick Mosteller
Harvard University

John W. Tukey
Princeton University and Bell Laboratories

This chapter sets the stage for the three chapters that follow.

As has become evident in the preceding chapters, exploratory data analysis makes broad use of the median, a simple summary whose resistance is easy to understand. Similarly, the fourth-spread provides a measure of spread or scale. Our discussion has not touched upon the variability associated with either of these summaries. Instead, we have tried to ensure that unusual behavior such as wild observations would not distort whatever analysis concerns us.

Often, we must take a further step, from exploring to consolidating what we can learn from the data. In pursuing this objective, an effective approach may assume that a statistical model, at least approximately, represents the process leading to the data. Then we generally need a reliable estimate of one or more parameters in such a model. At the same time, we prefer to avoid strong assumptions about the behavior of the fluctuations in the data. Thus we seek *robustness*, thought of as insensitivity to underlying assumptions—for example, about the shape of the distribution of measurements.

To take a specific example, we may feel safe in behaving as if the data constitute a sample from an approximately symmetric distribution, whose center we then wish to estimate, but we are unwilling to assume any particular symmetric distribution, such as a Gaussian distribution. Still, we would like our estimate of the center to be close to the true value, not just for one symmetric distribution, but for each of many symmetric distributions. For example, we might want to use an estimator that has relatively small variance for each of many distributions. Admittedly, many measures of closeness compete for attention.

In thinking about varied sorts of closeness, we could consider the more general notion of *efficiency*, a vague concept which can be made precise in various ways.* To illustrate for estimation, we would gain greater efficiency if we could make such improvements as decreasing the variance of an estimator, decreasing the mean squared error of an estimator, or producing a shorter confidence interval. Or, in testing a hypothesis, we gain efficiency if we can increase the power of the test while keeping the significance level fixed.

Contemporaneously with the development of exploratory data analysis, research in statistics has focused substantial effort on robust estimation, where we want high efficiency in a variety of situations. The most thoroughly investigated aspect has been estimating the center of a symmetric distribution. Section 9B explains why this emphasis has occurred. Chapters 10 and 11 discuss in detail some simple and some more refined estimators for the center of symmetry. Both discussions include comparative performance in small samples.

Even in a symmetric distribution, estimation of scale is not a well defined problem because it is not clear precisely what characteristic of the distribution we should estimate. We turn to this issue in Chapter 12, where we also discuss the role of a scale estimator in constructing interval estimates.

In the remainder of the present chapter, Section 9A explains the standard methods of studying estimators. Section 9B discusses the reasons for the emphasis on symmetry, and Section 9C treats the role of sample size in studying and choosing estimators. Because the highly refined estimators that we discuss in Chapter 11 can be approached in several ways, Section 9D takes a preliminary look at them. Finally, recent research has brought an understanding of robust estimation by following three separate approaches: experimental sampling and two kinds of asymptotic analysis. Section 9E sketches this important background.

---

*Some discussions in a more technical vein use the term *stringency* for this vague concept.

9A. VARIOUS APPROACHES TO ESTIMATION

Without writing a history of estimation, we can say that statisticians have for a long time tried to choose estimators of, say, location and scale that retrieve a great deal of information from the sample. Before any systematic theory for producing estimators had been developed, Gauss was comparing various measures of spread for their own reliability. Until almost 1950, these comparisons were largely limited to estimation in the family of Gaussian distributions.

When two statistics for estimating the same quantity have Gaussian distributions, they are especially easy to compare because then their properties can be completely summarized by their means and variances. In the special case where the two statistics are unbiased, the ratio of their variances has an easy interpretation as relative efficiency. The idea is that we can compare sample sizes required for equivalent accuracy of the two statistics. This simplicity is possible because the distributions of the statistics depend on only the two parameters. For example, in samples from a normal distribution, the sample mean is the best estimator of the population mean and itself is normally distributed. The median is also an unbiased estimator, but the median, which is approximately normally distributed, has larger variance. The ratio of the variances is $\text{var(mean)}/\text{var(median)} = 2/\pi$, approximately. Thus the sample median is said to be about 64% efficient compared with the sample mean for estimating the population mean of a normal distribution. In terms of sample sizes, because var(mean) and var(median) both behave like a constant multiple of $1/n$, the mean would need a sample only 64% as large to achieve the same performance as the median.

When we retreat from such an ideal situation, complications arise. The attempt through such approaches as maximum likelihood to obtain good estimators for parameters in other circumstances usually still leaves one hitched to the family of specific distributions whose shape one assumes. At the same time, everyone agrees that, in practice, we would not know the exact shape of a distribution, even for fairly broad families.

People wanted to develop estimators that would be accurate for collections of distributions, and so out of the many studies of nonparametric methods for constructing tests of significance, some methods of estimation were devised. These methods could be used to get estimates for, say, the median of any distribution whatsoever. And, of course, they also have the corresponding weakness that they may not be very strong against the kinds of distributions that we expect to see in the practical situation because they attempt to cope with such a broad family. It would take considerable space for us to discuss examples of nonparametric estimation, and so we shall not

do this except to say that the methods are oriented toward all continuous distributions.

Thus we have the two extremes: ideal estimators for narrow families of distributions such as the normal and nonparametric estimators that can be used against any continuous distribution without needing to assume a distributional form. What was missing was the concept of robustness and resistance—essentially the idea of accurate estimators against the families and situations that we think might arise in practice but that are not neatly summarized in the mathematical manner of the normal distribution.

We apply four approaches to find the properties of estimators. Since the mathematics of robustness and efficiency becomes ugly very early, the first method based on deriving exact properties is not much used. For modest sample sizes, the tendency has been to study the behavior of estimators across distributions for a fixed sample size using the second approach of experimental sampling. A sample is drawn from a hypothetical distribution of measurements, and the estimator is applied to the sample to give the value of the estimate. This process is repeated many times for a specific situation, and we obtain empirical information about the properties of the distribution of the estimator being studied for that parent distribution.

A third, more mathematical, approach deals with the study of very large samples, and this is called the asymptotic approach. It tells us a good deal about the properties of an estimator when the sample size grows large. We still have the problem of making the connection between these large samples and the smaller samples we actually use. The connection is primarily made through experimental sampling results. This approach has often given us good guidance in the past.

A fourth approach applies asymptotics to special families composed of distributions that are near members of a standard family. This makes it possible for us to see how well estimators work over "nearby" distributions we think resemble our data, while taking out insurance that substantial differences from the standard may occur. From these results, we develop the idea of robustness across families of distributions and of efficiency across the families. For example, if the standard distribution were a uniform distribution [Figure 9-1(a)], we might consider all distributions whose cumulatives $F(x)$ were within .1 of the cumulative of the standard. Thus instead of the standard, we would admit all distributions whose cumulatives were between the upper and lower curves of Figure 9-1(b). The method of describing neighborhoods of distributions illustrated here is not the only one that could be used, and, of course, the family of uniform distributions would rarely be the standard from which we start in practical work.

Chapters 10 and 11 use combinations of these methods to study estimators of location, and Chapter 12 studies estimators of scale and their use in

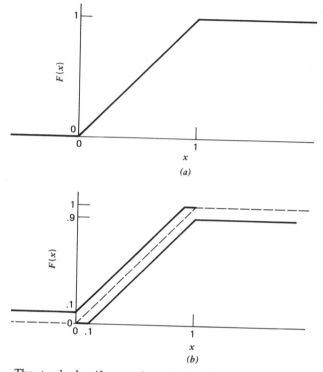

Figure 9-1. The standard uniform and nearby distributions. (*a*) Cumulative for the standard uniform distribution. (*b*) Bounds for the cumulatives within .1 of the standard uniform. The dashed line represents the cumulative of the standard uniform.

setting confidence limits. We do not treat the method based on asymptotics for neighborhoods of distributions, and so we refer the reader to Huber (1981).

9B. WHY THE SYMMETRIC CASE?

In much of scientific work we have no standard way to assess losses arising from errors of estimation. For location estimates, therefore, we

Choose population quantities, called estimands, that we think it helpful to estimate, such as the mean, median, or 10% point of a probability distribution,

Consider possible estimators of the estimands, such as the sample mean or median, and

Select measures of variability or efficiency for these estimators to help us choose among them.

Sometimes, we find estimators themselves rather natural, and we may allow them to determine the estimand as, say, the median or mean of the distribution of the estimator. With so many possibilities for estimators and estimands for the set of all probability distributions, we would expect that some special cases would capture our attention, and the symmetric probability distribution has captured it for the problem of estimating location. Because of its natural center, we are prepared to set aside many asymmetrical options.

Most of the study of refined estimators of location has focused on samples from symmetric probability distributions or from more general symmetric situations such as each sample having one observation drawn from a symmetric distribution with large variance. Two simple reasons help explain this emphasis:

1. When we are prepared to treat the data in a symmetric way as coming from a symmetric source, we know the estimand for location—namely, the center about which the distribution is symmetric.
2. Then, when we treat the data in a symmetric way so that no bias arises, we need not trade off bias and variability, as would otherwise be necessary.

If we have a sample from an almost symmetric distribution, all of that distribution's natural targets for location, including its mean (if this exists), median, midsummaries (described in Chapter 2), and midmean (the mean of that part of the distribution between its 25-percent points), almost *coincide*.

This agreement also holds if we want to think of a more complicated symmetric situation, such as:

A collection of symmetric distributions, all with the same center, though with different shapes or spreads, one observation to come from each; or

A basic symmetric distribution and two skew distributions, symmetric with each other around the center of the symmetric distribution, with $n - k$ observations to come from the basic distribution and k from *one* of the skew distributions, that one chosen, for each sample, at random from the two.

Skew Situations

If, on the other hand, we admit that we face a definitely skew situation, the potential targets for location—both those listed above and their relatives, as well as any others that might be relevant—are all likely to differ from one another. Which should we be trying to estimate? This is not a question a statistician alone should try to resolve because the answer surely depends on the subject matter.

For example, if we measure surface tension, both experience and sound evidence based on thermodynamic theory lead us to expect both larger and more frequent negative deviations from the correct value for the pure liquid than positive ones. Our target must then be something above the median, which is itself above the mean. But the proper combination of physics and statistics in this problem and, more generally, of subject matter knowledge and insight, statistical insight, and empirical evidence (which might tell us which such target to choose) has not been assembled to give that answer.

In insurance-like situations, where "losses" are almost always distributed with a heavy (stretched) tail to the right and where we expect to face at least a moderate number of such losses in the future period for which we are planning, it seems much more reasonable to take the "mean loss" as our target than to take the "median loss." Indeed, we may wonder whether a target even further into the tail might be desirable.

In general, then, the proper target in a skew situation will depend on subject matter considerations. We need to find which estimator to use for each of the possible range of targets. Until we have clear targets, it will be very hard, if not impossible, to decide which estimates perform well.

Of course, once some reasonable targets have been worked out, we will still have to face the combination of bias in our estimates (in the average or median over samples) and variability of them from one sample to another. In a few kinds of instances (contractual or other legal ones, particularly) it may be appropriate to begin with bias, requiring it to be zero or miniscule. In most instances, however, the natural requirement is for the estimate to be as "close" to the target as we can make it. In doing this, we must at least balance bias against variance in some quantitative way. The mean squared error, which adds the square of the bias to the variance of the estimator, is one example of such a balancing, but often that choice of balance has no justification beyond a desire to take both systematic error and sampling error into account. Again proper balance will, it would seem, depend on the subject matter. Even then, however, we still may have no natural loss function. Again the effort required to try to choose a reasonable balance between bias and variability has not been exerted.

Reformulating the Problem

One way to define our problem is to choose what is to be estimated and how closeness is to be assessed. Instead we could call for a more complicated unified effort in which subject matter skills, statistical insight, and empirical evidence combine to produce a way of judging "closeness" between a distribution of estimates and an unspecified summary for the distribution that was sampled. In many asymmetrical situations, we have no natural target.

9C. THE DOMINANT ROLE OF SAMPLE SIZE

In thinking about refined estimators of location, it helps to consider seven ranges of sample size briefly commented on in Table 9-1.

The gradual transfer of attention from variability to bias as the sample size grows occurs for two reasons:

Bias effects for well-chosen estimators are, to a first approximation, usually unaffected by sample size, whereas variability decreases steadily as sample size increases.

Symmetry is likely, in practice, to be only approximate; we can act as if it were exact when our estimates are highly variable, but we may not be able to continue to do this once our estimates are highly precise.

TABLE 9-1.   **Ranges of sample size important for location.**

Range	Comments
1 and 2	Little choice
3 and 4	Median seems to be the preferred estimator
5 to 9	Not thoroughly studied
10 to 50	Has been the main emphasis
about 500[a]	
about 10,000[a,b]	
about 1,000,000[b]	

[a]Somewhere in these ranges, questions of bias begin to dominate questions of variability, if they have not already done so at smaller sample sizes.
[b]Somewhere in these ranges, ease of computation, questions of bias, and the most careful attention to measurement details are the primary issues. Reduction in variability is no longer a major issue.

9D. INTRODUCTION TO w- AND M-ESTIMATORS

In much of robust estimation, the numerical values of the estimates can be obtained only after an iterative process because the estimators do not have closed forms like the mean or variance. Instead, they come equipped with an algorithm for producing the value of the estimate—for example, by minimizing a function. Usually one must choose a starting value, say T_0, and then compute to get a new estimate, say T^*. Then this new estimate can become the starting value for another round, and the process continues until further iterations would make little difference.

Two classes of estimators provide most of the highly refined estimators of location of current interest and use. Both can be described in terms of relative deviation of each residual

$$y_i - T,$$

where T can be regarded as the estimate of location at the current iteration. This deviation is assessed in comparison with the general size of all the residuals, $y_1 - T, y_2 - T, \ldots, y_n - T$. This general size, analogous to a multiple of the standard deviation, is the product of a measure of spread S calculated from the residuals and a tuning constant c. Most refined estimators use a measure of spread like the MAD (median absolute deviation from the median) or one-half the fourth-spread. (The factor of one-half makes these two choices for S about the same size, thus maintaining a fixed interpretation for c. Loosely, c can be regarded as a way of relating to the standard deviation. We delay interpreting c further.)

The measure of relative deviation is then taken to be

$$u_i = \frac{y_i - T}{cS}.$$

w-Estimators

A w-estimator starts with T_0 equal to the median, M, of the observations and involves *one* further step that could be extended to an iteration. (If all possible further steps were taken, we would have an M-estimator.) The new (and for w-estimators the final) estimate is given by

$$T^* = \frac{\Sigma w(u_i) \cdot y_i}{\Sigma w(u_i)}$$

where $w(u)$ is a symmetric weighting function conventionally taken to give value 1 at $u = 0$ and generally decreasing as $|u|$ becomes larger.

M-Estimators

To get *M*-estimates, we iterate this step until convergence, which would require infinitely many steps in principle, though only a finite number for practical accuracy. At convergence, we would have $T^* = T$—that is, a further step produces no change—so that

$$0 = T^* - T = \frac{\Sigma w(u_i) y_i}{\Sigma w(u_i)} - \frac{\Sigma w(u_i) T}{\Sigma w(u_i)}$$

$$= \frac{cS}{\Sigma w(u_i)} \Sigma w(u_i) \frac{y_i - T}{cS}$$

$$= \frac{cS}{\Sigma w(u_i)} \Sigma w(u_i) \cdot u_i$$

Thus at convergence

$$\Sigma w(u_i) u_i = 0.$$

As we discuss below, this condition generalizes the familiar requirement for the sample mean: choose the value of A so that

$$\Sigma (y_i - A) = 0.$$

This result gives us a natural way to lead into *M*-estimators. Let us introduce

$$\psi(u) = w(u) u$$

for which $\psi(-u) = -\psi(u)$ and $\psi'(0) = 1$, giving $\Sigma w(u_i) u_i = 0$ the form

$$\Sigma \psi(u_i) = 0;$$

that is, we want to find the value of T so that

$$\Sigma \psi \left(\frac{y_i - T}{cS} \right) = 0.$$

Estimators so defined by choice of ψ, c, and S and the summation condition have, in practice, to be approximated by iteration, using either the w-iteration just discussed or another.

If we can treat S and c as fixed from iteration to iteration, as we obviously can when we are concerned with location, and we use either the MAD or half the fourth-spread for S, the condition

$$\sum \psi\left(\frac{y_i - T}{cS}\right) = 0$$

arises naturally from minimizing

$$\sum \rho\left(\frac{y_i - T}{cS}\right),$$

where

$$\frac{d\rho(u)}{du} = \psi(u).$$

This interpretation has nice links with the classical arithmetic-mean estimator, for which

$$w(u) \equiv 1$$

$$\psi(u) = u$$

$$\rho(u) = \frac{u^2}{2},$$

and we can think of minimizing, in this special case,

$$\frac{1}{2}\sum\left(\frac{y_i - T}{cS}\right)^2 = \frac{1}{2c^2S^2}\sum(y_i - T)^2.$$

Minimizing this leads to the sample mean.

When we treat more general estimation problems such as regression, we cannot, at least so far, make effective use of one-step estimators. (This may be because we don't know how to choose a good starting point.)

In the location case, however, which is this chapter's concern, the performance of

one-step-from-the-median *w*-estimators

is essentially as good as that of

fully-iterated *M*-estimators.

(We choose the value of c that is best for the one-step estimator.) Practically, then, we may often use w-estimators. Theoretically, we may find advantages in working with M-estimators.

9E. TECHNICAL APPROACHES

We turn next to ways of studying the performance of location estimators in the heavily studied range of sample size, 10 to 50.

Aside from exact results derived mathematically in a few special circumstances, the technical approaches taken fall into three types:

Experimental sampling,
Individual asymptotics, and
Collective asymptotics.

We wish we could have finite-sample results for every sample size and every distribution; but, as a practical matter, we can have experimental sampling results for only a few of each. We can have asymptotic results for nearly any distribution of interest. The asymptotic approaches differ from experimental sampling because they emphasize limits as the sample size becomes large. Because individual asymptotics works with one distribution or situation at a time, it is closer in spirit to experimental sampling than to collective asymptotics. The latter emphasizes the worst performance in a neighborhood of some standard distribution. The discussions in Chapters 10, 11, and 12 focus primarily on experimental sampling, although Chapter 10 draws on exact small-sample results and Chapter 11 develops some individual asymptotics. The remainder of this section explains the nature of experimental sampling and of asymptotics.

Experimental Sampling

In principle, an experimental-sampling study is simple in structure, and its results are easy to interpret. Basically, it involves choosing:

A number, usually small, of distributions or more general sampling situations to be studied;
Procedures using the computer to generate n-tuples of numbers that can be taken as reasonable facsimiles of random samples from each of the chosen distributions or more general situations; and
A collection of estimators whose performance is to be assessed.

Having made these choices, we tell the computer to evaluate each estimator

for each sample and then to combine these evaluations to see how well each estimator performs in each situation. Although one might reasonably fear that it would be an inadequate measure, experimental samplers have found that the estimated variance of the sample of simulated estimates is a satisfactory description of variability, at least for estimators that perform relatively well across a variety of situations or distributions. If variance should turn out not to be an appropriate measure, then we can use the detail of the empirical distribution to adopt some more sophisticated measure of variability or loss.

Our experimental-sampling results are thus the entries in a table of variances for pairings of one estimator with one distribution or of an estimator with one situation. We offer these comments on this approach:

1. Although our results are only for a particular collection of N samples of size n for each situation, N is very large and we look at diverse situations, and so we may have a very effective comparison.
2. Our results are for only a few situations. Unless they have been chosen carefully, they will not adequately represent the situations where we plan to apply the estimator.
3. We have to be as ingenious as we can in choosing the estimators to be studied. If we omit all the good ones, we may never know what estimator we ought to use. (New techniques of "configural polysampling," not discussed here, can overcome this difficulty.)

Subject to these limitations and to the variability inevitable in an assessment by sampling, this approach gives firm, specific results. If we fail to choose appropriately diversified situations or to include good enough estimators, we may be misled.

Collective Asymptotics

The flavor of asymptotic approaches is different, emphasizing mathematical theorems and limits as the sample size n approaches infinity. Although individual asymptotics deals with only one distribution at a time, collective asymptotics produces results applying to all distributions whose "distance" from some basic standard distribution is small. The collective approach has led to useful precise notions and, particularly in the hands of Peter Huber and Frank Hampel, to deep insights about the estimators to include in any competition. The reader may wonder about difficulties because:

1. Its results are stated in terms of $n \to \infty$.
2. Treating computationally simple estimators such as the one-step w-estimators is not as simple as treating the completely iterated M-estimators.

(As long as computation is inexpensive, this need not trouble us because the M-estimators are at least as good as the w-estimators.)
3. Results typically apply either to rather narrow neighborhoods (in the space of distributions) or to rather broad neighborhoods whose shapes may not reflect those of the real distributions about which we care.

If the answers for n between 10 and 50, say, differ from those we would use for large n, an asymptotic "as $n \to \infty$" approach can still be useful. It merely calls upon us to be extra careful. In choosing the details of how things are set up, we must concentrate on the sample size we plan to use and not just on n very large. Then we can go on to the usual process—do $n \to \infty$, use the result for the finite n in which we are interested, and hope the approximation is good enough. It often is, down to $n = 20$ and sometimes beyond.

The major argument for this approach is that we get results for "*all* distributions close to the standard," so that we do not have any local "holes" in our coverage. The corresponding counterargument is that we may use too small a distance and cover too little, or we may use too large a distance and cover situations we do not want to cover. Still, no method is likely to be perfect.

Whichever approach we use, we want to confine our efforts to gain high relative performance for those distributions and situations that resemble those we might find in practice. If we get good performance for other situations as a consequence, well and good. But to demand it elsewhere is, almost inevitably, to lose quality of performance where we do want it.

REFERENCE

Huber, P. J. (1981). *Robust Statistics*. New York: Wiley.

Additional Literature

Bickel, P. J. (1976). "Another look at robustness: a review of reviews and some new developments (with discussion)," *Scandinavian Journal of Statistics*, 3, 145–168.

Relles, D. A. and Rogers, W. H. (1977). "Statisticians are fairly robust estimators of location," *Journal of the American Statistical Association*, 72, 107–111.

Tukey, J. W. (1979). "Study of robustness by simulation: particularly improvement by adjustment and combination." In R. L. Launer and G. N. Wilkinson (Eds.), *Robustness in Statistics*. New York: Academic, pp. 75–102.

CHAPTER 10

Comparing Location Estimators: Trimmed Means, Medians, and Trimean

James L. Rosenberger
Pennsylvania State University

Miriam Gasko
University of Chicago

The sample mean is the most common summary statistic of a batch of data. When the data come from a symmetric distribution, the mean gives an estimate of the location of the center of that distribution. Other simple estimators, such as the median, also do this. How should we choose among them? We prefer estimation procedures (estimators) that perform well for the conditions actually underlying the data. Theory gives us estimators that are best for particular narrowly specified conditions, such as the sample mean for the Gaussian distribution. In practice, however, we never know the underlying conditions precisely, if only because of possible disturbances in the data. Thus we seek estimators that perform well for a variety of underlying conditions.

In this chapter we discuss simple estimators of the location of a symmetric distribution. At this stage, we emphasize symmetry because it brings simplicity and clarity to an analysis, because theoretical work often relies on it, and, especially, because it is clear that the center of symmetry best describes the distribution's location. We elaborate this heuristic argument by showing the equivalence of the mean, median, and center of symmetry for symmetric distributions. A class of estimators, called L-estimators, is defined as linear combinations of the order statistics. This class includes the

sample mean, median, and trimmed means as special cases. Lack of precise knowledge about the true underlying conditions leads us to consider various alternative symmetric shapes for the assumed underlying distribution.

The alternative distributions considered here vary from neutral-tailed (Gaussian) to very heavy-tailed (slash and Cauchy). We evaluate the performance of these *L*-estimators for the set of distributions considered. The ratio of variance of the best estimator for a given distribution to the variance of a given estimator provides a measure of the efficiency of the estimator. An estimator with high efficiency for a broad class of distributions has robustness of efficiency. Robustness guarantees that an estimator is good for a collection of distributions without necessarily being best for any particular one.

In addition to choosing a robust estimator, we discuss whether a subset of perhaps two or three alternative distributions would provide sufficient guidance for selecting a good estimator.

Chapter 11 considers more complicated procedures for estimating location. Those estimators are more robust and efficient than the estimators considered here, but they require more extensive calculations.

10A. MAIN CONCEPTS

A location parameter indexes a family of distributions of fixed shape in the following sense: where the corresponding probability density functions all have the same shape and width but are shifted relative to each other, a parameter that specifies the shift of a specific one serves as a location parameter.* For example, the density of the Gaussian distribution with mean θ and variance σ^2 is given by

$$f(x; \theta, \sigma) = \frac{1}{\sqrt{2\pi}\,\sigma} e^{-(x-\theta)^2/(2\sigma^2)} \qquad \begin{array}{l} \sigma > 0, \; -\infty < \theta < \infty, \\ -\infty < x < \infty. \end{array} \qquad (1)$$

Graphs of $f(x; \theta, \sigma)$ for $\sigma = 1$ and three values of θ appear in Figure 10-1. We see that all three graphs have the same shape and are simply translations of each other, so that θ is a location parameter.

Notice that, in particular, the density (1) can be written as $h(y; \sigma)$, which eliminates dependence on θ by taking $y = x - \theta$:

$$h(y; \sigma) = \frac{1}{\sqrt{2\pi}\,\sigma} e^{-y^2/2\sigma^2} \qquad \sigma > 0, \; -\infty < y < \infty. \qquad (2)$$

*A parameter that measures the shift of one distribution in a family relative to another is sometimes called a *slippage* parameter.

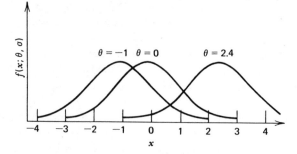

Figure 10-1. Density functions for Gaussian distributions with $\sigma = 1$ and three values of θ.

Formally, a location parameter is defined as follows:

DEFINITION: *Location parameter.* Let $f(x; \theta, \lambda)$ be the density function of a random variable X. The parameter θ is a *location parameter* if the density $f(x; \theta, \lambda)$ can be written as a function of $x - \theta$; that is, $f(x; \theta, \lambda) = h(x - \theta; \lambda)$ for some function $h(\cdot; \lambda)$, and $h(\cdot; \lambda)$ does not depend on θ.

From this definition of a location parameter, it follows immediately that θ is a location parameter for a random variable X if the distribution of $X - \theta$ does not depend on θ.

Although the center of a symmetric distribution is often a convenient location parameter, other quantities can determine a distribution's location. For example, the upper inflection point of a Gaussian density function specifies the location of the distribution. Denoting this location parameter by η, the density function is

$$g(x; \eta, \sigma) = \frac{1}{\sqrt{2\pi}\,\sigma} e^{-(1/2)[(x-\eta+\sigma)/\sigma]^2}.$$

Letting $y = x - \eta$, the function $g(x; \eta, \sigma)$ takes the form $h(y; \sigma)$. Thus η is a location parameter; it differs from the center of symmetry θ by a shift of size σ; that is, $\eta = \theta + \sigma$.

Symmetric Distributions

Visually, the graph of the density of a symmetric distribution has a symmetric shape. Figure 10-1 illustrates that the Gaussian distribution is

symmetric around θ, and from equation (1) it is immediate that the random variables $X - \theta$ and $-(X - \theta)$ are identically distributed.

DEFINITION: *Symmetric distribution.* The distribution of a random variable X is *symmetric* around the center of symmetry c if the random variables $X - c$ and $-(X - c)$ are identically distributed.

We explore the relationship between the center of symmetry and two other location parameters of symmetric distributions: the mean and the median. The median of a Gaussian distribution is equal to its mean and, as we saw above, is the center of symmetry. In the following lemma we show that for every symmetric distribution with a finite mean, the mean, median, and center of symmetry coincide. When the mean of a symmetric distribution is not finite, it is still true that both the center of symmetry and the median coincide.

By the definition of a symmetric distribution,

$$F_{X-c}(\cdot) = F_{-(X-c)}(\cdot), \tag{3}$$

where $F_X(\cdot)$ is the cumulative distribution function of the random variable X. The *median* of a random variable X is a value $x_{.5}$ that satisfies

$$P\{X < x_{.5}\} \leq \tfrac{1}{2} \leq P\{X \leq x_{.5}\}. \tag{4}$$

LEMMA 1: Let X be a random variable with distribution symmetric around c, with mean EX and median $x_{.5}$. Then $c = x_{.5}$ and if EX is finite, then $c = x_{.5} = EX$.

PROOF: We first show that $c = x_{.5}$. By definition,

$$F_{X-c}(y) = P\{X - c \leq y\} = P\{X \leq c + y\}.$$

From symmetry, equation (3) can be written

$$F_{X-c}(y) = F_{-(X-c)}(y) = P\{c - X \leq y\}$$

$$= P\{-X \leq y - c\} = P\{X \geq c - y\}.$$

But

$$P\{X \geq c - y\} = 1 - P\{X < c - y\}.$$

Therefore

$$P\{X \leq c + y\} + P\{X < c - y\} = 1$$

holds for all y and must therefore be true for $y = 0$, yielding $P\{X \leqslant c\} + P\{X < c\} = 1$. Since $P\{X \leqslant c\} \geqslant P\{X < c\}$, this implies both that $2P\{X \leqslant c\} \geqslant 1$ and $2P\{X < c\} \leqslant 1$, or equivalently

$$P\{X < c\} \leqslant \tfrac{1}{2} \leqslant P\{X \leqslant c\}.$$

Therefore the center of symmetry, c, is the median $x_{.5}$ from equation (4) above.

We now show that if EX is finite, then $c = EX$. By symmetry, the random variables $X - c$ and $-(X - c)$ are identically distributed and, in particular, their expected values are equal. Thus since

$$E(X - c) = EX - c$$

and

$$E[-(X - c)] = -EX + c,$$

if EX is finite, then $EX - c = -EX + c$ implies $EX = c$.

Lemma 1 provides a threefold heuristic basis for defining the location parameter of a symmetric distribution as its mean, median, and center of symmetry. Lemma 1 both enriches the meaning of location parameter for symmetric distributions and provides a starting point in the search for its robust estimator among the analogous sample statistics.

Asymmetric distributions do not have a "natural" location parameter with the same threefold interpretation as the center of symmetry of a symmetric distribution. A location parameter may describe an endpoint of the range of an asymmetric distribution as in the gamma and exponential distributions. Sometimes the location parameter may be a central value, but it will not, in general, coincide with either the mean or the median, which are different for an asymmetric distribution. The mean and the median describe the center of gravity and the center of probability, respectively, of the distribution.

When dealing with an underlying asymmetric distribution, the data analyst must determine the appropriate quantities to estimate for the problem at hand. In many settings, a transformation of the data produces sufficient symmetry in the transformed scale to justify proceeding in the same way as if the re-expressed data had come from a symmetric distribution.

Robustness

On the rare occasion when the data analyst is fortunate enough to know a mathematical formula that describes the underlying distribution—or is

willing to act as if such a distribution were known exactly—the location estimator that optimizes some chosen criterion can often be determined. The purpose of this chapter, on the other hand, is to select a simple procedure that behaves well for a variety of possible underlying distributions. Restricting the allowable distributions to be symmetric is not sufficient to determine a generally best procedure. We demonstrate that the best estimate of location for neutral-tailed distributions such as the Gaussian is not good for a heavy-tailed distribution like the slash (or the Cauchy).

When estimating the location of a Gaussian or normal distribution, the sample mean is well known to be the best estimator according to many criteria. However, the Gaussian model is not appropriate for many situations. For instance, frequently a few large errors infect the data so that the tails of the underlying distribution are heavier than those of the Gaussian distribution. In this situation, the sample mean is no longer a good estimate for the center of symmetry because all the sample observations contribute equally to the value of the mean; estimators that attach less emphasis to extreme values do better. Both the slash and Cauchy distributions have heavy tails, and the sample median is a much better estimator for their location than is the sample mean. However, although the sample median is determined by ranking all the observations, only one or two of the central observations provide its numerical value. Therefore, it neglects some of the information contained in the sample. The median also responds sharply to the presence of small errors in the centermost observations that may result from rounding or grouping. The effect of such errors diminishes when an estimator averages over several observations.

A robust estimator should be relatively insensitive to at least two types of anomalies encountered in sampling:

A few large deviations in the data, often thought of as outliers; and
Many rather small deviations in the data (rather small, but large enough to be at least comparable with the spacing between adjacent ordered observations), for example, as a result of rounding or grouping.

The above discussion about possible deficiencies of the sample mean and median suggests looking for a robust location estimator among those that utilize the values in a central part of the ordered observations.

Order Statistics

The order statistics of a sample are the observations rearranged in order of increasing magnitude. For example, the order statistics of the sample $(3, 0, -7, 2)$ are $(-7, 0, 2, 3)$.

TABLE 10-1.   **Twenty samples of size three, each drawn from a standard Gaussian distribution, and their order statistics.**

Sample Number	Unordered Sample			Ordered Sample		
	x_1	x_2	x_3	$x_{(1)}$	$x_{(2)}$	$x_{(3)}$
1	−0.73	−1.60	−1.04	−1.60	−1.04	−0.73
2	−0.28	1.93	−1.19	−1.19	−0.28	1.93
3	−0.16	1.54	−0.01	−0.16	−0.01	1.54
4	−0.34	−1.47	0.17	−1.47	−0.34	0.17
5	0.30	−0.49	0.18	−0.49	0.18	0.30
6	−1.33	2.05	1.53	−1.33	1.53	2.06
7	0.60	0.28	2.01	0.28	0.60	2.01
8	1.24	−0.64	0.89	−0.64	0.89	1.24
9	0.69	0.14	−0.99	−0.99	0.14	0.69
10	0.45	−0.64	−0.15	−0.64	−0.15	0.45
11	−0.32	−0.05	0.01	−0.32	−0.05	0.01
12	1.24	0.34	0.57	0.34	0.57	1.24
13	−1.63	−1.88	0.00	−1.88	−1.63	0.00
14	−0.69	0.01	−1.99	−1.99	−0.69	0.01
15	0.54	−1.30	−0.86	−1.30	−0.86	0.54
16	−0.01	0.52	−1.48	−1.48	−0.01	0.52
17	0.33	1.55	−0.02	−0.02	0.33	1.55
18	−0.70	1.91	0.12	−0.70	0.12	1.91
19	1.76	0.27	−0.01	−0.01	0.27	1.76
20	−0.02	0.47	−0.36	−0.36	−0.02	0.47
average	0.05	0.15	−0.13	−0.80	−0.02	0.88
variance	0.73	1.46	0.93	0.50	0.49	0.69

DEFINITION: *Order statistics.*   Let $X_1, X_2, \ldots, X_n$ be a sample of size n. The observations rearranged in ascending order of magnitude, denoted by $X_{(1)} \leqslant X_{(2)} \leqslant \cdots \leqslant X_{(n)}$, are called the *order statistics* of the sample, and $X_{(i)}$ is called the *ith order statistic*.

When we want to be explicit about the sample size, the notation $X_{i|n}$ denotes the ith order statistic.

In the following simple example, we demonstrate some features of the order statistics that are not shared by the unordered observations. Specifically, we look at means, variances, and correlation coefficients. These features motivate the use of order statistics in constructing location estimates.

TABLE 10-2. Correlation coefficients of ordered and unordered observations in the 20 samples of size three from the Gaussian distribution presented in Table 10-1.

Observations	Unordered Observations	Order Statistics
First and second	−.026	.532
First and third	.098	.497
Second and third	.132	.643

Table 10-1 shows 20 samples, each of size three, from a Gaussian distribution with mean 0 and variance 1 and the corresponding order statistics. The last two rows of the table contain averages and variances of the unordered and ordered observations. Table 10-2 shows, for the 20 samples of three, the correlation coefficients for pairs of observations from the original sample and for pairs of order statistics.

Some Features of Order Statistics

From the data in Tables 10-1 and 10-2 describing averages, variances, and correlation coefficients of unordered observations and order statistics, we compare the following:

Average values of the unordered observations and the average values of the order statistics

Variances of the unordered observations and the variances of the order statistics

Correlation coefficients between unordered observations and the correlation coefficients between the ordered observations.

Average Values

In the original unordered samples, the average values (over the 20 samples) of the three observations are $\bar{x}_1 = 0.05$, $\bar{x}_2 = 0.15$, and $\bar{x}_3 = -0.13$, numbers close to zero, the true population mean, with no apparent structure among them. The average values (over the 20 samples) of the order statistics are $\bar{x}_{(1)} = -0.80$, $\bar{x}_{(2)} = -0.02$, and $\bar{x}_{(3)} = 0.88$. These values are in increasing order of magnitude and close to the theoretical averages of the three order statistics from the Gaussian: namely, -0.846, 0.0, and 0.846 (Harter, 1970, p. 426).

Variances

The sample variances of the unordered observations are $s_1^2 = 0.73$, $s_2^2 = 1.46$, and $s_3^2 = 0.93$, again close to the population values of 1.00. The sample variances of the order statistics are $s_{(1)}^2 = 0.50$, $s_{(2)}^2 = 0.49$, and $s_{(3)}^2 = 0.69$, all smaller than those for the unordered observations. The smaller observed variability of the order statistics reflects the fact that an order statistic is less variable than a random observation. The theoretical variances of the three order statistics for a Gaussian sample of three are 0.559, 0.449, and 0.559 (Sarhan and Greenberg, 1956).

Correlations

From Table 10-2 we see that the sample correlation coefficients between pairs of unordered observations are close to 0. This is their theoretical value because the observations in a random sample are independent and hence uncorrelated. However, the sample correlation coefficients between the pairs of order statistics are .532, .497, and .643, very different from 0. The theoretical values of these correlations are .550, .329, and .550. Ordering the observations introduces correlations between the results. We have to keep this correlation in mind when we evaluate variances of estimators that are functions of the order statistics.

In the last example we observed a symmetry between the first and last (the third) order statistics. They are similar in magnitude but of opposite sign. Theoretically they are symmetric around 0, the center of symmetry of the underlying Gaussian distribution. This feature of symmetry is a special case of a more general distributional property of order statistics at equal depths from the extremes of a sample from a symmetric distribution. This property is described formally as follows:

Let $X_{(1)} \leqslant X_{(2)} \leqslant \cdots \leqslant X_{(n)}$ be the order statistics of a sample of size n from a distribution symmetric around θ. The distributions of order statistics at equal depths from the extreme, say of $X_{(i)}$ and $X_{(n+1-i)}$, denoted by $F_{(i)}(\cdot)$ and $F_{(n+1-i)}(\cdot)$, respectively, are mirror images of each other around θ; that is,

$$F_{(i)}(\theta - x) = 1 - F_{(n+1-i)}(\theta + x) \qquad \text{for all } x. \qquad (5)$$

Figure 10-2 depicts the density functions of the two order statistics at depth i from the extremes and demonstrates the result of equation (5). We use this property to save calculation when we evaluate the variances of estimators that are functions of the order statistics. We consider here only linear combinations of the order statistics with symmetric weights. For symmetric

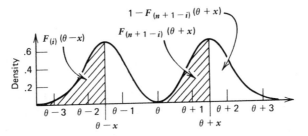

Figure 10-2. Density functions of the ith and $(n + 1 - i)$th order statistics. Shading indicates the cumulative distribution at points symmetric about θ, the center of symmetry. (Plot gives the densities of the extreme order statistics in samples of $n = 10$ from a Gaussian distribution with mean θ and $\sigma = 1$.)

distributions, the best linear combinations of order statistics fall within this class (Lloyd, 1952).

10B.   SIMPLE L-ESTIMATORS

We introduce several estimation procedures for the center of a symmetric distribution. Later we find the most robust estimator among these procedures for collections of distributions that vary in their elongation from neutral-tailed to heavy-tailed.

In the discussion of robustness, we motivated the use of functions of the order statistics rather than the unordered sample. Linear combinations of order statistics are called L-estimators. For example, the mean of a sample of size n is an L-estimator with all weights equal to $1/n$. The sample median is also an L-estimator, with all but one or two of the coefficients equal to 0.

DEFINITION: *L-estimator.* Let $X_{(1)} \leqslant X_{(2)} \leqslant \cdots \leqslant X_{(n)}$ be the order statistics of a sample of size n. Let $a_1, a_2, \ldots, a_n$ be real numbers, $0 \leqslant a_i \leqslant 1$, $i = 1, \ldots, n$, such that $\sum_{i=1}^{n} a_i = 1$. An *L-estimator* T with weights $a_1, a_2, \ldots, a_n$ is

$$T = \sum_{i=1}^{n} a_i X_{(i)}. \tag{6}$$

In Lemma 1 we showed that one location parameter of a symmetric distribution is the center of symmetry. This, combined with the corresponding symmetry properties of order statistics at equal depths from the ex-

TABLE 10-3.   Measurements of the passage time of light.
(Newcomb's measurements, recorded in millionths of
a second, are the given values times 10^{-3} plus 24.8.)

28	−44	29	30
26	27	22	23
33	16	24	29
24	40	21	31
34	−2	25	19

Source: Stephen M. Stigler (1977). "Do robust estimators work
with *real* data?" *Annals of Statistics*, **5**, 1055–1098 [data from Table
5 (Data Set 9), p. 1074].

tremes, leads us, when working on symmetric problems, to consider only
L-estimators with symmetric weights. Thus all estimators considered in this
chapter satisfy $a_i = a_{n+1-i}$, $i = 1,\ldots,n/2$ and therefore provide unbiased
estimates of θ, the center of symmetry. We note that the sample mean and
median have symmetric weights.

We will define a collection of simple *L*-estimators and illustrate their
computation on a set of nineteenth-century measurements of the speed of
light. Table 10-3 gives 20 observations from one of the experiments performed by Simon Newcomb in 1882 (see Stigler, 1977). A stem-and-leaf
display of these numbers (Figure 10-3) suggests the possibility of one or two
outliers. Otherwise, the data appear nearly symmetric.

Trimmed Means

The estimators considered in this chapter are almost exclusively trimmed
means. A trimmed mean is identified by the proportion that is trimmed off

$(-4 \mid 4 = -44.)$

```
−4 | 4
−3 |
−2 |
−1 |
−0 | 2
 0 |
 1 | 69
 2 | 12344567899
 3 | 0134
 4 | 0
```

Figure 10-3.   Stem-and-leaf display of Newcomb's data given in
Table 10-3. (Measurements in millionths of a second are the
given values times 10^{-3} plus 24.8.)

from each end of the ordered sample. Thus the 20%-trimmed mean of a sample of size 10 is the simple average of the six observations remaining after trimming off the two largest and two smallest observations.

The sample mean can be considered a 0%-trimmed mean, whereas the sample median is approximately a 50%-trimmed mean. We denote the trimmed mean with proportion α trimmed off each end by $T(\alpha)$.

EXAMPLES:

For Newcomb's data presented (in coded form) in Table 10-3, we compute the sample mean or 0%-trimmed mean, and the 5%, 10%, 20%, 30%, and 40%-trimmed means. The sample mean is

$$\overline{X} = T(0.0) = \frac{1}{20} \sum_{i=1}^{20} x_{(i)} = \frac{435}{20} = 21.75.$$

The trimmed means are:

$$T(.05) = \frac{1}{18} \sum_{i=2}^{19} x_{(i)} = \frac{439}{18} = 24.39$$

$$T(.10) = \frac{1}{16} \sum_{i=3}^{18} x_{(i)} = \frac{407}{16} = 25.44$$

$$T(.20) = \frac{1}{12} \sum_{i=5}^{16} x_{(i)} = \frac{308}{12} = 25.67$$

$$T(.30) = \frac{1}{8} \sum_{i=7}^{14} x_{(i)} = \frac{206}{8} = 25.75$$

$$T(.40) = \frac{1}{4} \sum_{i=9}^{12} x_{(i)} = \frac{102}{4} = 25.50.$$

These results suggest the instability of the sample mean caused by the influence of the largest and smallest observations. For these data, after trimming at least 10% to remove the two smallest (and two largest) values, the trimmed means are very similar and, one hopes, very stable.

The estimates given here should not be compared with an assumed true value for this quantity, 33.02, which is based on the currently accepted speed of light (see Figure 10-4 and Stigler, 1977). Although the 20% to

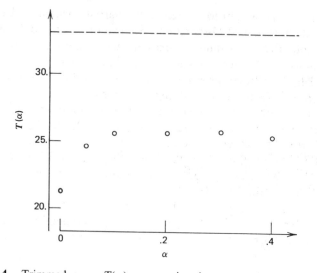

Figure 10-4. Trimmed mean $T(\alpha)$ versus trimming proportion α for Newcomb's data. Dashed line indicates currently accepted true value. (Measurements in millionths of a second are the given values times 10^{-3} plus 24.8.)

30%-trimmed means are closest to this true value, a systematic bias apparently existed in the measurements of this early experiment.

The discrepancy between our estimates and the assumed "true value" relates to the calibration and design of the measurement instrument rather than to the estimation procedure. Youden (1972) clearly demonstrates the impact of systematic errors on measurement experiments. He cites 15 historical measurements of the Astronomical Unit (the mean distance between the earth and the sun) and the experimenters' estimates of their error bounds. Each estimate lies *outside* the previous experimenters' error bounds. Clearly the experimenters' measurement techniques included biases or sources of variation omitted from the calculation of the reported error bounds. This series of experiments illustrates that a set of measurements can be precise (cluster tightly about some value) without being accurate. Accuracy is characterized by the observations clustering tightly about the true value. Such apparent inconsistencies often reflect changes in definition, rather than measurement biases.

Sometimes, in order to obtain a specified amount of trimming exactly, we need to trim a fraction of an observation; for example, a 5%-trimmed mean from a sample of size 10 requires trimming half of each of the largest and smallest observations. We allow for trimming a fraction of an observation

by giving fractional weight to the remaining partially trimmed observations relative to the untrimmed observations. Some authors trim only an integer number of observations from each extreme, where the integer is either the largest that does not exceed αn or the smallest that is not less than αn. However, neither of these procedures behaves smoothly as α or n changes, and the former does not trim anything at all for αn less than 1.

Figure 10-5 demonstrates these procedures by plotting the proportion actually trimmed for sample sizes through $n = 20$ for the case when $\alpha = .25$. Figure 10-6 shows the actual proportion trimmed for $n = 20$ when α varies. Both figures show the lack of smoothness by including the straight line for the procedure that partially trims an observation when αn is not an integer. We now define this procedure.

Let $X_{(1)} \leqslant X_{(2)} \leqslant \cdots \leqslant X_{(n)}$ be the order statistics from a sample of size n. Let $g = [\alpha n]$ denote the greatest integer less than or equal to αn, $0 \leqslant \alpha < .5$, and let $r = \alpha n - g$ be the fractional part of αn.

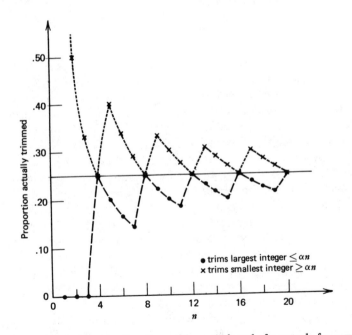

Figure 10-5. Proportion actually trimmed from each end of a sample for $n = 1(1)20$ and $\alpha = .25$ when using procedures that only trim the nearest integer number of observations.

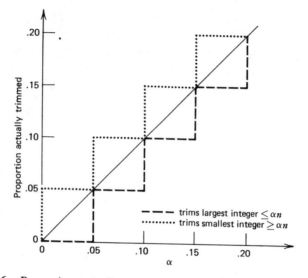

Figure 10-6. Proportion actually trimmed from each end for various trimming proportions α, for a sample of size 20, when using procedures that only trim the nearest integer number of observations.

DEFINITION: *α-trimmed mean.* The α-trimmed mean, denoted by $T(\alpha)$, is

$$T(\alpha) = \frac{1}{n(1-2\alpha)} \left\{ (1-r)\left[X_{(g+1)} + X_{(n-g)} \right] + \sum_{i=g+2}^{n-g-1} X_{(i)} \right\}. \quad (7)$$

Thus the α-trimmed mean is an L-estimator with weights a_i, $i = 1, \ldots, n$, given by

$$a_i = \begin{cases} 0 & \text{if } i \leq g \quad \text{or} \quad i \geq n - g + 1 \\ \dfrac{(1-r)}{n(1-2\alpha)} & \text{if } i = g + 1 \quad \text{or} \quad i = n - g \\ \dfrac{1}{n(1-2\alpha)} & \text{if } g + 2 \leq i \leq n - g - 1 \end{cases}$$

where $g = [\alpha n]$ and $r = \alpha n - g$.

Midmean

The average of the central half of the order statistics is called the midmean. This coincides exactly with the 25%-trimmed mean.

EXAMPLE:

We compute the midmean for Newcomb's data in Table 10-3. Since the sample size is 20, the midmean or $T(.25)$ is the average of the 10 central order statistics,

$$\text{midmean} = T(.25) = \frac{1}{10} \sum_{i=6}^{15.} x_{(i)} = \frac{257}{10} = 25.70.$$

Median

The median is an extremely simple L-estimator that puts 0 weight on all but the center one or two order statistics, depending on whether n is odd or even, respectively.

DEFINITION: *Median*. The median is the central order statistic for n odd, and the average of the central two order statistics for n even.

We denote the median by M. The median can be considered a variably trimmed mean with trimming proportion depending on n and equal to $\frac{1}{2} - 1/(2n)$.

Broadened Median

The broadened median attempts to preserve the resistance of the median to outliers while also achieving insensitivity to rounding and grouping of the observations. It accomplishes this by averaging the median and one or two neighboring order statistics on each side of the median. The exact number depends on n.

An example demonstrates the sensitivity of the sample median to rounding and grouping errors in the data. Blood pressure is often recorded to the nearest 5 mmHg although the underlying measured quantity varies continuously. For the ordered data

$$110, 115, 120, 120, 125, 130, 130, 135, 140$$

the median is 125 mmHg. However, if a single observation below 125 were instead above 125, the median would jump 5 mmHg to 130. This sensitivity to rounding and grouping can occur even for a much larger sample when using the median. The BMED for these data is the average of 120, 125, and 130, which is 125. Again moving a small value to a large one could cause at most a change in the BMED from 125 to the average of 125, 130, and 130,

which is $128\frac{1}{3}$. Thus the change in the BMED caused by this change in a single observation is $3\frac{1}{3}$ compared with a change of 5 for the median.

Thus the broadened median, suggested by Tukey (Andrews et al., 1972, p. 36), is primarily resistant to outliers and secondarily insensitive to rounding and grouping.

DEFINITION: *Broadened median.* For *n* odd, the *broadened median* is the average of the three central order statistics for $5 \leqslant n \leqslant 12$; the five central order statistics for $n \geqslant 13$. For *n* even, the broadened median is a weighted average of the central four order statistics for $5 \leqslant n \leqslant 12$ with weights $\frac{1}{6}, \frac{1}{3}, \frac{1}{3}$ and $\frac{1}{6}$; for $n \geqslant 13$, it is the weighted average of the central six order statistics with weights $\frac{1}{5}$ to the central four and weights $\frac{1}{10}$ to the end ones of the six.

We denote the broadened median by BMED. The broadened median can be thought of as a variably trimmed mean with trimming proportion

$$\left(.5 - \frac{1.5}{n}\right) \qquad \text{for } 5 \leqslant n \leqslant 12$$

and

$$\left(.5 - \frac{2.5}{n}\right) \qquad \text{for } n \geqslant 13.$$

For $n = 5$, BMED is a 20%-trimmed mean; for $n = 10$, a 35%-trimmed mean; for $n = 15$, a 33.3%-trim; and for $n = 20$, a 37.5%-trimmed mean.

EXAMPLE:

Again using the Newcomb data in Table 10-3, the median and broadened median estimates are:

median $= \frac{1}{2}(25 + 26) = 25.50$

BMED $= \frac{1}{10} \cdot 24 + \frac{1}{5}(24 + 25 + 26 + 27) + \frac{1}{10} \cdot 28 = 25.60.$

Trimean

Of the estimators considered here, only the trimean cannot be viewed as an example of a trimmed mean. We introduce it largely for its ease of calculation from the order statistics. The trimean is motivated by the desire to include sample information farther from the center by making use not

only of the median but also of a few additional order statistics, initially the
fourths along with the median.

DEFINITION: *Trimean.* Let F_L and F_U denote the lower and upper fourths
of the sample (approximately the quartiles). The trimean, denoted by TRI,
is TRI $= \frac{1}{4}(F_L + 2M + F_U)$.

EXAMPLE:

For Newcomb's data, displayed in Figure 10-2, we calculate the weighted
average of the median, with weight 0.5, and the fourths, each with weight
0.25. The sample median is 25.5, as shown earlier. The lower fourth is the
average of the fifth and sixth order statistics, here $\frac{1}{2}(21 + 22) = 21.50$; the
upper fourth is the average of the fifteenth and sixteenth order statistics,
here $\frac{1}{2}(29 + 30) = 29.5$. Thus the trimean is calculated as

$$\text{TRI} = \frac{1}{4}(21.5 + 29.5) + \frac{1}{2}(25.5) = 25.50.$$

In Table 10-4, we summarize the collection of estimates for Newcomb's
data presented in Table 10-3. After trimming off 10 to 20% of the data, the
estimates remain fairly constant. Figure 10-7 displays the estimates (except

**TABLE 10-4.   Summary of estimates for
Newcomb's data.**

Estimator[a]		Estimate
Mean	(0.0)	21.75
$T(.05)$		24.39
$T(.10)$		25.44
$T(.20)$		25.67
Midmean	(.25)	25.70
$T(.30)$		25.75
BMED	(.375)	25.60
$T(.40)$		25.50
Median	($\geqslant .45$)	25.50
Trimean		25.50

[a]For estimators that belong to the class
of trimmed means, the number in
parentheses is the trimming proportion,
which depends on n for the median and
broadened median (BMED).

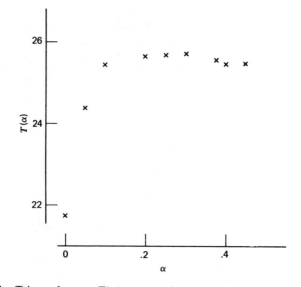

Figure 10-7. Trimmed mean $T(\alpha)$ versus trimming proportion α for Newcomb's measurements of the passage time of light. (Measurements in millionths of a second are the given values times 10^{-3} plus 24.8.)

for the trimean) plotted against the trimming proportion. Although all the estimates are less than the presently accepted value of 33.02 as stated earlier, this appears to be due to some systematic bias in the experiment, not to the choice of these estimators.

Variance of *L*-Estimators

From the definition of an *L*-estimator in equation (6), it follows that we can express its variance as a function of the weights a_i associated with the order statistics $X_{(i)}$, $i = 1, 2, \ldots, n$, and of the covariances between pairs of order statistics, as follows:

$$\text{var}\left[\sum_{i=1}^{n} a_i X_{(i)}\right] = \sum_{i=1}^{n} \sum_{j=1}^{n} a_i a_j \text{cov}\left[X_{(i)}, X_{(j)}\right]. \tag{8}$$

We need only know the variances and covariances of order statistics from the distribution. From the symmetry property of the distributions of order statistics at equal depths from the extremes for symmetric distributions, it follows that

$$\text{var}\left[X_{(i)}\right] = \text{var}\left[X_{(n+1-i)}\right], \qquad i = 1, 2, \ldots, \frac{n}{2},$$

and for $i \neq j$,

$$\text{cov}\left[X_{(i)}, X_{(j)}\right] = \text{cov}\left[X_{(n+1-i)}, X_{(n+1-j)}\right].$$

These identities, together with the symmetric weights ($a_i = a_{n+1-i}$, $i = 1, 2, \ldots, n/2$), simplify the computation of the variances of these estimators.

In summary, our choice of simple estimators for the location parameter of a symmetric distribution includes the following estimators: mean, 5%, 10%, 20%, 30%, and 40%-trimmed means, midmean, trimean, median, and broadened median.

In Chapter 11 we consider additional estimators called M-estimators, derived by minimizing various objective functions. These are usually more complicated to compute than the estimators described here because iterative procedures are involved. Hogg (1974) reviews other complex location estimators. Some, called adaptive estimators, use the sample itself to choose the estimation procedure; for example, some "adaptive trimmed means" determine the amount of trimming according to a sample estimate of the tail heaviness of the underlying distribution, whereas others attempt to minimize the estimated variance of the estimator.

10C. DISTRIBUTIONS

Various distributions and sampling situations have been suggested to represent the shape of the underlying sampled population. Ordinarily, the exact shape is simply not known. Occasionally, we believe that a Gaussian distribution adequately describes the idealized population; but, for various reasons, the actual data may have extreme observations occurring with a frequency many times that expected from a Gaussian. Thus even when a neutral-tailed distribution like the Gaussian might have been thought, in advance, to be the correct model, a more elongated distribution may more appropriately describe the data if large errors are possible.

We consider seven alternative distributions or situations that vary in shape and in tail weight from neutral-tailed (Gaussian) to stretch-tailed (Cauchy). We hope that these distributions span the range of reasonable situations. Our objective is to choose a location estimator from among the estimators introduced in Section 10B that is robust for subsets of these distributional situations. This approach will give the data analyst a basis for selecting a simple location estimator when only vague information about the underlying distribution of the data is available.

Five distributions considered in this chapter are: the Gaussian, logistic, double exponential, slash, and Cauchy. The distribution functions are given in Exercise 3. The slash distribution is defined by a standard Gaussian random variable divided by an independent uniform random variable on the interval $(0, 1)$. In addition, we consider two sampling situations called 1-wider situations, where $n - 1$ observations come from a standard Gaussian distribution [Gau(0, 1)] and one observation comes from a Gaussian with variance 9 or 100 [Gau(0, 9) or Gau(0, 100), respectively].

The arguments that suggest the usefulness of the Gaussian shape are more potent in the center of a distribution than in the tails. Thus we feel inclined to focus on distributions that are "Gaussian in the middle," such as the logistic and slash. However, we also give results for some distributions that do not have this property, for example, the double exponential and Cauchy, not because we think they are realistic, but because other studies have frequently used them or because they are especially tractable. In summarizing, we focus on those that seem most nearly realistic.

Some readers may be more interested in an overall choice of robust estimator than in the details of how the estimators we are studying perform at the individual distributions and situations. The summary in Section 10E presents our conclusions.

Comparison of 1-Wider Situations and Mixtures of Normal Distributions

The robustness literature has utilized both the 1-wider sampling situation (David et al., 1977) and mixtures of Gaussian distributions called contaminated normal distributions (Gastwirth and Cohen, 1970) as models for robustness studies. Both models combine observations from the standard Gaussian and a small fraction from a Gaussian with a larger standard deviation, say $K = 3$ or 10 times as large. Since the 1-wider situation takes exactly one observation from the wider Gaussian for each n observations in the sample, sampling from a single univariate distribution function cannot represent such observations. The contaminated normal distribution, however, represents a mixture of observations taken from a standard Gaussian with probability $1 - \alpha$ and from the wider Gaussian (with scale K and the same center) with probability α. The distribution function for such a contaminated normal distribution, denoted by CN(α; K), is

$$F(x) = (1 - \alpha)\Phi(x) + \alpha\Phi\left(\frac{x}{K}\right)$$

where $\Phi(x)$ is the cumulative distribution function for the standard Gaussian.

TABLE 10-5.   Means and variances of the three largest order statistics from the 1-wider situation (David et al., 1977) and the contaminated normal (CN) distribution (Gastwirth and Cohen, 1970).[a]

$n = 10$	CN ($\gamma = .10, K = 3$)		1-wider ($K = 3$)[b]	
	Mean	Variance	Mean	Variance
$X_{10\mid10}$	2.0647	1.7448	2.1036	1.7728
$X_{9\mid10}$	1.1423	.3857	1.1159	.2932
$X_{8\mid10}$	.7216	.2287	.7144	.2124

$n = 20$	CN ($\gamma = .05, K = 3$)		1-wider ($K = 3$)[b]	
	Mean	Variance	Mean	Variance
$X_{20\mid20}$	2.3211	1.4401	2.3535	1.4622
$X_{19\mid20}$	1.5319	.2819	1.5119	.2135
$X_{18\mid20}$	1.1983	.1568	1.1929	.1449

[a]Underlining indicates whether CN or 1-wider has larger mean and variance.
[b]Often specified as "one-out."

Arguments exist for the realism of both models. If data arise from a fixed number of sources (for example, from n laboratories, n technicians, or n machines producing a product), then the 1-wider model seems appropriate to represent one source with greater variance. In situations where the outliers occur from unstructured phenomena such as random keypunch errors, the contaminated normal model may seem more compelling.

Another way to look at the comparison is more rewarding. The mixture distributions are themselves mixtures of J-wider situations, where J follows a binomial distribution. For $n = 20$ and $\alpha = .05$, for example:

$$\text{prob}\{J = 0\} = (.95)^{20} = 35.8\%$$

$$\text{prob}\{J = 1\} = (.95)^{19}(.05)20 = 37.7\%$$

$$\text{prob}\{J \geqslant 2\} = \text{rest} = 26.4\%.$$

Experience indicates that 2-wider or more-wider situations are not as challenging as 1-wider ones. And the none-wider situation is not at

all challenging. Thus the mixture situation is less than 65% made up of challenging *J*-wider situations, which do not themselves average as challenging as the 1-wider situation. In some very real sense then, mixture situations are only a fraction as challenging as 1-wider ones.

Table 10-5 compares the expectations and variances of the 1-wider situation for $n = 20$ and $n = 10$ with scale $K = 3$ for the wider Gaussian and the corresponding mixture with 5% and 10% contamination from a Gaussian distribution with scale $K = 3$. The extreme (largest) order statistic in the 1-wider situation has larger expectation and variance than that of the contaminated normal. However, the second and third largest order statistics of the 1-wider situation have smaller means and variances than those of the contaminated normal.

The trimmed mean that has the smallest variance for a given sampling situation is called the "best trim" or "optrim." Comparing the best trimmed mean for the contaminated normal distribution with that for the 1-wider situation shows that the contaminated normal requires more trimming and results in higher variance (see Table 10-6) than the 1-wider situation.

TABLE 10-6. Variances of trimmed means for the 1-wider situation and the contaminated normal (CN) distribution.

	$n = 10$	
Estimator	CN ($\gamma = .10, K = 3$)	1-Wider ($K = 3$)[a]
Mean	.1800	.1800
$T(.10)$	.1384	.1296
$T(.20)$	.1379	.1339
$T(.30)$	.1468	.1438
Best trim	.1364	.1295
(Trim %)	(16.1%)	(13.3%)

	$n = 20$	
Estimator	CN ($\gamma = .05, K = 3$)	1-Wider ($K = 3$)[a]
Mean	.07000	.07000
$T(.05)$	.05943	.05782
$T(.10)$	.05891	.05827
$T(.20)$	.06198	.06164
$T(.30)$	.06706	.06677
Best trim	.05881	.05776
(Trim %)	(8.7%)	(6.4%)

[a]Often specified as "one-out."

Although this suggests that the contaminated normal model provides a stiffer challenge for trimmed means, other arguments indicate the opposite. The measure of efficiency defined in Section 10D shows that the mean and the 20% and 30% trimmed means for samples from the 1-wider situation result in lower efficiency than those from the contaminated normal mixture.

Because the differences between these models appear small, in this chapter we use the mixture distributions to compare percentiles, which are not defined for the 1-wider situations, and we use the 1-wider situation for the robustness studies because order-statistic covariances are readily available for it (David et al., 1977).

Comparison of Tail Length

To understand the tail length of the distributions, we compare their percentiles with those of other known distributions. This comparison is meaningless, however, without some method of first matching or equating the scales of the various distributions. There are several alternatives.

Central-density matching requires each distribution to be scaled such that the density function at the center of location is equal to a fixed constant, say that of the standard Gaussian; that is, $f(x; \theta, \lambda) = 1/\sqrt{2\pi}$ at $x = \theta$, where $f(x; \theta, \lambda)$ is the density function of the distribution with location θ and

TABLE 10-7. Percentiles of distributions scaled for central-density matching.

Distribution[a]	50	$50 + \varepsilon$[b]	60	75	90	95	98	99	99.9	99.99
Gaussian	0	(.251)	.253	.674	1.28	1.64	2.05	2.33	3.09	3.72
Logistic	0	(.251)	.254	.688	1.38	1.85	2.44	2.88	4.33	5.77
CN(.05; 3)	0	(.251)	.253	.677	1.31	1.72	2.26	2.82	5.96	8.34
CN(.10; 3)	0	(.251)	.254	.681	1.34	1.80	2.60	3.60	6.51	8.65
CN(.20; 3)	0	(.251)	.254	.688	1.41	2.06	3.34	4.28	6.70	8.55
D-Exp.	0	(.251)	.280	.869	2.02	2.89	4.03	4.90	7.79	10.7
CN(.05; 10)	0	(.251)	.254	.680	1.33	1.79	2.93	8.04	19.6	27.5
CN(.10; 10)	0	(.251)	.254	.686	1.40	2.11	7.66	11.7	21.2	28.1
CN(.20; 10)	0	(.251)	.255	.702	1.68	5.53	10.5	13.5	21.1	27.0
Slash	0	(.251)	.256	.735	2.00	3.99	9.97	19.9	199.	1995.
Cauchy	0	(.251)	.259	.798	2.46	5.04	12.7	25.4	254.	2540.

(Header spanning 60 through 99.99: **Percent**)

[a]Ordered by a sum of percentiles: the 90th, 95th, and 99th percentiles have weight 1 and the 99.9th percentile has weight 1/20. CN(α; K) is the contaminated normal mixture having proportion α of Gaussian with scale K times that of the remaining Gaussian.

[b](50 + ε)th percentile is near $(\varepsilon/10) \times$ (entry) = .0251ε.

scale λ (Rogers and Tukey, 1972). This corresponds to matching the $(50 \pm \varepsilon)$th percentiles for $\varepsilon \to 0$.

Quartile matching is achieved by choosing the scale parameter λ for each distribution such that the quartiles (25th and 75th percentiles) of the distributions, and therefore the interquartile range, match those of the standard Gaussian. The matched distributions then all have 75th percentiles equal to .6745, the upper quartile of the standard Gaussian.

Tables 10-7 and 10-8 present various percentiles (50, 50 + ε, 60, 75, 90, 95, 98, 99, 99.9, 99.99) of the distributions described above. In Table 10-7 matching is by equating the central density, in Table 10-8 by equating the quartiles.

The percentiles in Tables 10-7 and 10-8 show the relative tail length of the distributions, ordered arbitrarily in the table by a sum of percentiles. The distributions range from the neutral tails of the Gaussian to the heavy tails of the slash and Cauchy. The logistic, double exponential, and contaminated normal distributions are all intermediate as seen by the ordering and the size of the percentiles in Tables 10-7 and 10-8.

Matching could be based on other percentiles or on other measures of spread that depend only on the central portion of the density. Using

TABLE 10-8.   Percentiles of distributions scaled for quartile matching.

Distribution[a]	50	50 + ε[b]	60	75	90	95	98	99	99.9	99.99
Gaussian	0	(.251)	.253	.674	1.28	1.64	2.05	2.33	3.09	3.72
Logistic	0	(.246)	.249	.674	1.35	1.81	2.39	2.82	4.24	5.65
CN(.05; 3)	0	(.249)	.252	.674	1.30	1.71	2.25	2.80	5.93	8.30
CN(.10; 3)	0	(.248)	.251	.674	1.32	1.79	2.58	3.56	6.45	8.57
CN(.20; 3)	0	(.246)	.249	.674	1.38	2.01	3.27	4.19	6.56	8.36
D-Exp.	0	(.195)	.217	.674	1.57	2.24	3.13	3.81	6.05	8.29
CN(.05; 10)	0	(.249)	.252	.674	1.32	1.78	2.91	7.98	19.5	27.2
CN(.10; 10)	0	(.246)	.250	.674	1.37	2.08	7.53	11.5	20.8	27.5
CN(.20; 10)	0	(.241)	.245	.674	1.61	5.31	10.1	13.0	20.3	25.9
Slash	0	(.230)	.235	.674	1.83	3.66	9.15	18.3	183.	1861.
Cauchy	0	(.212)	.219	.674	2.08	4.26	10.7	21.5	215.	2147.

[a] Ordered by a sum of percentiles: the 90th, 95th, and 99th percentiles have weight 1 and the 99.9th percentile has weight 1/20. CN(α; K) is the contaminated normal mixture having proportion α of Gaussian with scale K times that of the remaining Gaussian.

[b] $(50 + \varepsilon)$th percentile is near $(\varepsilon/10) \times$ (entry)

variance as a measure of spread is not useful because it is primarily influenced by the extreme tails of the distribution and is infinite for two of the distributions that we consider. For the same reason, measuring tail-length by kurtosis, another moment-based measure, provides no differentiation among distributions with infinite fourth moments.

The notably small values of the 60th percentiles for the double exponential and Cauchy distributions when matching by quartiles (Table 10-8) reveal how far these distributions are from being "Gaussian in the middle." Quartile matching, which depends on the width of the central half of the distribution, provides a comparison of the tail weight that is less sensitive to the specific shape of the central part of the density function.

Indices of Tail Weight

In vague terms, the concept of tail weight expresses how the extreme portion of the distribution spreads out relative to the width of the center. More specifically, we use the relative distances of the 99th percentile and the 75th percentile from the median. The ratio of these two distances provides a measure of tail weight. Dividing this ratio by its value for the Gaussian distribution (where it equals 3.46) creates an index, equal to 1.0 for the neutral-tailed Gaussian. Lighter-tailed distributions such as the uniform have index values less than 1.0; heavier-tailed distributions such as the contaminated normals and the slash have index values greater than 1.0. The definition of the index for distribution F is

$$\tau(F) = \frac{F^{-1}(.99) - F^{-1}(.5)}{F^{-1}(.75) - F^{-1}(.5)} \Big/ \frac{\Phi^{-1}(.99) - \Phi^{-1}(.5)}{\Phi^{-1}(.75) - \Phi^{-1}(.5)}$$

where $\Phi(\cdot)$ is the standard Gaussian cumulative distribution function. Neither location changes nor scale changes affect the value of $\tau(F)$. For the uniform and triangular distributions and the neutral- to heavy-tailed distributions used in this chapter, the values of $\tau(F)$ are as follows:

Distribution	$\tau(F)$
Uniform	.57
Triangular	.86
Gaussian	1.00
CN(.05; 3)	1.20
Logistic	1.21
D-Exponential	1.63
CN(.05; 10)	3.42
Slash	7.85
Cauchy	9.22

This index, $\tau(F)$, has a direct connection with the pseudovariances defined in Chapters 2 and 12. The $100p\%$-pseudovariance is

$$PV_p(F) = \left(\frac{F^{-1}(1-p) - F^{-1}(p)}{\Phi^{-1}(1-p) - \Phi^{-1}(p)} \right)^2$$

and thus

$$\tau(F) = \frac{\sqrt{PV_{.01}(F)}}{\sqrt{PV_{.25}(F)}}.$$

Sample estimates similar to this index are suggested by Hogg (1974). Let $\overline{U}(\beta)$ be the average of the largest $n\beta$ order statistics and $\overline{L}(\beta)$ the average of the smallest $n\beta$ order statistics, where fractional observations are used if $n\beta$ is not an integer. Then the sample estimate of a tail-weight index based on spread at the 90th percentile relative to the 75th percentile is

$$\frac{\overline{U}(.2) - \overline{L}(.2)}{\overline{U}(.5) - \overline{L}(.5)}.$$

We suggest an alternative which should be better because it avoids averaging over the extreme order statistics. We use a sample version of the index based on order-statistic estimates of the percentiles. As described in Chapter 2 [equation (10)], the *ideal* depth of the order statistic corresponding to the tail area p is $d = (n + \frac{1}{3})p + \frac{1}{3}$. When $p \leq \frac{1}{2}$ and d is an integer, we estimate the $(100p)$th percentile by

$$\hat{Q}(p) = X_{(d)}.$$

For noninteger d greater than 1 we use a weighted average of the two adjacent order statistics with depths bracketing d. Let $g = [d]$ be the largest integer less than or equal to d. Let $r = d - g$ be the fractional part of d. Then for $p \leq \frac{1}{2}$ we define

$$\hat{Q}(p) = (1 - r)X_{(g)} + rX_{(g+1)}$$

(and similarly for $p > \frac{1}{2}$). This reduces to the equation above when d is an integer. Our sample estimate of the tail-weight index based on the spread at the 90th percentile relative to the 75th percentile is

$$\frac{\hat{Q}(.90) - \hat{Q}(.10)}{\hat{Q}(.75) - \hat{Q}(.25)}.$$

10D. CHOOSING THE ROBUST ESTIMATOR

From the collection of simple location estimators described in Section 10B, we want to find one or more that perform well for the set of distributions and sampling situations described in Section 10C. We use the variance of an estimator to measure its performance for a given distribution. However, to compare estimators across a collection of distributions, we use a notion of relative efficiency, which we call optrim-efficiency. For a specified estimator, this is the ratio of the variance of the best trimmed mean (the optrim) for a given distribution to the variance of the specified estimator. We choose the robust estimator for a collection of distributions by using a "maximin" approach. That is, for each estimator we find the minimum optrim-efficiency across distributions. We then choose as most robust the estimator whose minimum optrim-efficiency is the maximum—hence "maximin."

We consider here only symmetric distributions, so that the distributional symmetry property of order statistics holds [see equation (5)]. The estimators considered are all symmetric functions of the order statistics; it follows immediately from the symmetry of the expectation of the order statistics that they are unbiased estimators of the center of symmetry, which coincides with the usual location parameter. Therefore, it is likely that the performance of these estimators can reasonably be judged from their variances. Tables 10-9, 10-10, and 10-11 show the variances of the estimators for samples of size 5, 10, and 20, respectively, from the seven proposed distributional situations. Comparing across the situations in these tables is misleading because no attempt was made to standardize or match the scales among them.

We calculate the variances according to equation (8), using the variances and covariances of order statistics given by Sarhan and Greenberg (1956) for the Gaussian; Shah (1966) and Gupta, Qureishi, and Shah (1967) for the logistic; Govindarajulu (1966) for the double exponential; and Barnett (1966) for the Cauchy distribution. Covariances for the 1-wider situation with $K = 3$, labeled here "one-out," were obtained from David, Kennedy, and Knight (1977); and for the slash distribution and the 1-wider situation with $K = 10$, labeled "one-wild," from Bruce (1980).

We note that for the two heaviest-tailed distributions, slash and Cauchy, the variances of estimators that involve the two smallest and the two largest order statistics are not finite. Also, entries for estimators that involve the extreme order statistics of the one-wild situation were not calculated because the covariances were not available.

For a single distribution, we could choose the preferred estimator by selecting the one with smallest variance. These are indicated in Tables 10-9, 10-10, and 10-11 by the underlined variances. However, to select the

TABLE 10-9. Variances of estimators based on a sample of size 5.

Estimator[a]	Distributions and Situations						
	Gauss	Logistic	One-Out[b]	One-Wild[c]	D-Exp	Slash	Cauchy
Best Trim	.2000	.1911	.3220	.3711	.3174	2.2288	1.2213
(Trim %)	(0%)	(13%)	(20%)	(25%)	(31%)	(40%)	(40%)
Mean(0%)	.2000	.2000	.5200	4.1600	.4000	∞	∞
T(10%)	.2038	.1918	.4075	?	.3516	∞	∞
BMED(20%)	.2271	.1985	.3220	.3719	.3229	∞	∞
Midmean(25%)	.2290	.1991	.3227	.3711	.3197	∞	∞
Trimean(30%)[d]	.2336	.2015	.3261	.3725	.3175	∞	∞
Median(40%)	.2868	.2401	.3860	.4295	.3512	2.2288	1.2213
BLUE	.2000	.1910	—	—	.3168	—	1.2213

[a] For each distribution and situation, the smallest variance among the estimators is underlined.
[b] One-out is 1-wider with $K = 3$ (i.e., one observation has scale 3 times that of the rest).
[c] One-wild is 1-wider with $K = 10$ (i.e., one observation has scale 10 times that of the rest.)
[d] Trimean and $T(30\%)$ coincide for $n = 5$.

preferred estimator for a collection of distributions, we must simultaneously take into account the variances of the estimators for each of the different distributions.

A well-known measure of the performance of an estimator for a given distribution is the *Cramér–Rao efficiency*, sometimes simply called efficiency. It is the ratio of the lower bound for the variance of all unbiased estimators of the parameter of interest to the variance of the considered estimator for a given distribution. That is, the Cramér–Rao efficiency of an unbiased estimator T of θ is

$$\frac{1/I_n(\theta)}{\text{Var}(T)}$$

where $I_n(\theta)$ is the Fisher information about θ in samples of size n from $f(x; \theta)$, defined by

$$I_n(\theta) = nE\left\{\frac{d}{d\theta} \log f(x; \theta)\right\}^2 = n\,\text{var}\left\{\frac{d}{d\theta} \log f(x; \theta)\right\}.$$

TABLE 10-10. Variances of estimators based on a sample of size 10.

Estimator[a]	Distributions and Situations						
	Gauss	One-Out[b]	Logistic	One-Wild[c]	D-Exp	Slash	Cauchy
Best Trim	.1000	.1295	.09398	.1416	.1403	.6995	.3362
(Trim %)	(0%)	(11%)	(13%)	(16%)	(34%)	(38%)	(40%)
Mean(0%)	.1000	.1800	.10000	1.0900	.2000	∞	∞
$T(10\%)$	.1053	.1296	.09428	.1432	.1617	∞	∞
$T(20\%)$	.1133	.1339	.09616	.1433	.1463	.9649	.5377
Trimean	.1136	.1348	.09709	.1448	.1503	1.1143	.6348
Midmean(25%)	.1164	.1366	.09750	.1454	.1424	.8389	.4498
$T(30\%)$	.1238	.1438	.10187	.1521	.1408	.7252	.3672
BMED(35%)	.1270	.1472	.10394	.1554	.1404	.7063	.3500
Median(40%)	.1383	.1596	.11200	.1679	.1452	.7048	.3362
BLUE	.1000	—	.09345	—	.1399	—	.3263

[a] For each distribution and situation, the smallest variance among the estimators is underlined.
[b] One-out is 1-wider with $K = 3$ (i.e., one observation has scale 3 times that of the rest).
[c] One-wild is 1-wider with $K = 10$ (i.e., one observation has scale 10 times that of the rest).

The lower bound measures the amount of information in the sample about the parameter of interest. It is well known (Rao, 1965, p. 283) that in many situations the lower bound is not attainable, even as a limit.

The best linear unbiased estimator (BLUE) for a given distribution is the L-estimator with smallest variance among all L-estimators (David, 1970). For finite samples from known distributions, Lloyd (1952) derived the coefficients of the BLUE in terms of the expectations and the variances and covariances of the order statistics. Although the Cramér–Rao lower bound is achieved asymptotically by the best L-estimators (BLUEs), for finite sample sizes the variance of the BLUE exceeds the lower bound (Gastwirth and Cohen, 1970, p. 957; Hoaglin, 1975). Because the Cramér–Rao lower bound is not attainable in finite samples, we consider other standards.

A reasonable measure of efficiency of an estimator T for the center of a given distribution is the ratio of the variance of the best estimator, var(BLUE, F), to the variance of the estimator T, denoted by var(T, F). This is referred to as relative efficiency by Gastwirth and Cohen (1970).

TABLE 10-11. Variances of estimators based on a sample of size 20.

Estimator[a]	Gauss	One-Out[b]	One-Wild[c]	Logistic	Slash	D-Exp	Cauchy
Best Trim	.05000	.05776	.06103	.04641	.3039	.06383	.1357
(Trim %)	(0%)	(6%)	(9%)	(12%)	(34%)	(37%)	(39%)
Mean	.05000	.07001	.29750	.05000	∞	.10000	∞
T(5%)	.05115	.05782	.06192	.04715	∞	.08541	∞
T(10%)	.05276	.05827	.06105	.04649	.6964	.07782	.4141
T(20%)	.05683	.06164	.06368	.04740	.3579	.06904	.1874
Trimean	.05756	.06250	.06464	.04818	.3849	.07020	.2045
Midmean(25%)	.05928	.06400	.06590	.04856	.3221	.06639	.1591
T(30%)	.06205	.06677	.06862	.05015	.3071	.06466	.1444
BMED(37.5%)	.06643	.07130	.07311	.05299	.3048	.06384	.1361
T(40%)	.06888	.07388	.07570	.05473	.3092	.06439	.1358
Median(45%)	.07344	.07865	.08059	.05811	.3229	.06662	.1395
BLUE	.05000	—	—	.04617	—	.06368	.1257

[a]For each distribution and situation, the smallest variance among the estimators is underlined.
[b]One-out is 1-wider with $K = 3$ (i.e., one observation has scale 3 times that of the rest).
[c]One-wild is 1-wider with $K = 10$ (i.e., one observation has scale 10 times that of the rest).

DEFINITION: *Relative efficiency.* The *relative efficiency* of an estimator T on samples from distribution F, denoted by reff(T, F), is

$$\text{reff}(T, F) = \frac{\text{var}(\text{BLUE}, F)}{\text{var}(T, F)}.$$

In this chapter we consider only a limited set of estimators—trimmed means, trimean, and median—and this set does not include the BLUE for each distribution (except the Gaussian, for which the mean is the BLUE). Therefore, we define a measure of efficiency of an estimator in terms of the variance of the best trimmed mean rather than of the BLUE. This measure, which we denote by optrim-efficiency, can always achieve 100% for members of the set of estimators we consider.

TABLE 10-12. Optrim-efficiency of estimators based on samples of size 5.

	Distributions and Situations						
Estimator	Gauss	Logistic	One-Out[a]	One-Wild[b]	D-Exp	Slash	Cauchy
Mean(0%)	100.0	95.5	61.9	8.9	79.4	0.0	0.0
T(10%)	98.1	99.6	79.0	?	90.3	0.0	0.0
BMED(20%)	88.1	96.3	100.0	99.8	98.3	0.0	0.0
Midmean(25%)	87.3	96.0	99.8	100.0	99.3	0.0	0.0
Trimean(30%)[c]	85.6	94.8	98.8	99.6	100.0	0.0	0.0
Median(40%)	69.7	79.6	83.4	86.4	86.4	100.0	100.0
BLUE	100.0	100.1	—	—	100.2	—	100.0

[a] One-out is 1-wider with $K = 3$ (i.e., one observation has scale 3 times that of the rest).
[b] One-wild is 1-wider with $K = 10$ (i.e., one observation has scale 10 times that of the rest).
[c] Trimean and $T(30\%)$ coincide for $n = 5$.

Let T be an estimator of location for distribution F and let $\mathrm{var}(T, F)$ denote its variance. Let $T(\alpha_0)$ denote the minimum-variance trimmed mean for distribution F, with variance $\mathrm{var}[T(\alpha_0), F]$; that is,

$$\mathrm{var}[T(\alpha_0), F] = \min_{\alpha} \mathrm{var}[T(\alpha), F].$$

DEFINITION: *Optrim-efficiency.* The optrim-efficiency of T on samples from distribution F, denoted by optrim-eff(T, F), is

$$\mathrm{optrim\text{-}eff}(T, F) = \frac{\mathrm{var}[T(\alpha_0), F]}{\mathrm{var}(T, F)} \times 100\%.$$

The optrim-efficiency of T is a measure of the performance of the estimator T relative to the performance of the best trimmed mean about the location of F. Optrim-efficiency provides a conceptually and computationally simple standard to use as a basis for comparing the sets of estimators considered in this chapter.

The first two rows of Tables 10-9, 10-10, and 10-11 give the variance of the best trimmed mean and the optimal trimming proportion for each distribution and situation. Tables 10-12, 10-13, and 10-14 show the optrim-efficiencies of the selected estimators. To understand these tables more easily, the estimators are arranged in ascending order of trimming proportion, with the trimean inserted where appropriate. The distributions and

TABLE 10-13. Optrim-efficiency of estimators based on samples of size 10.

Estimator	Distributions and Situations						
	Gauss	One-Out[a]	Logistic	One-Wild[b]	D-Exp	Slash	Cauchy
Mean(0%)	100.0	71.9	94.0	13.0	70.1	0.0	0.0
$T(10\%)$	94.9	99.9	99.7	98.9	86.8	0.0	0.0
Trimean	88.0	96.0	96.8	97.9	93.4	62.8	53.0
$T(20\%)$	88.3	96.7	97.7	98.8	95.9	72.5	62.5
Midmean(25%)	85.9	94.8	96.4	97.3	98.5	83.4	74.7
$T(30\%)$	80.8	90.0	92.3	93.0	99.6	96.5	91.6
BMED(35%)	78.7	87.9	90.4	91.1	99.9	99.0	96.1
Median(40%)	72.3	81.2	83.9	84.3	96.6	99.3	100.0
BLUE	100.0	—	100.6	—	100.3	—	103.0

[a]One-out is 1-wider with $K = 3$ (i.e., one observation has scale 3 times that of the rest).
[b]One-wild is 1-wider with $K = 10$ (i.e., one observation has scale 10 times that of the rest).

situations are arranged in ascending order of the trimming proportion for the best trimmed mean for each situation. This arrangement produces a strong diagonal pattern in the tables: we see high efficiencies from the upper left corner (using the mean with the Gaussian) to the lower right corner (using the median with the Cauchy).

One simple conclusion from Tables 10-12, 10-13, and 10-14 is that the ideal amount of trimming is related directly to the heaviness of the tails of the distribution from which the data are sampled. The most efficient estimator for data from the Gaussian is the sample mean (zero trimming). For slightly stretched tails, as exhibited by the logistic distribution and the 1-wider ($n = 10$ and 20) situations, the 10%-trimmed mean is most efficient. For moderately stretched tails, exhibited by the 1-wider ($n = 5$) situations, the midmean or 25%-trimmed mean is nearly most efficient. For heavy-tailed distributions such as the double exponential, slash, or Cauchy, the BMED or median is most efficient. Thus if one has an unusually good notion of the tail weight of the distribution underlying the data, the above remarks and Tables 10-12, 10-13, and 10-14 should suffice for choosing a relatively efficient estimator from this set.

Robustness of Efficiency (Maximin Criterion)

In many settings, we have only a vague notion of the distribution generating the data. What is needed, then, is not an estimator that is best for a specific

TABLE 10-14.   Optrim-efficiency of estimators based on samples of size 20.

Estimator	Distributions and Situations						
	Gauss	One-Out[a]	One-Wild[b]	Logistic	Slash	D-Exp	Cauchy
Mean(0%)	100.0	82.5	20.5	92.8	0.0	63.8	0.0
T(5%)	97.8	99.9	98.6	98.4	0.0	74.7	0.0
T(10%)	94.8	99.1	100.0	99.8	43.6	82.0	32.8
T(20%)	88.0	93.7	95.8	97.9	84.9	92.4	72.4
Trimean	86.9	92.4	94.4	96.3	79.0	90.9	66.4
Midmean(25%)	84.4	90.3	92.6	95.6	94.4	96.1	85.3
T(30%)	80.6	86.5	88.9	92.6	98.9	98.7	94.0
BMED(37.5%)	75.3	81.0	83.5	87.6	99.7	100.0	99.7
T(40%)	72.6	78.2	80.6	84.8	98.3	99.1	99.9
Median(45%)	68.1	73.4	75.7	79.9	94.1	95.8	97.3
BLUE	100.0	—	—	100.6	—	100.2	108.0

[a] One-out is 1-wider with $K = 3$ (i.e., one observation has scale 3 times that of the rest).

[b] One-wild is 1-wider with $K = 10$ (i.e., one observation has scale 10 times that of the rest).

situation, but rather one that is fairly good over a suitable range of situations. We want an estimator that has fairly high efficiency over a range of possible situations, hence the maximin estimator with respect to efficiency.

To keep the analysis simple, we consider the three sample sizes (5, 10, and 20) separately. For each estimator we find the minimum optrim-efficiency across the broad collection of realistic situations considered, which includes the Gaussian, one-out, logistic, one-wild, and slash. This minimum optrim-efficiency is then compared among estimators, and the estimator with the maximum (best) minimum optrim-efficiency is selected as the preferred estimator for that collection of distributions. The left panel of Table 10-15 presents the minimum optrim-efficiency for each estimator. The robust (maximin) estimator described above for the broad set of five realistic situations for $n = 5$, 10, and 20 is indicated by underlining. The maximin estimator trims 40% from each extreme for samples of size $n = 5$, 25% for samples of size $n = 10$, and 20% for samples of size $n = 20$. This suggests that the optimum trimming proportion changes appreciably with sample size when considering the entire spectrum of distributions from Gaussian to slash. In fact, trimming "the largest half-integer $\leqslant \sqrt{4n/5}$" observations from each tail reproduces our results.

TABLE 10-15. Minimum optrim-efficiencies for n = 5, 10, and 20 and various groups of distributions and situations.

	Broad Group[a]			Non-Gaussian[b]			Non-Slash[c]		
	$n = 5$	$n = 10$	$n = 20$	$n = 5$	$n = 10$	$n = 20$	$n = 5$	$n = 10$	$n = 20$
Mean	0.0	0.0	0.0	0.0	0.0	0.0	8.9	13.0	20.5
$T(5\%)$	0.0	0.0	0.0	0.0	0.0	0.0	?[d]	?	97.8
$T(10\%)$	0.0	0.0	43.6	0.0	0.0	43.6	?	94.9	94.8
$T(20\%)$	0.0	72.5	84.9	0.0	72.5	84.9	88.1	88.3	88.0
Midmean(25%)	0.0	83.4	84.4	0.0	83.4	90.3	87.3	85.9	84.4
$T(30\%)$	0.0	80.8	80.6	0.0	90.0	86.5	85.6	80.8	80.6
$T(40\%)$	69.7	72.3	72.6	79.6	81.2	78.2	69.7	72.3	72.6
Trimean	0.0	62.8	79.0	0.0	62.8	79.0	85.6	88.0	86.9
BMED	0.0	78.7	75.3	0.0	87.9	81.0	88.1	78.7	75.3
Median	69.7	72.3	68.1	79.6	81.2	73.4	69.7	72.3	68.1

[a]Gaussian, one-out, logistic, one-wild, slash. (Underscored values correspond to trimming "the largest half-integer $\leq \sqrt{4n/5}$" observations from each tail.)
[b]Broad group without Gaussian. (Underscored values correspond to trimming $\left[\sqrt{5n/4}\right]$ observations from each tail.)
[c]Broad group without slash. (Underscored values correspond to trimming one observation from each tail.)
[d]Unknown since variance of extreme order statistic is unknown for one-wild.

Restricted Situations

If we rule out the Gaussian as a possible distribution because we believe that it has unrealistically light tails, we can find the robust estimator for the remaining situations in an analogous fashion. We naturally expect to trim somewhat more, except for $n = 5$, where we already have trimmed to the median. The middle panel of Table 10-15 presents the results for $n = 5$, 10, and 20. The indicated trimming percentages are now 40% for $n = 5$, 30% for $n = 10$, and 25% for $n = 20$. Now we trim from each tail approximately "the largest integer $\leq \sqrt{5n/4}$" observations.

If we omit the slash distribution from consideration for having possibly unrealistically heavy tails for some circumstances, we expect to trim somewhat less than for the broad group. The right panel of Table 10-15 presents the minimum optrim-efficiency for each estimator with the maximin underlined. The indicated trimming percentages are now 20% for $n = 5$, 10% for $n = 10$, and 5% for $n = 20$.

These percentages result in trimming exactly one observation from each tail—just enough to remove the outlier from the one-wild situation. We need to remember that we might reasonably have included more intermediate situations between the slash and the one-wild, so that these trimming percentages may be too small. (If we were unrealistic enough to allow the double exponential distribution to remain in the set of nonslash distributions, then the suggested trimming proportion would be 20% for $n = 5$, 10, and 20.)

If we want to simplify the above results further, we could consider the following simple rule:

1. For $n \leqslant 6$ use the median.
2. For $n = 7$ trim two observations from each tail.
3. For $n \geqslant 8$ trim 25% from each tail.

The performance of this rule for the sample sizes we have investigated is shown in Table 10-16.

The performance of this simple rule should be satisfactory as long as we consider a very heavy-tailed distribution (represented here by the slash) a likely model for the data. If we eliminate the slash distribution as unrealistic, then trimming less than 25% should be satisfactory.

The collection of distributions and situations considered here includes a variety of symmetric shapes, spans a wide range of tail weights from Gaussian to Cauchy, and includes the 1-wider sampling situations. Nevertheless, the worst case for efficiency of the estimators occurs at one of the extreme distributions as ranked on the tail weight spectrum. Thus as suggested by Hogg (1974), an estimator of the center of a symmetric

TABLE 10-16.   **Performance of the simple rule[a] compared to the best rule[b] for each group of distributions.**

	Minimum Optrim-Efficiency					
	Broad Group		Non-Gaussian		Non-Slash	
	Simple	Best	Simple	Best	Simple	Best
$n = 5$	69.7	69.7	79.6	79.6	69.7	88.1
$n = 10$	83.4	83.4	83.4	90.0	85.9	94.9
$n = 20$	84.4	84.9	90.3	90.3	84.4	97.8

[a]Simple rule is Median for $n \leqslant 6$. Trim maximum of {two observations or 25%} for $n \geqslant 7$.
[b]Best rule is the maximin estimator indicated in Table 10-15.

distribution that performs well for a broad class of distributions can usually be found by selecting the maximin estimator for two or three extreme distributions of the class.

10E. SUMMARY

The estimators considered here are all linear functions of the ordered observations. The task of ordering the observations is not burdensome for small sample sizes, which are our focus here, and can conveniently be aided by the stem-and-leaf technique described in Chapter 1. Despite the relatively simple calculations required, the performance of these estimators can be quite good. The optrim-efficiency of the midmean, for $n = 20$, remained above 84% for all distributional situations considered.

Generally when heavy-tailed distributions are anticipated, and also for samples less than 20, slightly more than 25% trimming is preferred. When tails as heavy as those of the slash and Cauchy are not reasonable, slightly less trimming is required, and we recommend the 20%-trimmed mean. However, for the broad class of distributions considered here the midmean, which is the 25%-trimmed mean, should provide an excellent estimate of the center of location.

REFERENCES

Andrews, D. F., Bickel, P. J., Hampel, F. R., Huber, P. J., Rogers, W. H., and Tukey, J. W. (1972). *Robust Estimates of Location: Survey and Advances.* Princeton, NJ: Princeton University Press.

Barnett, V. D. (1966). "Order statistics estimators of the location of the Cauchy distribution," *Journal of the American Statistical Association*, **61**, 1205–1218.

Bruce, A. (1980). "Tables of order statistics and their use in robust estimation." A. B. Thesis, Department of Statistics, Princeton University.

Crow, E. L. and Siddiqui, M. M. (1967). "Robust estimates of location," *Journal of the American Statistical Association*, **62**, 353–389.

David, H. A. (1970). *Order Statistics.* New York: Wiley.

David, H. A., Kennedy, W. J., and Knight, R. D. (1977). "Means, variances, and covariances of normal order statistics in the presence of an outlier." In D. B. Owen and R. E. Odeh (Eds.), *Selected Tables in Mathematical Statistics*, Vol. 5. Providence, RI: American Mathematical Society.

Gastwirth, J. L. and Cohen, M. L. (1970). "Small sample behavior of some robust linear estimators of location," *Journal of the American Statistical Association*, **65**, 946–973.

Govindarajulu, Z. (1966). "Best linear estimates under symmetric censoring of the parameters of a double exponential population," *Journal of the American Statistical Association*, **61**, 248–258.

Gupta, S. S., Qureishi, A. S., and Shah, B. K. (1967). "Best linear unbiased estimators of the parameters of the logistic distribution using order statistics," *Technometrics*, **9**, 43–56.

Harter, H. L. (1970). *Order Statistics and Their Use in Testing and Estimation*, Vol. 2. Washington, DC: U.S. Government Printing Office.

Hoaglin, D. C. (1975). "On the small-sample variance of the Pitman location estimators," *Journal of the American Statistical Association*, **70**, 880–888.

Hogg, R. V. (1974). "Adaptive robust procedures," *Journal of the American Statistical Association*, **69**, 909–921.

Huber, P. J. (1964). "Robust estimation of a location parameter," *Annals of Mathematical Statistics*, **35**, 73–101.

———— (1972). "Robust statistics: a review," *Annals of Mathematical Statistics*, **43**, 1041–1067.

Lloyd, E. H. (1952). "Least-squares estimation of location and scale parameters using order statistics," *Biometrika*, **39**, 88–95.

Rao, C. R. (1965). *Linear Statistical Inference and Its Applications*. New York: Wiley.

Rogers, W. H. and Tukey, J. W. (1972). "Understanding some long-tailed symmetrical distributions," *Statistica Neerlandica*, **26**, 211–226.

Sarhan, A. E. and Greenberg, B. G. (1956). "Estimation of location and scale parameters by order statistics from singly and doubly censored samples, I," *Annals of Mathematical Statistics*, **27**, 427–451.

Shah, B. K. (1966). "On the bivariate moments of order statistics from a logistic distribution," *Annals of Mathematical Statistics*, **37**, 1002–1010.

Stigler, S. M. (1973). "The asymptotic distribution of the trimmed mean," *Annals of Statistics*, **1**, 472–477.

———— (1977). "Do robust estimators work with *real* data?" *Annals of Statistics*, **5**, 1055–1098.

Youden, W. J. (1972). "Enduring values," *Technometrics*, **14**, 1–11.

Additional Literature (for Chapters 10 and 11)

Hogg (1979) gives a general overview of *L*-estimation, *M*-estimation (discussed in Chapter 11), and *R*-estimation (estimation based on rank tests).

Two papers give small-sample results for robust location estimators, matching them with scale estimators to produce robust confidence intervals. De Wet and van Wyk (1979) consider adaptive trimmed means (according to an earlier proposal by Hogg) for sample sizes of 20 and above. Gross (1976) reports the results of a Monte Carlo study of 25 pairs (combining a location estimator and a scale estimator) for small samples from various distributional situations.

This chapter has concentrated on results for symmetric distributions. Carroll (1979) shows how heavy skewness of errors can seriously bias estimates of the variance of robust location estimators. D'Agostino and Lee (1977) study the effect of changes in kurtosis and tail-thickness on trimmed means, medians, and Winsorized means for the exponential-power and *t*-distribution families, finding that $T(.25)$ performs well. Collins (1976) develops a method of robust estimation in the face of asymmetric departures from normality. Lee and Krutchkoff (1980) discuss the problem of estimating location and scale for a truncated variable. Stigler (1976) offers the reassuring news that trimmed means are less influenced by outliers than might be expected in cases of asymmetric contamination. Gastwirth and Rubin (1975) investigate the effect of serial dependence in the data on the efficiency of certain *L*-estimators. Prescott and Hogg (1977) discuss other properties of trimmed means.

A great deal of work along many lines has focused on techniques for robust estimation of location. Harter, Moore, and Curry (1979) propose a two-step adaptive procedure for location estimation in which the analyst first classifies the population distribution by its tail thickness and then uses the maximum-likelihood estimator for the chosen population. Chan and Rhodin (1980) suggest an estimator for symmetric distributions based on a few order statistics, optimally spaced. Tukey (1978) introduces a new location estimator called the ninther. Parr and Schucany (1980) demonstrate the robustness properties of minimum-distance estimation with asymptotic and Monte Carlo results for symmetric distributions. Pollak (1979) also includes Monte Carlo results in his discussion of a robust class of estimators possessing properties of Frechet-differentiability.

Brown, B. M. (1981). "Symmetric quantile averages and related estimators," *Biometrika*, **68**, 235–242.

Carroll, R. J. (1979). "On estimating variances of robust estimators when errors are asymmetric," *Journal of the American Statistical Association*, **74**, 674–679.

Chan, L. K. and Rhodin, L. S. (1980). "Robust estimation of location using optimally chosen sample quantiles," *Technometrics*, **22**, 225–237.

Collins, J. R. (1976). "Robust estimation of a location parameter in the presence of asymmetry," *Annals of Statistics*, **4**, 68–85.

D'Agostino, R. B. and Lee, A. F. S. (1977). "Robustness of location estimators under changes of population kurtosis," *Journal of the American Statistical Association*, **72**, 393–396.

David, H. A. (1979). "Robust estimation in the presence of outliers." In R. L. Launer and G. N. Wilkinson (Eds.), *Robustness in Statistics*. New York: Academic, pp. 61–74.

De Wet, T. and van Wyk, J. W. J. (1979). "Efficiency and robustness of Hogg's adaptive trimmed means," *Communications in Statistics*, **A8**, 117–128.

Gastwirth, J. L. and Rubin, H. (1975). "Behavior of robust estimators on dependent data," *Annals of Statistics*, **3**, 1070–1100.

Gross, A. M. (1976). "Confidence interval robustness with long-tailed symmetric distributions," *Journal of the American Statistical Association*, **71**, 409–416.

Harter, H. L., Moore, A. H., and Curry, T. F. (1979). "Adaptive robust estimation of location and scale parameters of symmetric populations," *Communications in Statistics*, **A8**, 1473–1492.

Hogg, R. V. (1979). "An introduction to robust estimation." In R. L. Launer and G. N. Wilkinson (Eds.), *Robustness in Statistics*. New York: Academic, pp. 1–18.

Lee, L. and Krutchkoff, R. G. (1980). "Mean and variance of partially-truncated distributions," *Biometrics*, **36**, 531–536.

Parr, W. C. and Schucany, W. R. (1980). "Minimum distance and robust estimation," *Journal of the American Statistical Association*, **75**, 616–624.

Pollak, M. (1979). "A class of robust estimators," *Communications in Statistics*, **A8**, 509–532.

Prescott, P. and Hogg, R. V. (1977). "Trimmed and outer means and their variances," *The American Statistician*, **31**, 156–157.

Spjøtvoll, E. and Aastveit, A. H. (1980). "Comparison of robust estimators on data from field experiments," *Scandinavian Journal of Statistics*, **7**, 1–13.

Stigler, S. M. (1976). "Effect of sample heterogeneity on linear functions of order statistics, with applications to robust estimation," *Journal of the American Statistical Association*, **71**, 956–960.

Tukey, J. W. (1978). "The ninther, a technique for low-effort robust (resistant) location in large samples," In H. A. David (Ed.), *Contributions to Survey Sampling and Applied Statistics, in Honor of H. O. Hartley*. New York: Academic, pp. 251–258.

EXERCISES

1. *Central-Density Matching*
    Derive the scale parameter value (λ) required to achieve central-density matching of each of the following densities with the standard normal density. Since the densities are each centered at zero, find λ such that

    $$f(0; 0, \lambda) = \frac{1}{\sqrt{2\pi}}.$$

    (a) Logistic:

    $$f(x; \theta, \lambda) = \frac{(1/\lambda)e^{-(x-\theta)/\lambda}}{[1 + e^{-(x-\theta)/\lambda}]^2}$$

    (b) Double exponential (or Laplace):

    $$f(x; \theta, \lambda) = \frac{1}{2\lambda}e^{-|x-\theta|/\lambda}$$

    (c) Cauchy:

    $$f(x; \theta, \lambda) = \frac{1}{\pi}\frac{\lambda}{\lambda^2 + (x - \theta)^2}$$

    (d) Slash:

    $$f(x; \theta, \lambda) = \frac{1 - e^{-(x-\theta)^2/2\lambda^2}}{[(x - \theta)^2/\lambda^2]\sqrt{2\pi}} \qquad x \neq \theta$$

    $$= \frac{1}{2\lambda\sqrt{2\pi}} \qquad x = \theta$$

2. Central-density matching for mixtures of two Gaussian densities, called the contaminated normal distribution $CN(\alpha; K)$, is achieved by finding λ, the scale parameter, such that the central density $f(x = \theta; \theta, \lambda)$ is equal to $1/\sqrt{2\pi}$, the central density of the standard Gaussian. The

density of the mixture distribution is

$$f(x; \theta, \lambda) = (1 - \alpha)g(x; \theta, \lambda) + \alpha g(x; \theta, \lambda K)$$

where

$$g(x; \theta, \lambda) = \frac{1}{\lambda\sqrt{2\pi}} \exp\left\{-\frac{(x - \theta)^2}{2\lambda^2}\right\}.$$

The scale for the contaminating distribution is usually $K = 3$ or $K = 10$. Show that central-density matching leads to

$$\lambda = (1 - \alpha) + \frac{\alpha}{K}.$$

3. Quartile matching of distributions is accomplished by letting the scale parameter λ be fixed such that the 75th percentiles (or 25th) of the distributions are all equal. Having thus matched the central half of the distribution, relative tail weight can easily be assessed by comparing percentiles larger than the 75th.

Find the scale parameter value λ for each of the following distributions such that the 75th percentile of the scaled distributions matches that of the standard normal, $z_{.75} = .6745$; that is, find λ such that $.75 = F(.6745; 0, \lambda)$.

(a) Logistic:

$$F(x; \theta, \lambda) = [1 + e^{-(x-\theta)/\lambda}]^{-1}$$

(b) Double-exponential:

$$F(x; \theta, \lambda) = 1 - .5e^{-(x-\theta)/\lambda} \qquad x > \theta$$

$$= .5e^{(x-\theta)/\lambda} \qquad x \leqslant \theta$$

(c) Cauchy:

$$F(x; \theta, \lambda) = \frac{1}{\pi}\left[\arctan\left(\frac{x - \theta}{\lambda}\right) + \frac{\pi}{2}\right]$$

(d)* Slash:

$$F(x; \theta, \lambda) = \Phi\left(\frac{x - \theta}{\lambda}\right) - \left(\frac{x - \theta}{\lambda}\right)f\left(\frac{x - \theta}{\lambda}\right)$$

*Hint: This requires an iterative solution.

where

$$f(y) = \frac{1 - e^{-y^2/2}}{y^2\sqrt{2\pi}} \qquad y \neq 0$$

$$= \frac{1}{2\sqrt{2\pi}} \qquad y = 0$$

and $\Phi(y)$ is the standard Gaussian cdf.

(e)* Mixture Distributions:

$$F(x; \theta, \lambda) = (1 - \alpha)G(x; \theta, \lambda) + \alpha G(x; \theta, \lambda K),$$

where

$$G(x; \theta, \lambda) = \int_{-\infty}^{x} \frac{1}{\lambda\sqrt{2\pi}} \exp\left\{ -\frac{(y - \theta)^2}{2\lambda^2} \right\} dy.$$

4. Using tables of variances and covariances for order statistics from the Gaussian(0, 1) distribution, verify the variances for each location estimator in Table 10-4 as given in Tables 10-9, 10-10, and 10-11 for

   (a) $n = 5$
   (b) $n = 10$
   (c) $n = 20$.

5. Using tables, calculate the tail-weight index based on the 90th percentile relative to the 75th percentile for the

   (a) Uniform
   (b) Gaussian
   (c) Logistic

   distributions. Compare with results for the index based on the 99th percentile.

6. Using schematic plots, tail-weight ratios, and the tables of this chapter,

   (a) Determine the best location estimator for the menstrual cycle data of Chapter 1.
   (b) Compare your estimator in (a) with the "simple rule" estimator (see Table 10-16).

7. Do as in Exercise 6 for the tumor data in Chapter 1.

8. Fill out Table 10-4 for the data in Exercises 6 and 7. How do the best estimators compare with the others? Is there much difference? When would you expect to see sizable differences among the location estimators?

*Hint: This requires an iterative solution.

CHAPTER 11

M-Estimators of Location: An Outline of the Theory

Colin Goodall
Harvard University

A discussion of more refined estimators necessarily brings us into more systematic contact with theoretical principles in estimation. We study and compare whole classes of estimators, each class based on a specific approach or criterion, and we measure the performance of individual estimators in order to choose a few that perform well in a variety of situations. In Chapter 10 we have made some use of the family of trimmed means, which includes the mean and the median as limiting cases. Modern research on robust methods offers even better performance if we can accept more complicated estimators of location. The present chapter provides an introduction to the theory associated with M-estimators, the class of estimators that offers the greatest advantages in performance, flexibility, and convenience.

Three classes—L-estimators, R-estimators, and M-estimators—have played a prominent role in recent research on robust estimation. We discussed L-estimators (linear combinations of the ordered observations) in Chapter 10. Although simple to calculate, they may sacrifice resistance by giving weight to extreme observations, or, conversely, they may sacrifice efficiency by placing too little weight on end observations that are not extreme, as would happen for a trimmed mean with a fixed amount of trimming.

R-estimators are derived from rank tests for a shift between two samples, estimating the shift by moving one sample along until the test is least able to

detect a shift. In estimating location, the second sample is the mirror image of the actual sample, reflected about the estimate, so that an *R*-estimator of location minimizes the shift between the sample and its mirror image, as measured by the rank test. Because *R*-estimators of location do not perform as well as the best *M*-estimators in small to moderate samples, and because they are not as easy to work with, we do not discuss them further.

As the early sections of the chapter explain, *M*-estimators minimize functions of the deviations of the observations from the estimate that are more general than the sum of squared deviations or the sum of absolute deviations. In this way the class of *M*-estimators includes the mean and the median as special cases. Viewed in another way, *M*-estimators generalize the idea of the maximum-likelihood estimator of the location parameter in a specified distribution. Thus it is reasonable to expect that a suitably chosen *M*-estimator will have good robustness of efficiency in large samples. In fact, the original theoretical development was motivated by achieving robustness in a neighborhood of the normal distribution.

A simple reformulation of *M*-estimators yields a weighted mean in which the weights depend on the data, thus providing both intuitive and computational support for this approach. The resulting *W*-estimators provide a straightforward way of modifying the familiar least-squares method, particularly in regression problems, where they are the basis for the technique of iteratively reweighted least squares.

Among the theoretical tools for studying the resistance and robustness of location estimators, several apply very simply to *M*-estimators. In showing how an estimator responds to the introduction of a new observation, the influence curve is especially revealing because it mimics the ψ-function defining the *M*-estimator. Thus one can readily construct an *M*-estimator whose influence curve has chosen characteristics.

In this chapter we introduce the basic theory of *M*-estimators, emphasizing qualitative features that help to explain the robustness of good estimators in this class, and we examine in detail several examples that illustrate the diversity available.

Most *M*-estimators of location require that we also give attention to the scale of the sample by employing an auxiliary estimate of scale. Section 11G discusses this aspect of scale, and Chapter 12 takes up the problem of estimating scale for its own sake.

Computational details play an important role in practical applications of *M*-estimators and *W*-estimators; Section 11K examines these issues.

Finally, the advantage of any robust estimator in routine use depends more on its efficiency in small samples than on its optimality in large samples. The small-sample results assembled in Section 11L serve to bridge much of the gap between these two ways of assessing performance.

11A. *M*-ESTIMATORS

M-estimators minimize objective functions more general than the familiar sum of squared residuals associated with the sample mean. Instead of squaring the deviation of each observation x_i from the estimate t, we apply a function $\rho(x; t)$ and form the objective function by summing over the sample: $\sum_{i=1}^{n} \rho(x_i; t)$. Often $\rho(x; t)$ depends on x and t only through $x - t$, so that we could write $\rho(x - t)$; for the moment we retain the greater generality of treating x and t as separate arguments. The nature of ρ determines the properties of the *M*-estimator.

DEFINITION: The *M-estimate* $T_n(x_1, \ldots, x_n)$ for the function ρ and the sample $x_1, \ldots, x_n$ is the value of t that minimizes the objective function $\sum_{i=1}^{n} \rho(x_i; t)$. Often we simply write T_n when the name of the sample is not essential. When we know the derivative of ρ with respect to t, a function which (except for a multiplicative constant) we denote by ψ, we may find it more convenient to calculate T_n by finding the value of t that satisfies

$$\sum_{i=1}^{n} \psi(x_i; t) = 0. \tag{1}$$

(We have implicitly assumed that ρ has a derivative with respect to t at all values of t. For some ρ, however, the derivative may fail to exist at a finite number of points. Ordinarily we expect ρ to be continuous.)

The most familiar *M*-estimate is the sample mean, the least-squares estimate of location. For least-squares estimation, ρ is the square of the residual:

$$\rho(x; t) = (x - t)^2.$$

Thus we minimize $\sum_{i=1}^{n}(x_i - t)^2$. Differentiating the objective function with respect to t and dropping the constant 2 lead to the equation

$$\sum_{i=1}^{n}(x_i - t) = 0.$$

Because $t = \sum_{i=1}^{n} x_i / n$ solves this equation, T_n is indeed the sample mean. Figure 11-1 shows the functions ρ and ψ for the sample mean.

A second example is the sample median. (To fit this formalism, when n is even we accept *any* answer between the two middle observations.) The

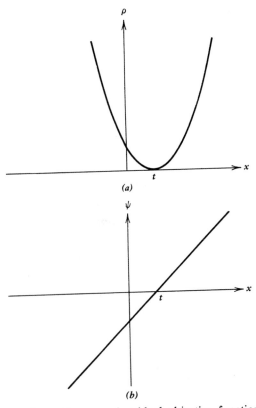

Figure 11-1. Estimation with squared-residual objective function. (*a*) Objective function, $\rho(x; t) = (x - t)^2$. (*b*) ψ-function, $\psi(x; t) = x - t$.

objective function is the absolute value of the residual,

$$\rho(x; t) = |x - t|,$$

and the corresponding ψ-function is

$$\psi(x; t) = \text{sgn}(x - t),$$

where

$$\text{sgn}(u) = \begin{cases} +1 & u > 0 \\ 0 & u = 0 \\ -1 & u < 0. \end{cases}$$

[Technically, $|u|$ does not have a derivative at $u = 0$, but it is reasonable to accept the value from the customary definition of $\text{sgn}(u)$, and the result agrees with the behavior of other ψ-functions.] The expression

$$\sum_{i=1}^{n} \psi(x_i; t) = \sum_{i=1}^{n} \text{sgn}(x_i - t)$$

counts each observation above t as $+1$ and each observation below t as -1, so that $t = $ median yields a sum of zero. Figure 11-2 displays ρ and ψ for the absolute-residual objective function.

Through the choice of objective functions, *M*-estimation generalizes least-squares estimation. However, ψ-functions are more convenient to work with than ρ, so we emphasize them, occasionally mentioning ρ and, in Sections 11I and 11J, some related functions.

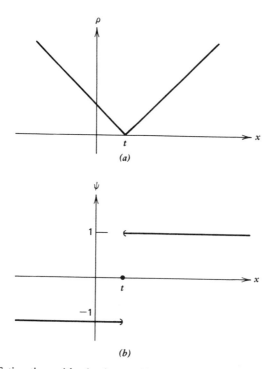

Figure 11-2. Estimation with absolute-residual objective function. (*a*) Objective function, $\rho(x; t) = |x - t|$. (*b*) ψ-function, $\psi(x; t) = \text{sgn}(x - t)$.

Equivariance and Invariance

Some technical terms can help describe the ways that estimators respond to systematic changes in the sample.

When we shift the whole sample by an amount a, any reasonable estimator of location should follow by the same amount. Specifically, we want

$$T_n(x_1 + a, \ldots, x_n + a) = T_n(x_1, \ldots, x_n) + a. \tag{2}$$

Such an estimator is said to be *location-equivariant* (Huber, 1981).

It is straightforward to see that an *M*-estimator of location is location-equivariant if the argument of the objective function and ψ-function takes the simple form $u = x - t$, so that $\psi(x; t) = \psi(x - t)$. When T_n is the value of t that yields

$$\sum_{i=1}^{n} \psi(x_i - t) = 0,$$

$T_n + a$ is the value of t that satisfies

$$\sum_{i=1}^{n} \psi(x_i + a - t) = 0.$$

Therefore, *M*-estimators of location with $\psi(x; t) = \psi(x - t)$ are location-equivariant.

Often we may multiply the whole sample by a nonzero constant b and then shift the result by a. Again, the estimator of location should follow this simultaneous change in location and scale:

$$T_n(bx_1 + a, \ldots, bx_n + a) = bT_n(x_1, \ldots, x_n) + a. \tag{3}$$

Such estimators are said to be *location-and-scale-equivariant*. Another way of writing equation (3) is sometimes more suggestive:

$$T_n(x_1, \ldots, x_n) = BT_n\left(\frac{x_1 - A}{B}, \ldots, \frac{x_n - A}{B}\right) + A.$$

By straightforward checking, we can see that *L*-estimators, which we discussed in Chapter 10, are location-and-scale-equivariant. Most *M*-estimators, however, achieve this property only by incorporating some measure of the scale of the sample, which we now denote by S_n. It is reasonable to

require that shifting the whole sample leaves the value of S_n unchanged (S_n is *location-invariant*),

$$S_n(x_1 + a, \ldots, x_n + a) = S_n(x_1, \ldots, x_n),$$

and that S_n follow changes in scaling:

$$S_n(bx_1, \ldots, bx_n) = |b| S_n(x_1, \ldots, x_n); \tag{4}$$

that is, S_n is *scale-equivariant*. The absolute value of b appears on the right-hand side of equation (4) because measures of scale are nonnegative.

Our need in this chapter is primarily for measures of scale that behave in a suitable way. Chapter 12 discusses more careful estimation of scale.

Allowing for Scale

In general, an M-estimator of location must take account of the scale of the sample in order to be location-and-scale-equivariant. Two exceptions are the mean and the median. The sample mean has $\psi(x; t) = \psi(x - t) = x - t$, so that $\psi(bx + a; bt + a) = b\psi(x; t)$. The sample median has $\psi(x; t) = \mathrm{sgn}(x - t)$, and hence $\psi(bx + a; bt + a) = \mathrm{sgn}(b)\psi(x; t)$. For each of these estimators, $\Sigma \psi(bx_i + a; bt + a) = 0$ whenever $\Sigma \psi(x_i; t) = 0$.

The other M-estimators of location that we meet depend on the scale of the arguments of ρ and ψ. Therefore, we choose an auxiliary estimator of scale S_n which is a function of $x_1, \ldots, x_n$ and use this, together with a constant c, to rescale the $x_i - t$. We then have the centered and rescaled observations

$$u_i = \frac{x_i - t}{cS_n}.$$

T_n is a value of t that minimizes $\Sigma_{i=1}^n \rho(u_i)$ or satisfies

$$\sum_{i=1}^n \psi(u_i) = 0.$$

If S_n is scale-equivariant, then T_n is location-and-scale-equivariant. Not all choices of ρ or ψ lead to a unique T_n; those associated with the median serve as a convenient example (when n is even). We mention this minor difficulty again only when it requires specific attention.

In general, an M-estimator of location involves a fixed measure of scale S_n. The constant c in the definition of u_i matches the basic scale of ψ or ρ to

the scale of the data, measured in units of S_n. An inherent part of the definition of the M-estimator, c is known as the *tuning constant* because it can be chosen to fine-tune the estimator so that it has a specified asymptotic efficiency at a chosen distribution (usually the Gaussian). The ψ-functions for the mean and the median do not reveal the need for S_n and c. More commonly, however, the ψ-function is curved or is composed of several linear pieces, and some ψ-functions are identically zero outside an interval. As we shall see for the biweight estimator in Section 11B, it is often convenient to take $(-1, +1)$ as this interval. Thus an M-estimator of location is actually a family of estimators, all involving the same scale measure or auxiliary scale estimator; the value of the tuning constant determines the individual member of the family.

We discuss auxiliary scale estimators further in Section 11G. For the present we simply mention that the ones most often used are:

The median absolute deviation, $\text{MAD} = \text{med}_i \{ | x_i - \text{med}_j \{ x_j \} | \}$

The fourth-spread (d_F, the difference between the lower fourth and the upper fourth, discussed in Chapter 2) or its close relative, the interquartile range.

Simultaneous Estimation of Location and Scale

Instead of using a fixed initial estimate of scale, we could estimate location and scale simultaneously. To calculate a scale estimate, we first need a preliminary estimate of location. This location estimate must be necessarily simple—for example, the mean or median—unless we estimate location and scale simultaneously. Then the location estimate is used in computing the scale estimate and vice versa.

This problem of simultaneous estimation is familiar from classical theory, where a location-scale family consists of densities $(1/\sigma)f[(x - \theta)/\sigma]$, with θ and σ being, respectively, the location and scale parameters. The joint likelihood of the random sample $x_1, \ldots, x_n$ is $\prod_{i=1}^{n}(1/\sigma)f[(x_i - \theta)/\sigma]$. Maximum-likelihood estimates $\hat{\theta}$ and $\hat{\sigma}$ of θ and σ are chosen to maximize this likelihood or, equivalently, its logarithm. If we differentiate the log-likelihood with respect to θ and σ, we obtain two simultaneous equations for $\hat{\theta}$ and $\hat{\sigma}$:

$$\sum_{i=1}^{n} \psi \left(\frac{x_i - \hat{\theta}}{\hat{\sigma}} \right) = 0$$

$$\sum_{i=1}^{n} \left[\left(\frac{x_i - \hat{\theta}}{\hat{\sigma}} \right) \psi \left(\frac{x_i - \hat{\theta}}{\hat{\sigma}} \right) - 1 \right] = 0.$$

(5)

To emphasize the parallel with *M*-estimation of location, ψ in these equations is the negative of the score function:

$$\psi(u) = -\frac{d}{du} \ln f(u) = -\frac{1}{f(u)} \frac{df(u)}{du}. \tag{6}$$

For simultaneous *M*-estimation of location and scale, we simply generalize this pair of equations, incorporating the tuning constant c to obtain

$$\sum_{i=1}^{n} \psi\left(\frac{x_i - T_n}{cS_n}\right) = 0 \quad \text{and} \quad \sum_{i=1}^{n} \chi\left(\frac{x_i - T_n}{cS_n}\right) = 0.$$

We choose ψ and χ to give T_n and S_n the desired properties. Usually ψ is an odd function, $\psi(-u) = -\psi(u)$, and χ is an even function, $\chi(-u) = \chi(u)$, as in maximum-likelihood estimation when f is symmetric. As we discussed in Chapter 9, we make this choice because we do not understand well enough what we should estimate in asymmetric situations. Section 11E discusses criteria for the choice of ψ-functions and looks further at this connection between *M*-estimators and maximum-likelihood estimation.

For estimating only the scale S_n, assuming location is zero, the appropriate defining equation is

$$\sum_{i=1}^{n} \chi\left(\frac{x_i}{cS_n}\right) = 0.$$

Again, c is the tuning constant, and χ is usually an even function.

11B. EXAMPLES

We survey more *M*-estimators of location in Section 11I. Here we briefly discuss the robustness of three estimators—the mean, the median, and the biweight—to give a heuristic background for our discussion of the choice of ψ in Section 11F.

The *mean* has $\psi(x_i - T_n) = x_i - T_n$. It is equally sensitive to all observations and, in particular, is adversely affected by outliers. The ψ-function is a straight line unbounded in both directions, as illustrated in Figure 11-1.

The *median* is the solution of $\sum_{i=1}^{n} \text{sgn}(x_i - T_n) = 0$. The median is insensitive to outliers but is sensitive to the values of the middle one or two

observations. The ψ-function is bounded but has a step at 0, as in Figure 11-2.

The *biweight*, or bisquare, estimator of location is the solution T_n of $\sum_{i=1}^{n} \psi(u_i) = 0$, where

$$\psi(u) = \begin{cases} u(1 - u^2)^2 & |u| \leqslant 1 \\ 0 & |u| > 1 \end{cases}$$

and

$$u_i = \frac{x_i - T_n}{cS_n}.$$

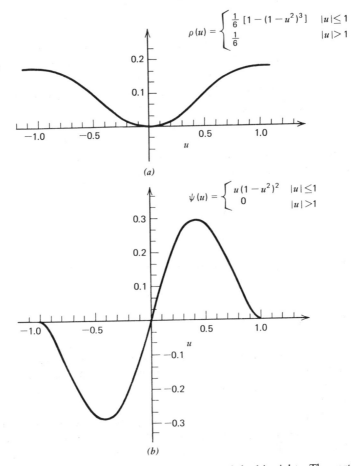

$$\rho(u) = \begin{cases} \frac{1}{6}[1 - (1 - u^2)^3] & |u| \leq 1 \\ \frac{1}{6} & |u| > 1 \end{cases}$$

(a)

$$\psi(u) = \begin{cases} u(1 - u^2)^2 & |u| \leq 1 \\ 0 & |u| > 1 \end{cases}$$

(b)

Figure 11-3. Objective function and ψ-function of the biweights. The vertical scale is 3 times the horizontal scale. (a) Objective function, $\rho(u)$. (b) ψ-function, $\psi(u)$.

The corresponding objective function is

$$\rho(u) = \begin{cases} \frac{1}{6}\left[1 - (1 - u^2)^3\right] & |u| \leq 1 \\ \frac{1}{6} & |u| > 1. \end{cases}$$

Figure 11-3 shows these ρ and ψ functions. The auxiliary estimator of scale S_n is usually the median absolute deviation or half the fourth-spread. The tuning constant c typically lies in the range 6 to 12; we discuss the choice of c in Section 11L. Outliers do not affect the biweight because $\psi(u) = 0$ if $|u|$ is sufficiently large. Moreover, the estimator is not as sensitive to small changes in the data values as is the median. Since $\psi(u) \approx u$ for small u, near the center of the sample the biweight behaves like the mean. (This is essential for high performance against distributions that are "Gaussian in the middle.")

Notice that these three location estimators have odd ψ-functions: $\psi(-u) = -\psi(u)$.

11C. RESISTANCE AND ROBUSTNESS OF EFFICIENCY

Two properties required of a robust estimator are resistance and robustness of efficiency. These are discussed in Huber (1972), Hampel (1974), and Mosteller and Tukey (1977).

An estimator is *resistant* if it is affected to only a limited extent either by a small number of gross errors or by any number of small rounding and grouping errors. An estimator is resistant to gross errors if a small subset of the sample cannot have a disproportionate effect on the estimate. (A single observation can dominate the mean of a sample.) An estimator is resistant to rounding and grouping errors if it responds continuously to small errors and, furthermore, if the estimate is not determined by rounding or grouping of a small fraction of the observations. (A small error in the median observation of a sample of odd size gives an equal change in the sample median.) Ordinarily we fear the effects of gross errors more than those of rounding and grouping, and so we routinely use the median, as illustrated in other chapters. For more refined work we prefer an estimator that responds more smoothly to rounding and grouping while remaining resistant to gross errors.

An estimator has *robustness of efficiency* over a range of distributions if its variance (or, for biased estimators, its mean squared error) is close to the minimum for each distribution. In Chapter 10, and later in this chapter, we formalize this by looking at the minimum efficiency of an estimator,

compared to the best estimator from a prescribed class of estimators, for the set of distributions considered.

Our experience with real data tells us that such data are often inconsistent with sampling from a Gaussian distribution. It is therefore inadequate to consider only the efficiency of an estimator at that distribution. In addition to the Gaussian we consider heavier-tailed distributions.

The extreme observations associated with sampling from a heavy-tailed distribution suggest the inconsistency of the data with an underlying Gaussian distribution. Sampling from a light-tailed distribution produces no comparable indication of inconsistency. In Section 7B we showed that a mixture of Gaussian distributions with differing variances but identical locations is heavier-tailed. We included this situation in Chapter 10. A mixture of Gaussian distributions with identical variances but differing locations is light-tailed (Tukey, 1960). But then it may be difficult to agree on what location parameter to estimate.

Robustness of efficiency guarantees that the estimator is good when repeated samples are drawn from a distribution that is not known precisely. Additionally, the estimate should change only a little when the sample is contaminated. Contamination may be either by gross errors (outliers) or by rounding and grouping errors among the observations.

We consider contamination separately from ideas of probability and the underlying distribution. A number of gross errors may have occurred as an event with small probability associated with sampling from the tails of the distribution.

11D. THE INFLUENCE CURVE

We now explore how to choose a ψ-function for good resistance and robustness of efficiency. Huber (1981) finds estimators, discussed further in Section 11H, that have optimum robustness of efficiency close to the Gaussian. He argues, using a theorem of Hampel (1971), that resistance and robustness of efficiency are equivalent asymptotically. Our approach is first to consider resistance by studying the estimator's sensitivity curve, influence curve, and change-of-value curve. The sensitivity curve shows the effect on an estimate of adding or deleting an observation. The influence curve extends this notion from sample to distribution. The change-of-value curve, which we discuss in Section 11I, and, less directly, the sensitivity curve show the effect of varying the value of an observation.

The Sensitivity Curve

Suppose we have an estimator, not necessarily an *M*-estimator, that is defined for samples of any size n. For a sample of size $n - 1$, $x_1, \ldots, x_{n-1}$,

the estimate is $T_{n-1}(x_1,\ldots,x_{n-1})$. The change in the estimate when an nth observation equal to x is included is $T_n(x_1,\ldots,x_{n-1}, x) - T_{n-1}(x_1,\ldots,x_{n-1})$. We can make comparisons among sample sizes when we take into account the proportionate change in the size of the sample. We divide the change in the estimate by $1/n$ or, equivalently, we multiply by n. The result is the sensitivity curve.

DEFINITION: The *sensitivity curve* of the estimator T_n, defined for $n = 2, 3, \ldots$, at the sample $x_1,\ldots,x_{n-1}$ is

$$SC(x; x_1,\ldots,x_{n-1}, T_n)$$

$$= n\{T_n(x_1,\ldots,x_{n-1}, x) - T_{n-1}(x_1,\ldots,x_{n-1})\}. \qquad (7)$$

Here we regard the sensitivity curve primarily as a function of the added observation x, but it also depends on the sample and the form of the estimator. An abbreviated notation is $SC(x)$.

EXAMPLE:

Suppose that $n = 2m + 1$ is odd and that the estimator is the median. Let $x_{(1)} < \cdots < x_{(n-1)}$ be the order statistics of the sample $x_1,\ldots,x_{n-1}$. Then

$$T_{n-1}(x_1,\ldots,x_{n-1}) = \tfrac{1}{2}[x_{(m)} + x_{(m+1)}],$$

and

$$SC(x) = \begin{cases} n\{x_{(m)} - \tfrac{1}{2}[x_{(m)} + x_{(m+1)}]\} \\ \quad = \dfrac{n}{2}[x_{(m)} - x_{(m+1)}] & \text{if } x < x_{(m)} \\[2mm] n\{x - \tfrac{1}{2}[x_{(m)} + x_{(m+1)}]\} & \text{if } x_{(m)} \leqslant x \leqslant x_{(m+1)} \\[2mm] n\{x_{(m+1)} - \tfrac{1}{2}[x_{(m)} + x_{(m+1)}]\} \\ \quad = \dfrac{n}{2}[x_{(m+1)} - x_{(m)}] & \text{if } x > x_{(m+1)}. \end{cases}$$

Thus an observation at x has one of two constant effects on the sample median unless x lies between the two median observations of the original sample. These constant effects are proportional to the distance between the median observations. We graph the sensitivity curve for the median in Figure 11-4.

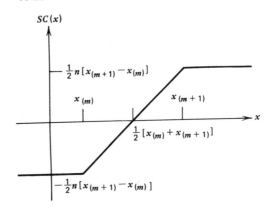

Figure 11-4. The sensitivity curve of the median. The vertical scale is n times the horizontal scale.

The sensitivity curve describes the effect on an estimator of an additional observation at x. Therefore, it describes the effect a gross error in the sample may have. The rounding or grouping of an observation is conceptually the same as the removal of the observation followed by its reintroduction elsewhere. Hence the sensitivity curve shows how rounding and grouping affect an estimator. Therefore, the sensitivity curve gives us a way of studying both aspects of the resistance of an estimator.

The Influence Curve

The sensitivity curve is a realistic summary of resistance, but it is inconvenient because it is tied to a sample. To remove this dependence, we let the sample size tend to infinity. The sample gives way to the underlying distribution, and the sensitivity curve becomes the influence curve. This technique, introduced by Hampel (1968, 1974), provides a single summary curve of the effect of contamination for each estimator and for each distribution. We give a definition of the estimator T_n that emphasizes its connection with the parameter $T(F)$, and then we develop the influence curve.

With the assumption that $x_1, x_2, x_3, \ldots$ are independent and identically distributed, an estimator T_n usually approaches a parameter $T(F)$ of the underlying distribution F. For example, the sample mean estimates the population mean. We require that T_n is a consistent estimator of $T(F)$:

$$T_n \to T \qquad \text{as} \qquad n \to \infty.$$

For M-estimators and for other estimators, T_n is a function of the empirical cumulative distribution function F_n. The equation

$$\sum_{i=1}^{n} \psi\left(\frac{x_i - T_n}{cS_n}\right) = 0$$

can be written

$$\int_{-\infty}^{\infty} \psi\left(\frac{x - T_n}{cS_n}\right) dF_n(x) = 0. \tag{8}$$

If the parameters $T(F)$ and $S(F)$ correspond to the M-estimator of location T_n and the scale estimator S_n, then $T(F)$ is defined by

$$\int_{-\infty}^{\infty} \psi\left(\frac{x - T(F)}{cS(F)}\right) dF(x) = 0. \tag{9}$$

When the underlying density $f(x)$ exists, we can substitute $f(x)\,dx$ for $dF(x)$ in equation (9).

As n grows large, F_n approaches F. From equation (8) and equation (9) we see that T_n may be a consistent estimator of T, provided we also establish, either jointly with the consistency of T_n or separately, that S_n is consistent for $S(F)$.

The median provides an example that does not involve auxiliary scale estimation. As n increases, the solution $t = T_n$ of

$$\sum_{i=1}^{n} \text{sgn}(x_i - t) = 0$$

approaches the solution $t = T(F)$ of

$$\int_{-\infty}^{\infty} \text{sgn}(x - t)f(x)\,dx = 0. \tag{10}$$

The solution of equation (10) is the population median M. It satisfies the equation

$$\int_{-\infty}^{M} f(x)\,dx = \int_{M}^{\infty} f(x)\,dx.$$

To derive the influence curve, we consider what happens to the sensitivity curve as n tends to infinity, assuming T_n is consistent for T. We introduce

into the underlying distribution a point contamination δ_x at x with probability mass ε. The contaminated distribution is $(1 - \varepsilon)F + \varepsilon\delta_x$. By analogy with the sensitivity curve, we find the difference between population parameters and take into account the proportionate change ε in the distribution. We divide $T[(1 - \varepsilon)F + \varepsilon\delta_x] - T(F)$ by ε. As n increases to infinity, the proportionate change in the sample by adding an observation, $1/n$, decreases to 0. Correspondingly, the influence curve is the limit as ε decreases to 0 of the adjusted change in population parameters. This also removes the dependence on ε.

DEFINITION: The *influence curve* is the limit

$$IC(x; F, T) = \lim_{\varepsilon \downarrow 0} \frac{T[(1 - \varepsilon)F + \varepsilon\delta_x] - T(F)}{\varepsilon}, \qquad (11)$$

if the limit exists.

We now derive the influence curve of the median from the sensitivity curve. As the sample size increases, the central part of the sensitivity curve of the median, shown in Figure 11-4, becomes steeper, whereas the tail sections remain flat. For well-behaved distributions, where the density f is continuous and nonzero at the population median M, the distance $x_{(m+1)} - x_{(m)}$ decreases to 0 and the sample points $x_{(m)}$ and $x_{(m+1)}$ approach M. The ratio of the number of sample points in a short interval of fixed length containing M, to the length L of the interval, tends to $f(M)$ as the sample size increases to infinity. The number of sample points in the interval is approximately $nLf(M)$, so the average distance between points tends to $1/nf(M)$. Therefore, $\frac{1}{2}n[x_{(m+1)} - x_{(m)}]$ tends to the limit $1/2f(M)$. The sensitivity curve of the median approaches a sign function, which, apart from the scale factor $1/2f(M)$, is the ψ-function of the median, shown in Figure 11-2(b).

Alternatively, we may calculate the influence curve of the median from the definition, equation (11). When $x = M$, the median of the contaminated distribution $(1 - \varepsilon)F + \varepsilon\delta_x$ is again M. When $x > M$ and the density f is continuous at M, then, for sufficiently small ε, the change in the median, $T[(1 - \varepsilon)F + \varepsilon\delta_x] - T(F)$, corresponds to a shift of $\varepsilon/2$ in the mass of F. Therefore, the median shifts a distance $\varepsilon/2f(M)$. Similarly, when $x < M$ the median shifts a distance $-\varepsilon/2f(M)$. Therefore, dividing by ε, the influence curve is the same sign function,

$$IC(x; F, T) = \text{sgn}(x - M)\frac{1}{2f(M)}, \qquad (12)$$

as we deduced from the sensitivity curve.

Properties

In large samples, an important property of an estimator is its *asymptotic variance*, defined as the limit, as n becomes infinite, of $n\,\mathrm{var}(T_n)$ (if this limit exists). The sample mean provides the simplest possible example: when each observation has variance σ^2, $\mathrm{var}(\bar{x}) = \sigma^2/n$, so that $n\,\mathrm{var}(\bar{x}) = \sigma^2$ and, of course, $\lim_{n \to \infty}[n\,\mathrm{var}(\bar{x})] = \sigma^2$. Thus the asymptotic variance of the sample mean is σ^2 regardless of the distribution underlying the samples. In general, both an estimator's variance in finite samples and its asymptotic variance depend on the distribution of the data. In finite samples, the variance of the sample median does not reduce to a closed-form expression. The asymptotic variance of the median can be calculated, however; for samples from a Gaussian distribution with variance σ^2 it is $\pi\sigma^2/2$, for samples from the (standard) Cauchy distribution it is $\pi^2/4$, and for the (standard) slash distribution it is 2π.

A simple relationship links the asymptotic variance and the influence curve of an estimator. For M-estimators of location and many other estimators, the variance decreases approximately in proportion to $1/n$ as n increases. For these estimators, $n\,\mathrm{var}(T_n \mid F)$ tends to a limit, the asymptotic variance of T_n. We write

$$\lim_{n \to \infty} n\,\mathrm{var}(T_n \mid F) = A(F, T).$$

A theorem relating the influence curve and asymptotic variance is

THEOREM 1: Under appropriate regularity conditions, the asymptotic variance of the consistent estimator T_n of T is

$$A(F, T) = \int_{-\infty}^{\infty} IC(x; F, T)^2 f(x)\, dx. \tag{13}$$

The proof is in Huber (1981, Chapter 3).

For the median, for example, using equation (12) in equation (13),

$$\int_{-\infty}^{\infty} IC(x; F, T)^2 f(x)\, dx = \int_{-\infty}^{\infty} \left\{ \frac{1}{2f(M)} \,\mathrm{sgn}(x - M) \right\}^2 f(x)\, dx$$

$$= \frac{1}{4f(M)^2}.$$

This formula for the asymptotic variance of the median can be obtained in other ways (David, 1981; Kendall and Stuart, 1977).

Thus the influence curve is related to the large-sample variance of the estimator and, therefore, to its robustness of efficiency. A second theorem shows that the influence curve and ψ have the same shape—as we have already seen for the median. For this theorem we return to the original description of ψ as a function with two arguments, $\psi(x; t)$. The parameter $T(F)$ is defined by

$$\int_{-\infty}^{\infty} \psi[x; T(F)] f(x)\, dx = 0.$$

THEOREM 2: The influence curve of an M-estimator T_n with defining function $\psi(x; t)$ and underlying distribution F is

$$IC(x; F, T) = \frac{\psi[x; T(F)]}{-\int_{-\infty}^{\infty} (d/dt)[\psi(x; t)] f(x)\, dx},$$

where the derivative $(d/dt)[\psi(x; t)]$ is evaluated at $t = T(F)$.

The effect of a scale parameter is to leave unchanged the shape of the influence curve for an M-estimator of location, provided ψ is odd and F is symmetric.

COROLLARY TO THEOREM 2: The influence curve of an M-estimator of location T_n with defining function ψ such that $\psi(-u) = -\psi(u)$, auxiliary scale S, tuning constant c, and underlying distribution F symmetric about the location T, is

$$IC(x; F, T, S) = \frac{cS(F)\psi\left[\dfrac{x - T(F)}{cS(F)}\right]}{\displaystyle\int_{-\infty}^{\infty} \psi'\left[\dfrac{y - T(F)}{cS(F)}\right] f(y)\, dy}, \tag{14}$$

where

$$\psi'(u) = \frac{d}{du}\psi(u).$$

The proofs of Theorem 2 and the Corollary are in Huber (1981). One implication of the corollary is that the asymptotic variance of an M-estimator of location depends in a direct way on the scale.

The Corollary to Theorem 2 also tells us that

$$\text{influence curve} = (\text{constant})(\psi\text{-function})$$

where the constant, and therefore the size but not the shape of the influence curve, depends on the distribution. Given an influence curve, we can find a ψ-function which is a constant multiple of it. In Section 11E we discuss desirable features of an influence curve, based on considerations of resistance and robustness of efficiency. We use these properties to choose a shape for the ψ-function of an M-estimator. The corollary then shows that the influence curve of the estimator has the prescribed features for every distribution.

A further consequence of the corollary is that M-estimators are distinguished by having proportional influence curves for any two distributions. Moreover, any estimator with this property is asymptotically equivalent, though perhaps very different for finite samples, to an M-estimator. Therefore, asymptotically, we can regard M-estimators as the results of compromising on a single shape in place of the different shapes of the influence curve desirable for different distributions. For large samples we might want to give up this compromise, but we must then forgo M-estimators.

The influence curve tells us how an infinitesimal proportion of contamination affects the estimate in large samples. In fact, the influence curve is often useful for samples of size 20 or perhaps even smaller. To get an idea of the amount of contamination for which the curve is useful, we need the concept of breakdown of an estimator.

Breakdown Bound

An estimator is resistant if it is altered to only a limited extent by a small proportion of outliers. The estimator breaks down if the proportion becomes too large.

DEFINITION: The *breakdown bound* or breakdown point (Hampel, 1968) of an estimator is the largest possible fraction of the observations for which there is a bound on the change in the estimate when that fraction of the sample is altered without restriction.

An estimator is resistant only if its breakdown bound is greater than 0. As a single observation is made larger, the mean increases without bound. Therefore, the breakdown bound of the mean is 0. The breakdown bound of the median (Section 5E) is the largest possible for a location estimator that treats observations on each side of the estimate symmetrically. It is $1/2 - 1/n$ for even n, and $1/2 - 1/(2n)$ for odd n. The breakdown bound of any estimator that treats observations equivariantly cannot exceed 0.5. There do exist estimators with breakdown bound greater than 0.5. For example, an

estimator of location with breakdown bound 1 is $\Sigma_{i=1}^{n} y_i$, where for fixed c and d,

$$y_i = \begin{cases} x_i & c \leqslant x_i \leqslant d \\ \dfrac{c+d}{2} & x_i < c \quad \text{or} \quad x_i > d. \end{cases}$$

Essentially, this estimator handles out-of-bounds observations by pushing them to the center of the interval.

The influence curve tells us about the effect of a mass ε of contamination at x in the limit as $\varepsilon \downarrow 0$. In practice, one, two, or more observations are contaminated. Thus the mass of contamination in the sample is in discrete amounts of $1/n$. A rough rule is that the influence curve of an estimator is of use in assessing the effect of contamination in the sample, provided that the contamination does not exceed 25 to 50% of the breakdown bound.

M-estimators with symmetric ψ-function have breakdown bound close to 50%, provided that the auxiliary scale estimator has equal (or better) breakdown bound.

11E.   THE SHAPE OF ψ

We now discuss criteria for the shape of ψ. The first three criteria principally measure the resistance of the estimator.

Gross-Error Sensitivity

The gross-error sensitivity (g.e.s.) expresses, asymptotically, the maximum effect a contaminated observation can have on the estimator T_n. It is the maximum absolute value of the influence curve. Figure 11-5, the influence curve for the biweight when $T = 0$, shows that the g.e.s. of the biweight is finite.

DEFINITION: The *gross-error sensitivity* (Hampel, 1974) of a consistent estimator T_n of T at distribution F is

$$\text{g.e.s.} = \sup_{x} |IC(x; F, T)|. \tag{15}$$

The supremum (sup) of $|IC(x; F, T)|$ is the smallest number that $|IC(x; F, T)|$ does not exceed for any x. In Figure 11-5,

$$\text{g.e.s.} = \max(G, -G').$$

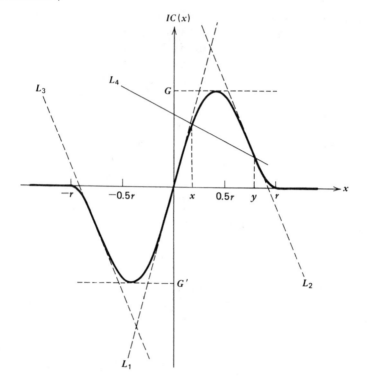

Figure 11-5. The influence curve of the biweight estimators; g.e.s. = max(G; $-G'$), l.s.s. = maximum absolute slope of L_1, L_2, L_3; rejection point = $r = cS$.

Because the influence curve in Figure 11-5 is odd—that is, $IC(-x) = -IC(x)$—we have $G = -G' = $ g.e.s.

The asymptotic bias of an estimator is simply related to the g.e.s. The distribution function of a distribution F with a proportion ε of contamination is $(1 - \varepsilon)F + \varepsilon H$, where H is the distribution of the contamination. The maximum bias from the contamination is, asymptotically,

$$\sup_{H} | T[(1 - \varepsilon)F + \varepsilon H] - T(F) | .$$

From the definition of the influence curve, equation (11), the maximum bias is approximately the g.e.s. times ε.

An estimator has robustness of efficiency and is resistant only if the g.e.s. is bounded. For a resistant estimator, we would like the g.e.s. to be as small

as possible. However, we face a conflict of goals: At a given distribution, the g.e.s. can be decreased beyond a certain point only if the asymptotic variance is allowed to increase. Figure 11-1 shows that the g.e.s. of the mean is infinite, because the influence curve and ψ-function are proportional. Figure 11-2 shows that the g.e.s. of the median is finite.

Local-Shift Sensitivity

The effect on the estimator of the removal of mass ε at y and its reintroduction at x is asymptotically, as $n \to \infty$ and $\varepsilon \downarrow 0$, $IC(x) - IC(y)$. Therefore, the influence curve tells us the effect on an estimator of rounding and grouping errors. The magnitude of the perturbation introduced by rounding and grouping depends on the distance through which the observation is shifted. Thus we standardize the difference $IC(x) - IC(y)$ by the shift distance $x - y$.

The quantity $|IC(x) - IC(y)|/|x - y|$ has a ready geometrical interpretation. In Figure 11-5, with the x and y shown, it is the absolute value of the slope of the line L_4. The sensitivity of the estimator to rounding and grouping is the supremum of this standardized difference over all choices of x and y.

DEFINITION: The *local-shift sensitivity* is the supremum of the absolute slopes of chords joining all pairs of distinct points on the influence curve:

$$\text{l.s.s.} = \sup_{x \neq y} \frac{|IC(x) - IC(y)|}{|x - y|}. \tag{16}$$

The Mean Value Theorem tells us that for each $x \neq y$ there is an x^* between x and y for which, provided the influence curve is differentiable in that interval,

$$IC(x) - IC(y) = IC'(x^*)(x - y).$$

Thus if the influence curve is continuous, and differentiable except at a finite set of points, then the local-shift sensitivity is simply $\sup_x |IC'(x)|$. Because $IC(x)$ is differentiable for the biweight, we consider only tangents to the curve in Figure 11-5. The local-shift sensitivity is the maximum of the absolute slopes of the tangent lines L_1, L_2, and L_3 shown. The line L_1 has maximum absolute slope.

Figure 11-2 shows that the l.s.s. of the median is infinite. We mentioned in Section 11D that the central section of the sensitivity curve of the median (see Figure 11-4) has asymptotically infinite slope. The median is determined by only one or two observations, so it reflects any rounding and

grouping of those points (and, especially, any systematic rounding or grouping errors). Asymptotically, the proportion of the sample in which rounding and grouping errors determine the median is 0. Therefore, the median is not resistant, at least in large samples, to systematic rounding and grouping errors, and it has infinite l.s.s.

For the highest resistance, we would require that the l.s.s. be bounded, but in some practical circumstances this condition is unnecessarily strict. It may be sufficient to require that the influence curve be moderately continuous. We think of moderate continuity in the sense of the modulus of continuity (Billingsley, 1968). Monomials x^α are increasingly discontinuous at $x = 0$ as $\alpha \to 0$ because the slope $x^{\alpha-1}$ of the chord from the origin increases without bound. The limiting value $\alpha = 0$ gives a step discontinuity, with infinite slope, and corresponds to the influence curve for the median. Thus this restriction would still exclude the median, but in some situations we may not need even moderate continuity, and thus we would be prepared to use the median. We discuss the median further in Section 11H.

Rejection Point

The ψ-function of the biweight is 0 for $|u|$ larger than 1. Thus in Figure 11-5, $IC(x) = 0$ for $|x| > cS$. We say that the rejection point is $r = cS$. Observations beyond the rejection point do not contribute to the value of the estimate except possibly through the auxiliary scale estimate. The rejection point of the median is infinity; when we find the median, we count all observations. For the biweight, observations beyond the rejection point are ignored once the scale estimate is calculated and the approximate location of the biweight is chosen.

DEFINITION: The *rejection point r* is the least distance from the location estimate beyond which observations do not contribute to the value of the estimate for a given auxiliary scale estimate.

Estimators whose ψ-functions have a finite rejection point (e.g., the biweight) are particularly well protected against sufficiently large outliers.

Maximum-Likelihood Estimation

A motivation for M-estimation is that some M-estimators are maximum-likelihood estimators. We now describe a connection between the ψ-function and the underlying density that allows us to choose ψ to give an asymptotically efficient estimator at a particular distribution.

If $F(\cdot\,;T)$ is a family of distributions with density $f(\cdot\,;T)$ parametrized by T, then the joint likelihood of the sample $x_1,\ldots,x_n$ is $\prod_{i=1}^{n} f(x_i; T)$. Taking logs and differentiating, the maximum-likelihood estimate T_n of T is the solution t of

$$\sum_{i=1}^{n} \frac{(d/dt)f(x_i; t)}{f(x_i; t)} = 0.$$

Taking ψ to be the negative of the score function,

$$\psi(x; t) = -\frac{1}{f(x; t)} \frac{d}{dt} f(x; t) = -\frac{d}{dt}[\log f(x; t)], \qquad (17)$$

we see that T_n is an M-estimate. The minus sign is present to satisfy the convention that ψ is positive for large x. A constant of proportionality may be freely inserted.

Therefore, the maximum-likelihood estimator for any distribution is an M-estimator; conversely, given any M-estimator, we can seek to solve equation (17) to find the distribution for which it is a maximum-likelihood estimator. We call the latter distribution, if it exists, the *target distribution* of the M-estimator. The target distribution has density

$$f(x; T) \propto \exp\left[-\int_T^x \psi(u; T)\, du\right]. \qquad (18)$$

For ψ-functions with finite rejection points, $\int_T^x \psi(u; T)\, du$ is bounded. Therefore, $f(x; T)$ is bounded away from 0 and cannot be a proper density. Thus M-estimators with finite rejection points have no target distributions. An example is the biweight.

When an M-estimator is related to a maximum-likelihood estimator, it is often minimum-variance at the corresponding distribution. Silvey (1970, p. 73) shows that when, in a regular finite-sample situation, there is an unbiased estimator whose variance attains the Cramér–Rao lower bound, that estimator is the maximum-likelihood estimator. Asymptotically, a stronger result is true.

THEOREM 3: Consider the density $f(\cdot\,;T)$, parametrized by T. Then under regularity conditions on f, the M-estimator of T for which

$$\psi(\cdot\,; t) \propto -\frac{d}{dt} \log[f(\cdot\,; t)]$$

has the minimum asymptotic variance at f among all estimators of T.

Three alternative proofs use maximum-likelihood estimation (Silvey, 1970, p. 77), the influence curve (Huber, 1981, p. 69), and ψ-functions and Fisher information (Huber, 1981, p. 77).

Theorem 3 and the associated finite-sample result suggest that if we have a strong belief in a particular underlying distribution, then there is a corresponding choice of ψ-function. This choice should be exercised with caution: the maximum-likelihood estimator need not be resistant and need not have robustness of efficiency. For example, the mean is the maximum-likelihood estimator for the Gaussian distribution, and the median is the maximum-likelihood estimator for the double-exponential distribution [whose density is $f(x; t) = \frac{1}{2} e^{-|x-t|}$]. Also, because an estimator with a finite rejection point does not have a target distribution, some well-performing estimators (e.g., the biweight) may be preferable from a robustness point of view to any maximum-likelihood estimator.

As we discussed in Section 10D, we can use the minimum-variance estimator to convert from asymptotic variance to efficiency. For example, at the standard Gaussian distribution the asymptotic variance of the mean is 1. Therefore, the asymptotic efficiency of an estimator is the reciprocal of its asymptotic variance.

Winsor's Principle

Winsor's principle, quoted by Tukey (1960, p. 457), states "all distributions are normal in the middle." We can apply this idea to M-estimators, asking that, in the middle, their ψ-functions resemble the one that is best for Gaussian data. The ψ-function of the maximum-likelihood estimator for the Gaussian distribution, the mean, is linear. Therefore, the ψ-functions for M-estimators of location should be linear near the origin:

$$\psi(u) \approx ku$$

for small $|u|$ where k is a nonzero constant, usually standardized to $k = 1$.

Winsor's principle is the empirical analog of the theoretical fact that, under the Central Limit Theorem, convergence is almost always most rapid near the mean. If we combine only a few different distributions, the convolution is usually closer to a Gaussian distribution near its mean than elsewhere.

Symmetry

For a symmetric underlying distribution, the objective function of an M-estimator of location should give equal weight to observations at equal

distances either side of the center of symmetry. Therefore, the ψ-function should be odd: $\psi(-u) = -\psi(u)$. If the distribution is not symmetric, then the definition of location is unclear. Often, particularly if the departure from symmetry is not too violent, we continue to use the same estimators that we have found satisfactory in symmetric situations.

Lemma 1 of Section 10A states that, in a symmetric distribution, the population median is the center of symmetry and is also the population mean if the mean is finite. The more general result is that an M-estimator with odd ψ-function is unbiased when the underlying distribution is symmetric.

THEOREM 4: Let the M-estimator of location T_n be the solution of

$$\sum_{i=1}^{n} \psi\left(\frac{x_i - T_n}{cS_n}\right) = 0,$$

where S_n, the auxiliary estimator of scale, is an even function of the $x_i - T_n$ and c is the tuning constant. If ψ is odd and F, the underlying distribution, is symmetric with center T, then T_n is an unbiased estimator of T.

PROOF: Since F is symmetric with center T,

$$E[T_n(X_1, \ldots, X_n)] = E[T_n(2T - X_1, \ldots, 2T - X_n)],$$

where $X_1, \ldots, X_n$ are the random variables underlying the sample $x_1, \ldots, x_n$. Therefore,

$$
\begin{aligned}
E[T_n(X_1, &\ldots, X_n)] \\
&= \tfrac{1}{2}\{E[T_n(X_1, \ldots, X_n)] + E[T_n(2T - X_1, \ldots, 2T - X_n)]\} \\
&= \tfrac{1}{2}E[T_n(X_1, \ldots, X_n) + T_n(2T - X_1, \ldots, 2T - X_n)].
\end{aligned}
$$

Because ψ is odd and S_n is an even function of the $x_i - T_n$, defining k by

$$T_n(x_1, \ldots, x_n) = T + k,$$

yields

$$T_n(2T - x_1, \ldots, 2T - x_n) = T - k.$$

Therefore,

$$T_n(x_1, \ldots, x_n) + T_n(2T - x_1, \ldots, 2T - x_n) = 2T,$$

and

$$E[T_n(X_1,\ldots,X_n)] = \tfrac{1}{2}E[2T] = T.$$

11F. SUMMARY OF CRITERIA

Having studied estimators and their influence curves, we would like the ψ-function of a robust M-estimator of the location of a symmetric underlying distribution to have the following properties:

1. The breakdown point of the estimator is large.
2. ψ is bounded (finite gross-error sensitivity).
3. ψ is moderately continuous (finite local-shift sensitivity).
4. ψ has finite rejection point (if resistance to very large outliers is important).
5. For efficiency at some target distribution with density f, ψ is proportional to $-(\log f)' = -f'/f$ (to be chosen with caution).
6. $\psi(u) \approx ku$, $k \neq 0$, for small u.
7. $\psi(-u) = -\psi(u)$.

In the next section we discuss the choice of an auxiliary estimator of scale. In Section 11H we present a selection of M-estimators of location and consider their adequacy under these criteria.

11G. AUXILIARY SCALE ESTIMATES

Three common scale estimators are the standard deviation, the fourth-spread (d_F), and the median absolute deviation (MAD). The sample standard deviation has breakdown point 0; it is not resistant. In fact, gross errors affect the standard deviation even more adversely than they affect the mean. We therefore do not use the standard deviation as an auxiliary scale for M-estimators.

The Corollary to Theorem 2 holds only for symmetric distributions. The importance of asymmetry should not be underestimated. When we believe that the sample is contaminated and drawn from an asymmetric distribution, a practical approach, discussed by Huber (1981), is to use a scale estimator with, in order of desirability, (a) large breakdown bound, (b) small bias, and (c) small (asymptotic) variance.

Table 12-5 compares the efficiencies of four scale estimators including the standard deviation, MAD, and d_F, for samples of size 20 drawn from

TABLE 11-1. *M*-estimators of location.[a]

Estimator with Tuning Constant(s)	Figure	Objective Function ρ	ψ-Function	ψ'	Weight Function w	Range of u	Commonly used Denominator of u
Mean	11-1	$\frac{1}{2}u^2$	u	1	1	$-\infty$ to $+\infty$	none
Median	11-2	$|u|$	$\mathrm{sgn}(u)$	$\delta(u)$[b]	$\dfrac{\mathrm{sgn}(u)}{u}$	$-\infty$ to $+\infty$	none
Huber (k) $0 < k$	11-8	$\frac{1}{2}u^2$ $k|u| - \frac{1}{2}k^2$	u $k\,\mathrm{sgn}(u)$	1 0	1 $\dfrac{k\,\mathrm{sgn}(u)}{u}$	$|u| \leq k$ $|u| > k$	normalized F-spread or MAD

Redescending Estimators (Finite Rejection Point)

		$\rho(u)$	$\psi(u)$	$\psi'(u)$	$w(u)$		MAD
Hampel (a, b, c) (three-part redescending) $0 < a \leqslant b \leqslant c$	11-10	$\dfrac{1}{2}u^2$	u	1	1	$\|u\| \leqslant a$	MAD
		$a\|u\| - \dfrac{1}{2}a^2$	$a\,\text{sgn}(u)$	0	$\dfrac{a\,\text{sgn}(u)}{u}$	$a < \|u\| \leqslant b$	
		$ab - \dfrac{1}{2}a^2 + (c-b)\dfrac{a}{2}\left[1 - \left(\dfrac{c-\|u\|}{c-b}\right)^2\right]$	$\dfrac{c - \|u\|}{c - b}\,a\,\text{sgn}(u)$	$-\dfrac{a}{c-b}\,\text{sgn}(u)$	$a\,\dfrac{c-\|u\|}{c-b}\,\dfrac{\text{sgn}(u)}{u}$	$b < \|u\| \leqslant c$	
		$ab - \dfrac{1}{2}a^2 + (c-b)\dfrac{a}{2}$	0	0	0	$\|u\| > c$	
Andrews' wave (c) $0 < c$	11-11	$\dfrac{1}{\pi^2}(1 - \cos \pi u)$	$\dfrac{1}{\pi}\sin \pi u$	$\cos \pi u$	$\dfrac{1}{\pi u}\sin \pi u$	$\|u\| \leqslant 1$	$c\,\text{MAD}$
		$\dfrac{2}{\pi^2}$	0	0	0	$\|u\| > 1$	
Tukey's biweight (c) $0 < c$	11-3	$\dfrac{1}{6}[1 - (1 - u^2)^3]$	$u(1 - u^2)^2$	$(1 - u^2)(1 - 5u^2)$	$(1 - u^2)^2$	$\|u\| \leqslant 1$	$c\,\text{MAD}$
		$\dfrac{1}{6}$	0	0	0	$\|u\| > 1$	

[a]To each objective function may be added an arbitrary constant. As written, $\rho(u) = 0$ for $u = 0$. The multiplicative factors are chosen so that each ψ-function has derivative 1 at 0. Section 11J discusses w and Section 11I discusses ψ'.

[b]The Dirac delta function $\delta(u)$ takes the value ∞ at $u = 0$ and the value 0 for $u \neq 0$.

three neutral to heavy-tailed symmetric distributions. The standard deviation has small efficiencies at the heavy-tailed distributions, and d_F has slightly higher efficiencies than the MAD.

The breakdown bound of the fourth-spread, 0.25, is smaller than that of the MAD, 0.50. A high breakdown bound indicates tolerance to sample asymmetry. The fourth-spread illustrates this: when the contamination is placed symmetrically, the breakdown bound increases from 0.25 to 0.50. The breakdown bound of a location estimator with auxiliary scale is the smaller of the breakdown bound for location and the breakdown bound for scale. An arbitrary scale may lead to the unwanted influence of outliers on the location estimate or to ignoring essentially all the sample. The breakdown bound of many *M*-estimators of location is 0.50. For these reasons MAD is often the favored scale estimate. Andrews et al. (1972) show convincingly the superiority of the MAD over d_F in some situations. We make our own comparisons in Chapter 12.

The fourth-spread and median absolute deviation may be normalized by dividing by the corresponding value for the standard Gaussian distribution. These divisors are 1.3490 and 0.6745, respectively. The *M*-estimator of location is unchanged, except that the tuning constant(s) of the ψ-function should be multiplied by the normalizing constant, For example,

$$c\,\mathrm{MAD} = (0.6745c)\,\frac{\mathrm{MAD}}{0.6745}.$$

As discussed in Section 2C, the square of the normalized fourth-spread is known as the 25%-pseudovariance.

11H.   EXAMPLES OF LOCATION ESTIMATORS

In this section we present examples of *M*-estimators of location and attempt to motivate their successively more complex ψ-functions. Table 11-1 lists these six estimates. We suggest that the reader keep in mind the criteria summarized in Section 11F. Table 11-2 checks the ψ-functions against these criteria. Table 11-3 gives the numerical robustness properties of the estimators at the standard Gaussian distribution. In Figures 11-6 and 11-7 we plot, respectively, the g.e.s. and l.s.s. against efficiency at the Gaussian distribution for a variety of estimators.

Mean

The mean is the classical estimator of location. The objective function and ψ-function are shown in Figure 11-1. It is the maximum-likelihood estimator

TABLE 11-2. Criteria for ψ.[a]

Estimator	Resistant (1)	Bounded (2)	Moderate Continuity (3)	Finite Rejection Point (4)	Linear at Origin (6)	Odd (7)
Mean	No	No	Yes	No	Yes	Yes
Median	Yes	Yes	No	No	No	Yes
Huber	Yes	Yes	Yes	No	Yes	Yes
Hampel	Yes	Yes	Yes	Yes	Yes	Yes
Wave	Yes	Yes	Yes	Yes	Yes	Yes
Biweight	Yes	Yes	Yes	Yes	Yes	Yes

[a]Column numbers refer to criteria in Section 11F.

for the Gaussian distribution. The variance of the sample mean at the Gaussian distribution is the minimum. The local-shift sensitivity is also the minimum because the observations contribute exactly equally to the estimate. The unboundedness of ψ is responsible for the lack of resistance of the mean (breakdown bound = 0).

Median

The median is the classical robust estimator. The objective function and ψ-function are shown in Figure 11-2. It has the maximum breakdown bound, close to 0.5. The gross-error sensitivity is low, but the asymptotic variance is high. Moreover, the median is sensitive to rounding and grouping errors of the middle observations. The median is the m.l.e. for the double-exponential distribution, which has density $\frac{1}{2}e^{-|x-t|}$.

Suppose that a proportion $(1 - \varepsilon)$ of observations comes from a symmetric unimodal distribution and a proportion ε are arbitrary. This is called the *contamination model*, with ε contamination. Huber (1981) argues that the median is the best estimator for *large* sample sizes, assuming the contamination model. Any estimator of location in a symmetric distribution will have a maximum bias over all choices of the contamination. As the sample size n increases, the variance of the estimator decreases as $1/n$, but the maximum bias does not change. Therefore, for large sample sizes, the bias is the property of importance. The median is the estimator with the smallest maximum bias for given ε. Therefore, it is the unique best estimator of

TABLE 11-3. Numerical robustness properties at the standard Gaussian for a selection of estimators.[a]

Estimator	Tuning Constant	Scale	Asymptotic Variance	Gross Error Sensitivity	Local Shift Sensitivity	Rejection Point	Breakdown Bound
Mean	none	none	1.000	∞	1.00	∞	0.00
Median	none	none	1.571	1.25	∞	∞	0.50
Huber	1.0	Normalized MAD	1.107	1.46	1.46	∞	0.50
	1.5	Normalized MAD	1.037	1.73	1.15	∞	0.50
	1.5	Normalized Fourth-spread	1.037	1.73	1.15	∞	0.25
	2.0	Normalized MAD	1.010	2.10	1.05	∞	0.50
Andrews' wave[b]	4.7	MAD	1.161	1.65	1.63	3.2	0.50
	6.6	MAD	1.042	1.82	1.28	4.4	0.50
Tukey's biweight	3	MAD	2.102	2.10	3.63	2.0	0.50
	6	MAD	1.094	1.68	1.45	4.0	0.50
	9	MAD	1.018	2.05	1.18	6.1	0.50
	12	MAD	1.006	2.54	1.10	8.1	0.50

Source: Hampel (1974) and author's calculations.

[a] The breakdown bound is the only robustness property among those tabulated that does not depend on the distribution.

The minimum asymptotic variance of any estimator is unity.

In general, for an estimator, as the tuning constant increases, the center of the ψ-function is increasingly linear, and the numerical robustness properties resemble more closely those of the mean.

The asymptotic variances of the last three estimators tabulated are not greatly higher than that of the mean. Gross-error sensitivities are finite, not infinite, as for the mean.

The use of fourth-spread instead of MAD in Huber's estimator gives lower breakdown bound with no change in other numerical properties. If the distribution were asymmetric, then this would not be true.

[b] Tuning constants are $1.5\pi = 4.7$ and $2.1\pi = 6.6$.

location for very large samples from an arbitrarily contaminated symmetric unimodal distribution.

We get a rough idea of the sample sizes under consideration by calculating the n at which the maximum bias for the median is equal to $1/\sqrt{n}$. This quantity, $1/\sqrt{n}$, expresses the asymptotic dependence of the standard deviation of the estimator on the sample size. Values of n at the ε-con-

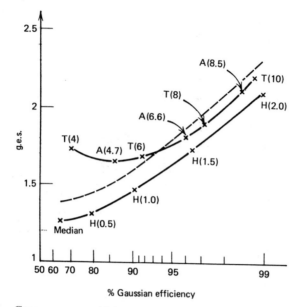

Figure 11-6. Gross-error sensitivity versus Gaussian efficiency for families of estimators: Hubers (H), Andrews' waves (A), Tukey's biweights (T). Waves and biweights lie on approximately the same curve. Tuning constants are given in parentheses. For the waves, $4.7 = 1.5\pi$, $6.6 = 2.1\pi$, and $8.5 = 2.7\pi$. Dashed line = g.e.s. for Hubers + 10%, for comparison. Efficiencies are on a log scale, with 100% efficiency at ∞.

taminated Gaussian distribution are:

ε	0.25	0.1	0.05	0.01
n	5	50	230	6300

For larger ε, n is quite small.

The mean and median do not require auxiliary scale estimators. The estimators we now discuss do require auxiliary scale, as well as associated tuning constant(s). Thus each example is a family of estimators.

Hubers

We have seen that the squared-residual objective function makes the estimator too sensitive to outliers. On the other hand, using the absolute residual

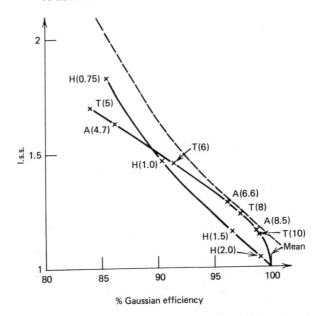

Figure 11-7. Local-shift sensitivity versus Gaussian efficiency for families of estimators: Hubers (H), Andrews' waves (A), Tukey's biweights (T). Waves and biweights lie on approximately the same curve. Tuning constants are given in parentheses. For the waves, $4.7 = 1.5\pi$, $6.6 = 2.1\pi$, and $8.5 = 2.7\pi$. Dashed line = l.s.s. for Hubers + 10%, for comparison.

makes the estimate too sensitive to the middle observations. A compromise is possible when we remember Winsor's principle. The objective function of a Huber estimator, drawn in Figure 11-8(a), is quadratic in the center and linear in the tails. An auxiliary scale estimator is now essential for the data to fix the point of transition from quadratic to linear.

The ψ-function of a Huber estimator, shown in Figure 11-8(b), is linear in the center and constant in the tails. The ψ-function is monotone, and Huber's estimators are examples of monotone M-estimators. The mean and median are extreme cases in Huber's family. At $k = 0$, the objective function is linear only, whereas as $k \to \infty$, the objective function becomes quadratic throughout.

Huber's estimators are the maximum-likelihood estimators for the *least favorable ε-contaminated* Gaussian distributions. They are the estimators that, in terms of efficiency, do the best possible for arbitrary choices of the

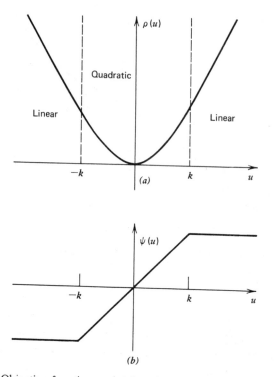

Figure 11-8. Objective function and ψ-function of Huber's estimators of location (formulas in Table 11-1). (*a*) Objective function, $\rho(u)$. (*b*) ψ-function, $\psi(u)$.

ε-contamination. The density of a least favorable distribution is

$$
f(x) = \begin{cases} \dfrac{1-\varepsilon}{\sqrt{2\pi}}\,e^{-x^2/2} & |x| \leq k \\[2ex] \dfrac{1-\varepsilon}{\sqrt{2\pi}}\,e^{+k^2/2-k|x|} & |x| > k. \end{cases} \tag{19}
$$

The parameter k is related to ε by

$$
\frac{2\phi(k)}{k} - 2\Phi(-k) = \frac{\varepsilon}{1-\varepsilon}, \tag{20}
$$

where Φ is the standard Gaussian cumulative distribution function and ϕ is its density.

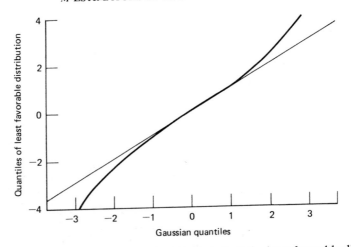

Figure 11-9. Gaussian probability plot (Q–Q plot) of the least favorable distribution for $k = 1.5$. The reference line has unit slope.

The Gaussian probability plot of the least favorable distribution, Figure 11-9, reveals its shape. The shape is a guide to the robustness of Huber's estimator. The weight of the tails, although greater than for the Gaussian distribution, does not provide for the outliers sometimes encountered. Consequently, Huber's estimator may not be resistant enough. On the other hand, Huber (1981) finds that the empirical distributions of large samples from what are supposed to be Gaussian distributions fit the least favorable distributions closely, with ε between 0.1 and 0.01, corresponding to $1.945 > k > 1.140$.

In practice, we choose the tuning constant k to give an estimator with reasonable performance over a range of situations. The relationship between k and ε suggests how we might select k on the basis of prior knowledge or guesses about the amount of contamination in the sample.

Redescending Estimators, Hampels

The influence curve of Huber's estimator is constant for all observations beyond a certain point. An M-estimator can be made more resistant by having the ψ-function, and hence the influence curve, return to 0. Outliers have diminishing effects on a redescending estimator. Apart from a possible effect on the auxiliary scale estimator, they have no effect at all beyond the rejection point. The *three-part redescending M-estimator* (Andrews et al., 1972), sometimes called a *Hampel*, has a piecewise-linear ψ-function, shown

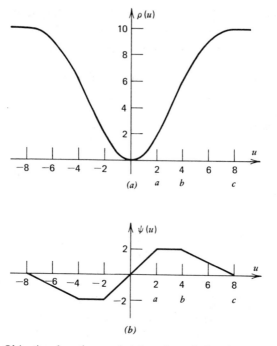

Figure 11-10. Objective function and ψ-function of the three-part redescending estimators of Hampel. The formulas for ρ and ψ appear in Table 11-1. Tuning constants are $(a, b, c) = (2, 4, 8)$. (*a*) Objective function, $\rho(u)$. (*b*) ψ-function, $\psi(u)$.

in Figure 11-10. This was the first redescending estimator tested for its robustness.

The three tuning constants of the Hampels, specified in Table 11-1, provide flexibility for tuning the estimator, or for indecision. There are some guidelines. We choose the constant a in the same way as the constant k for Huber's estimators, taking account of the nonnormalized scale convention-ally used with the Hampels. From Theorems 1 and 2, the asymptotic variance of the M-estimator defined by ψ is $E\psi^2/(E\psi')^2$. Probability mass on the redescending part of Hampel's ψ (or of any other redescending ψ-function) causes $E\psi'$ to decrease while $E\psi^2$ increases (because $\psi^2 > 0$), and this adversely affects the asymptotic variance. If the redescending part is omitted, taking $b = c$, then the estimator will not be resistant to rounding and grouping errors. Therefore, we choose the constant b so that few observations, on the average, lie outside the interval $(-b, b)$ for u. For large samples from the Gaussian distribution, less than $1\frac{1}{2}\%$ of the probability

mass is further than $2\frac{1}{2}$ standard deviations from the mean, corresponding to $b = 3.6$ with scale $=$ MAD. For heavier-tailed distributions than the Gaussian, the weight of the tails further out than a particular multiple of the MAD is greater.

However, simulations show (Section 11L) that, in the expression given for the asymptotic variance, the numerator $E\psi^2$ is relatively more important than the denominator $(E\psi')^2$. Therefore, contrary to the previous remarks, the tuning constant b, together with a, should be smaller for efficient estimation at heavier-tailed distributions. A general principle in robust estimation of location is that the tuning constant(s) should be smaller for heavier-tailed distributions (as we have already seen for the Hubers). This accords with the notion that closer attention to outliers is necessary when the sample is more outlier-prone.

Returning to the denominator $(E\psi')^2$, a rough rule is that the absolute slope of the redescending part of Hampel's ψ-function should be no greater than half the slope of the central part, which is 1 by convention. In Figure 11-10, $a = 2$, corresponding to $k = 1.35$, and $b = 4$. The rule for the redescending slope gives $c - b \geqslant 2a$. We choose $c - b = 4$ and thus $c = 8$.

Collins (1976) proposes a development of the Hampels that substitutes a smoothly descending hyperbolic tangent (tanh) function for the two sections a to b and b to c. Huber (1977) indicates that this estimator is optimal in a restricted form of the sense that Hubers are optimal, maximizing robustness of efficiency for the ε-contaminated Gaussian, subject to the additional constraint that the estimator redescends.

Andrews' Wave

The abrupt changes in slope of the three-part redescending estimators are intuitively unappealing because of the abrupt changes in the way data are used. Andrews' wave estimators, also called sine estimators, have a smooth redescending influence curve, shown in Figure 11-11. We see from Table 11-3 and Figures 11-6 and 11-7 how the choice of the tuning constant c affects the asymptotic variance and the parameters of the influence curve at the standard Gaussian distribution. Andrews et al. (1972) use $c = 2.1\pi$, Hogg (1979) suggests values of 1.5π and 2.0π, and Gross (1976) uses $c = 1.8\pi$ and $c = 2.4\pi$.

Biweight

Tukey's biweight estimators are a popular robust family. Both Andrews' wave estimators and the biweights have smooth redescending ψ-functions. Additionally, through the factor $(1 - u^2)^2$ in the formula in Table 11-1, the

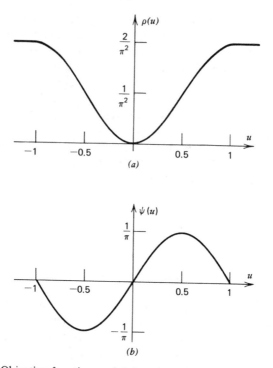

Figure 11-11. Objective function and ψ-function of Andrews' wave estimators of location (formulas in Table 11-1). (a) Objective function, $\rho(u)$. (b) ψ-function, $\psi(u)$.

slope of the biweight ψ-function is continuous at the rejection point $\psi(\pm 1)$ = 0, as shown in Figure 11-3. A desirable feature, from the discussion of the Hampels, is that the redescending part of the biweight ψ-function is, proportionately to the rejection point, longer than the corresponding part of the wave ψ-function, shown in Figure 11-11.

Figure 11-5 shows the influence curve of the biweights. For reasonable values of c, say $6 \leqslant c \leqslant 12$, the biweights have good overall performance (meaning robustness of efficiency) and are resistant. Apart from under-estimation of scale and multiple solutions, discussed in Section 11K, the biweight (for $6 \leqslant c \leqslant 9$) of a data set should always be a reasonable location. Although the discerning statistician may at times do better, the routine user of the biweight will not lose much on the average. Relles and Rogers (1977) compare the performances of statisticians and robust estima-tors.

Through the choice of tuning constant c, we select an estimator from the biweight family according to our requirements of robustness. For example, with scale = MAD and $c = 9$, the rejection point is $9(0.6745) \approx 6$ standard deviations from the mean for a sample approximating the Gaussian distribution.

Tukey proposed the biweight in the 1970s after the Princeton Robustness Study (Andrews et al., 1972) had compared a range of estimators including the Hubers and Andrews' wave estimators. However, the first known M-estimator, apart from the mean and median, is a nineteenth-century precursor of the biweight. In 1888, R. H. Smith (Smith, 1888) proposed an estimator of location that in our notation has ψ-function

$$\psi(u) = \begin{cases} u(1 - u^2) & |u| \leq 1 \\ 0 & |u| > 1 \end{cases}$$

and a subjectively chosen auxiliary scale. For additional details see Stigler (1980).

To this point, our discussion introduces four families of M-estimators in addition to the mean and median. The principal motivation of the choices of ψ-function is through the influence curve. Tables 11-2 and 11-3 summarize the heuristic and asymptotic properties of the estimators. We now return to specific finite-sample aspects: the change-of-value curve, computation, and finite-sample variances. The chapter concludes with a comparative discussion of the M-estimators of location.

11I. THE CHANGE-OF-VALUE CURVE

The local-shift sensitivity is perhaps the least interesting feature of the influence curve discussed in Section 11E. For the Huber, wave, and biweight families of estimators, the l.s.s. simply decreases monotonically as the tuning constant increases. On the other hand, the sample alternative to the influence curve, the sensitivity curve, depends too much on the sample for most M-estimators of location. An alternate way of using samples to study an estimator is the change-of-value curve, which corresponds to the slope of the sensitivity curve and is more useful and informative than the local-shift sensitivity.

DEFINITION: The *change-of-value curve* of the estimator T_n, with sample $x_1, \ldots, x_{n-1}$ and nth observation at x, is the rate of change of

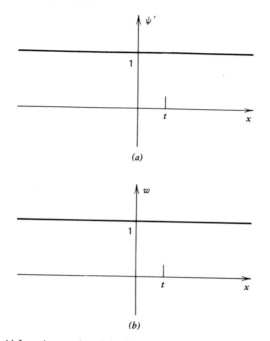

Figure 11-12. ψ'-function and weight function of the sample mean. (*a*) ψ'-function, $\psi'(x; t) = 1$. (*b*) Weight function, $w(x; t) = 1$.

$T_n(x_1, \ldots, x_{n-1}, x)$ with x. Symbolically,

$$CV(x; x_1, \ldots, x_{n-1}, T_n) = \frac{\partial}{\partial x} T_n(x_1, \ldots, x_{n-1}, x). \qquad (21)$$

Of course, for a sample of size n, an arbitrary observation can be designated as the nth, and the effect of varying the observation discovered from the change-of-value curve.

For M-estimators of location, we simply take the implicit equation for T_n,

$$\sum_{i=1}^{n} \psi\left(\frac{x_i - T_n}{cS_n}\right) = 0,$$

and differentiate with respect to x_n. Writing x for x_n to signify that the value x is not restricted to be equal to x_n, we then solve for $\partial T_n/\partial x$. In practice it is useful to make two approximations. First, we assume that $\partial S_n/\partial x = 0$. In fact, this is easily seen to be generally true for extreme x

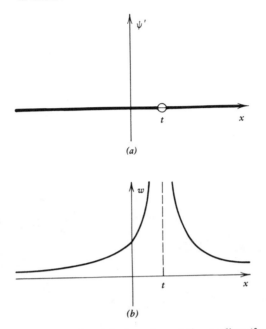

Figure 11-13. ψ'-function and weight function of the median (formulas in Table 11-1). (*a*) ψ'-function, $\psi'(x; t)$. (*b*) Weight function, $w(x; t)$.

when S_n is d_F or MAD. Then

$$CV(x) = \frac{\psi'(u)}{\psi'(u) + \sum_{i=1}^{n-1} \psi'(u_i)}, \tag{22}$$

where

$$u = \frac{x - T_n}{cS_n} \quad \text{and} \quad u_i = \frac{x_i - T_n}{cS_n}.$$

Second, we assume that the denominator in equation (22) is adequately approximated by $\sum_{i=1}^{n} \psi'(u_i)$ to give:

$$CV(x) = \frac{\psi'(u)}{\sum_{i=1}^{n} \psi'(u_i)}. \tag{23}$$

For Huber's estimator, the second approximation changes $CV(x)$ only by a scale factor.

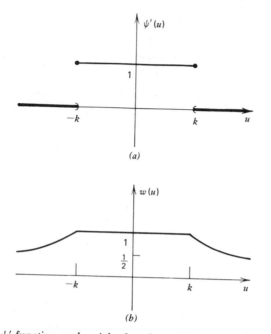

Figure 11-14. ψ'-function and weight function of Huber's estimators of location (formulas in Table 11-1). (*a*) ψ'-function, $\psi'(u)$. (*b*) Weight function, $w(u)$.

Thus the change-of-value curve is approximately proportional to $\psi'(u)$, with constant of proportionality $1/\Sigma_{i=1}^{n}\psi'(u_i)$ for the sample $x_1, \ldots, x_n$. Table 11-1 lists the ψ' functions for the six *M*-estimators of location. Figures 11-12 to 11-17 graph ψ', together with the weight function w, discussed in the next section. Tukey suggests using the constant of proportionality $\Sigma_{i=1}^{n} w[(x_i - T_n)/cS_n]$ in equation (23). This constant is smoother than $\Sigma \psi'(u_i)$.

11J. *W*-ESTIMATION

An alternative form of *M*-estimation is called *W*-estimation. The *M*-estimate T_n is defined by

$$\sum_{i=1}^{n} \psi\left(\frac{x_i - T_n}{cS_n}\right) = 0.$$

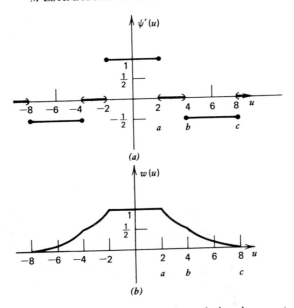

Figure 11-15. ψ'-function and weight function of the three-part redescending estimators of Hampel. The formulas for ψ' and w appear in Table 11-1. Tuning constants are $(a, b, c) = (2, 4, 8)$. (a) ψ'-function, $\psi'(u)$. (b) Weight function, $w(u)$.

When we define w according to $uw(u) = \psi(u)$ and substitute for $\psi(u)$, we get

$$\sum_{i=1}^{n} \left(\frac{x_i - T_n}{cS_n} \right) w \left(\frac{x_i - T_n}{cS_n} \right) = 0,$$

or, rearranging,

$$T_n = \frac{\sum_{i=1}^{n} x_i w[(x_i - T_n)/cS_n]}{\sum_{i=1}^{n} w[(x_i - T_n)/cS_n]}. \tag{24}$$

T_n is thus a weighted mean of the x_i. We call T_n, defined iteratively by equation (24), the *W-estimate* based on the weight function w. If ψ is an odd function, then w is even: $w(u) = w(-u)$.

A trivial example is the sample mean. We need no auxiliary scale, and the ψ-function is simply $\psi(u_i) = u_i$ with $u_i = x_i - T_n$. The weight function is

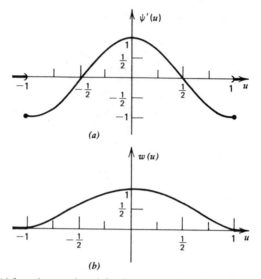

Figure 11-16. ψ'-function and weight function of Andrews' wave estimators of location (formulas in Table 11-1). (a) ψ'-function, $\psi'(u)$. (b) Weight function, $w(u)$.

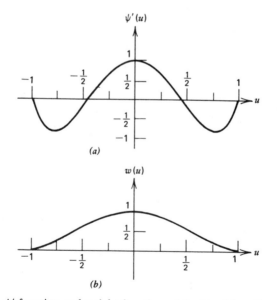

Figure 11-17. ψ'-function and weight function of the biweights (formulas in Table 11-1). (a) ψ'-function, $\psi'(u)$. (b) Weight function, $w(u)$.

identically equal to 1, and equation (24) becomes

$$T_n = \frac{1}{n} \sum_{i=1}^{n} x_i.$$

To motivate *W*-estimation, we consider the computational details. A direct algebraic solution of equation (24), such as we obtain for the mean, is rarely available. Equation (24) suggests how we can iterate to obtain a numerical solution. Let $T_n^{(k)}$ be the estimate at the kth iteration. Let

$$u_i^{(k)} = \frac{x_i - T_n^{(k)}}{cS_n}.$$

Then the iteration formula is

$$T_n^{(k+1)} = \frac{\sum_{i=1}^{n} x_i w\left[u_i^{(k)}\right]}{\sum_{i=1}^{n} w\left[u_i^{(k)}\right]}. \tag{25}$$

Equation (25) is an example of a general procedure known as *iteratively reweighted least-squares* (IRLS) estimation with weights $w_i^{(k)} = w[u_i^{(k)}]$. The ordinary least-squares (OLS) estimate T is the choice of t that minimizes $\sum_{i=1}^{n} (x_i - t)^2$, namely

$$T = \frac{1}{n} \sum_{i=1}^{n} x_i.$$

The weighted least-squares estimate T_w, based on *fixed* weights w_i, is the choice of t that minimizes $\sum_{i=1}^{n} w_i(x_i - t)^2$, namely

$$T_w = \frac{\sum_{i=1}^{n} w_i x_i}{\sum_{i=1}^{n} w_i}.$$

Iteratively reweighted least-squares estimation is a further development. Each weight, as we have seen, depends on the residual at the preceding iteration. Starting with a sensible initial estimate (for *W*-estimation of location the sample median is a good choice), we iterate until the sequence of estimates has converged to within our desired accuracy. The weights at each iteration correspond to the contribution of each observation to the estimate. For example, outliers may receive small or even zero weights. The weight functions for the six estimators of location are shown in Table 11-1 and graphed in Figures 11-12 to 11-17.

The advantage of W-estimation lies in equation (25), which permits straightforward computation. In most situations, the W-estimate calculated from a sample will be the same as the corresponding M-estimate. We return to this and to the computation of M-estimates and W-estimates in the next section.

The least-squares estimator is the maximum-likelihood estimator at the Gaussian distribution. In Section 11E we saw how, through the connection between density and objective functions, M-estimation may be regarded as a generalization of maximum-likelihood estimation. This is the origin of the term "M-estimator." Another generalization of least-squares estimation is to IRLS estimation and thus to W-estimation. It is illuminating to see that the two generalizations, M-estimation and W-estimation, are very closely related. The theory of M-estimation provides insight into iteratively reweighted least-squares estimation.

11K. COMPUTATION AND ONE-STEP ESTIMATORS

W-estimation provides a practical, relatively easy, solution to the problem of calculating an M-estimate. To calculate an M-estimate directly, we use the Newton–Raphson algorithm. Suppose we have a fixed auxiliary estimate of scale S_n. Then the M-estimate of location T_n is a solution of

$$\sum_{i=1}^{n} \psi\left(\frac{x_i - T_n}{cS_n}\right) = 0.$$

Usually we cannot find this solution explicitly. An exception is the mean, for which $\psi(x_i - T_n) = x_i - T_n$. Generally, we solve the equation iteratively. The Newton–Raphson algorithm seeks a zero of a function $h(t)$ by evaluating h and its derivative h' at an approximation $t^{(k)}$ to the zero. The next approximation $t^{(k+1)}$ is the point where the tangent line to h at $t^{(k)}$ intersects the t-axis. Figure 11-18 illustrates this process.

Let $h(T_n) = \sum_{i=1}^{n} \psi[(x_i - T_n)/cS_n]$. With the notation of Section 11J, the algorithm is described algebraically by

$$T_n^{(k+1)} = T_n^{(k)} - \frac{h\left[T_n^{(k)}\right]}{h'\left[T_n^{(k)}\right]}$$

$$= T_n^{(k)} + cS_n \frac{\sum_{i=1}^{n} \psi\left[u_i^{(k)}\right]}{\sum_{i=1}^{n} \psi'\left[u_i^{(k)}\right]}. \tag{26}$$

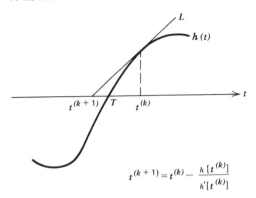

Figure 11-18. The Newton–Raphson algorithm. The $(k + 1)$th approximation $t^{(k+1)}$ to the root T of $h(t)$ is at the intersection of the line L, tangent to $h(t)$ at $t^{(k)}$, with the t axis. From the figure, the subsequent approximation $t^{(k+2)}$ will be very close to T.

An appropriate resistant starting value $T_n^{(0)}$ is the median. The M-estimate of location T_n is the limit of the sequence $T_n^{(k)}$.

One-Step Estimators

If the Newton–Raphson algorithm for calculation of an M-estimate takes only a single step, the resulting estimator is called a *one-step M-estimator* (*m-estimator*). Similarly, taking only a single step toward the calculation of a W-estimate gives a *one-step W-estimator* (*w-estimator*). (That is, the lower-case m or w conventionally denotes the one-step version.) In both instances, the choice of the starting value $T_n^{(0)}$ is important. Generally, we use $T_n^{(0)} =$ median. The choice of $T_n^{(0)} =$ mean gives a poor one-step estimator. The full and one-step (from the median) estimators tend to be almost equally robust (Andrews et al., 1972). (They are equivalent asymptotically, although this may not matter for finite n.)

Multiple Solutions

The iterations for M-estimation and W-estimation both converge to a solution T_n of

$$\sum \psi \left(\frac{x_i - T_n}{cS_n} \right) = 0. \tag{27}$$

For monotone ψ-functions (which include the Hubers), a simple argument shows that the solution of this equation is unique, provided that at least one observation lies on a strictly increasing part of the ψ-function. For redescending estimators, equation (27) may have multiple solutions. A trivial example is to take T_n so large that each observation has u_i less than the lower rejection point. Then T_n is a trivial solution. (This possibility rarely bothers us in practice.)

If a sample itself is symmetric, the clear choice for its location is the center of symmetry, which coincides with its mean and median. A nonsymmetric sample may force us to choose between two or more iterative solutions. We have three strategies. The first is to calculate all solutions and then to take one that gives the absolute minimum of $\Sigma_{i=1}^{n} \rho(u_i)$. However, the strategy is burdensome, as Barnett (1966) illustrates for maximum-likelihood estimation in the Cauchy distribution. The second approach is to take the solution closest to the median. The third strategy is to take the median as starting value for the iterations and then to use the resulting estimate. This is what is commonly done, both for the full iteration and for the one-step version.

If the solution of equation (27) is not unique, then the iterated M-estimate and the iterated W-estimate may differ, even when the starting value is the same. The Newton–Raphson method converges to any solution, however poor, if started sufficiently close. Birch (1980) discusses conditions under which the iterations for a W-estimate cannot converge to a preferred solution at the approximate center of the sample.

11L. FINITE-SAMPLE VARIANCES AND EFFICIENCIES

We use Monte Carlo experiments to compare the average behavior of estimators for repeated samples drawn from a collection of situations. The Princeton Robustness Study (Andrews et al., 1972) assesses the performance of some 65 estimators in 32 sampling situations which include simulated samples of sizes 5, 10, 20, and 40. Later results for the biweight (Tukey, 1981) supplement results from the Princeton study for the five other estimators introduced in Section 11H. We consider sample sizes 5 and 10, but principally sample size 20.

Rather than choose a large number of sampling situations supposedly representative of the majority of real applications, we select three situations that we hope delimit the range of actual situations. These three "corner" situations are the Gaussian distribution, the one-wild mixture of Gaussian distributions described in Chapter 10, and the slash distribution. The Gaussian distribution gives rise to fewer outliers than found in real data.

For balance, the slash distribution has very heavy tails. In Chapter 10 we indicated how distributions may be ordered according to tail weight. The choice of maximin L-estimator then depends critically on the choice of the two endpoint distributions. The one-wild situation has tails of intermediate weight. The single wild observation, which has variance 100, lies within the range ±2 (twice the standard deviation of the identically distributed observations) less than 16% of the time. Therefore, the wild observation can be easily identified almost always, and any resistant estimator of location may do well. On the other hand, the one-wild situation is realistic and is often appropriate for modeling single samples of real data. We want an estimator to do well at the one-wild situation, as well as at the Gaussian and slash distributions.

Each estimator has odd ψ-function, and each sampling situation is symmetric. Thus the estimators are unbiased. Consideration of pseudovariances (Andrews et al., 1972) shows that, for a given estimator and for the set of simulated samples from the given situation, the distribution of the estimates has only moderately heavy tails. Therefore the variance is an appropriate measure of performance. Thus, recalling that the variance decreases as $1/n$, we use n times the variance. For comparison of estimators across the three situations we use relative efficiencies.

TABLE 11-4. Sample size times variance for reference estimators at the Gaussian, one-wild, and slash situations.

Gaussian distribution
    For any sample size, $n \times \text{var(mean)} = 1$. The mean is the Pitman estimator, the m.l.e., and the best-trim estimator. The variance of the mean achieves the Cramér–Rao lower bound.

Estimator	Sample Size			
	5	10	20	∞
One-wild situation				
Minimum variance			1.125	
Best-trim	1.855	1.416	1.221	
Subsample mean	1.250	1.111	1.053	
Slash distribution				
Pitman	9.061	6.21	5.552	
m.l.e.	10.368	6.894		4.847
Minimum variance		6.31	5.78	
Best-trim	11.144	6.995	6.078	

Source: Andrews et al. (1972), Tukey (1981), author's calculations, and references listed in Chapter 10.

The *efficiency* of an estimator T relative to a reference estimator T_0 at a situation F is

$$\text{eff}(T \mid T_0, F) = \frac{\text{var}(T_0 \mid F)}{\text{var}(T \mid F)}.$$

We generally choose T_0 to be the estimator with the smallest variance for the given situation. Section 10D discusses the choice of T_0 and the use of the Cramér–Rao lower bound on the variance. Two other choices of T_0 are the best linear unbiased estimator (BLUE) and the best-trim estimator at each of the three situations. To calculate efficiencies, we use four other reference estimators: the Pitman estimator, the maximum-likelihood estimator, the minimum-variance estimator, and the subsample mean.

The *Pitman estimator* has the smallest mean-squared error (variance for symmetric distributions) among equivariant estimators. The *maximum-likelihood estimator* has, asymptotically, the smallest variance and may be highly efficient, relative to the Pitman estimator, for finite samples.

TABLE 11-5. Selected estimators and situations.

$$n = 20$$

Estimators (each situation): mean; median; one-step and fully iterated
   Hubers, including simultaneous scale estimation; Hampels; wave; one-step
   biweights.
Reference estimators: Gaussian—mean
                      One-wild—minimum-variance
                      Slash—Pitman

$$n = 10$$

Estimators (Gaussian and slash only): mean, median, fully iterated Hubers,
   Hampels, and wave; (each situation): one-step biweight.
Reference estimators: Gaussian—mean
                      One-wild—subsample mean
                      Slash—minimum-variance[a]

$$n = 5$$

Estimators: as for $n = 10$.
Reference estimators: Gaussian—mean
                      One-wild—subsample mean
                      Slash—Pitman

---

[a]The variance of the Pitman estimator became available too late to permit use of this estimator as the reference estimator. For efficiencies relative to the Pitman estimator, multiply the entries in the last column of Table 11-9 by 0.984.

The *minimum-variance estimator* for the given situation is the estimator with smallest variance that is included in the Princeton study or its continuation (Tukey, 1981). For the slash distribution, this estimator is, for $n = 10$, the Pitman estimator for the Cauchy distribution (Andrews et al., 1972, p. 26), and for $n = 20$, the Cauchy m.l.e. For the one-wild situation with $n = 20$, the one-step biweight *w*-estimator with tuning constant 8.8 has the smallest variance of those tried out.

For the one-wild situation, a notional estimator is the *subsample mean*, the mean of the subsample obtained by removing the wild observation, assuming knowledge of which observation is sampled from the long-tailed distribution. The mean is the efficient estimator for the subsample. Kafadar (Tukey, 1981) points out that the subsample mean provides an approximate lower bound on the variance, equal to $1/(n - 1)$.

TABLE 11-6.   Variances (times n) of selected estimators for the selected situations, sample size $n = 20$

Estimator	Type	Scale	Tuning Constant(s)	Situation		
				Gauss	One-Wild	Slash
Mean				1.000	6.485	∞
Median				1.498	1.555	6.60
Huber	*m*	Normalized MAD	1.5	1.051	1.222	8.80
	M		1.5	1.050	1.222	8.75
	M		2.0	1.019	1.273	10.52
	M	Simultaneous[a]	1.0	1.114	1.224	7.50
	M		1.5	1.036	1.214	11.41
	M		2.0	1.009	1.281	18.41
Hampel	*M*	MAD	1.7, 3.4, 8.5	1.130	1.166	6.76
	M		2.1, 4.0, 8.2	1.081	1.136	7.38
	M		2.5, 4.5, 9.5	1.046	1.127	8.01
Wave	*M*	MAD[b]	2.1π	1.070	1.131	7.74
Biweight	*w*	MAD	4.0	1.557	1.450	6.111
	w		6.0	1.158	1.177	6.790
	w		8.8	1.041	1.125	8.122

[a]Huber Proposal 2 (Huber, 1964). For simultaneous estimation of location and scale, see Section 11A.
[b]The scale, MAD, is updated from the residuals every third iteration.

Table 11-4 shows n times the variance for the Pitman, maximum-likelihood, minimum-variance, and subsample-mean estimators. To facilitate comparison of M-estimators with L-estimators, we also include the best-trim estimator $T(\alpha_0)$ used as the reference in Section 10D.

We assemble results of Monte Carlo simulations from the Princeton study and from various other studies (Tukey, 1981). The collection of results is fragmentary, as Table 11-4 illustrates, and the Princeton study does not consider the slash distribution at $n = 5$ as does Tukey (1981). Moreover, each result involves some variability and can be exactly reproduced only when the same random-number generator and computational procedure are used. Comparison within studies is easier than comparison between studies. The biweight variances for $n = 20$ come from subsequent unpublished waves of the Princeton Robustness Study, making comparisons with other estimators easier.

Table 11-5 lists the sampling situations, sample sizes, estimators, and reference estimators. We choose as reference estimator the estimator with the smallest variance. Therefore, the efficiencies are relative to the best estimator known. Tables 11-6 and 11-7 give the variances, and Tables 11-8 and 11-9 the efficiencies, for the selected estimators and situations.

TABLE 11-7. **Variances (times n) of selected estimators for the selected situations, sample sizes $n = 5$ and $n = 10$.**

Estimator	Type	Scale	Tuning Constant(s)	Situation and Sample Size		
				Gauss ($n = 5$)	Gauss ($n = 10$)	Slash ($n = 10$)
Mean				1.000	1.000	∞
Median				1.465	1.366	7.33
Huber	M	Normalized MAD	1.5	1.116	1.049	10.92
	M		2.0	1.074	1.023	13.06
Hampel	M	MAD	1.7, 3.4, 8.5	1.271	1.127	8.04
	M		2.1, 4.0, 8.2	1.231	1.089	8.77
	M		2.5, 4.5, 9.5	1.184	1.058	9.63
Wave	M	MAD[a]	2.1π	1.232	1.083	9.29
Biweight[b]	w	MAD	6	1.355	1.164	7.88

[a]Updated every third iteration.
[b]Additionally, for this biweight—one-wild ($n = 5$): 1.698; slash ($n = 5$): 11.87; one-wild ($n = 10$): 1.299.

Triefficiencies

The variances depend on the scaling of the distribution. However, as in Chapter 10, there is no need to match the distributions when efficiencies are the primary concern. Following Chapter 10, we look for the maximin estimator, the estimator with the largest minimum efficiency over the set of distributions. The *triefficiency* of an estimator, discussed by Beaton and Tukey (1974), is the minimum of its efficiencies for the Gaussian, one-wild, and slash situations. Table 11-10 shows triefficiencies for $n = 20$ obtained from Table 11-8. Inspection of Table 11-8 reveals that the minimum efficiency is at the slash distribution, except for the biweight with smallest tuning constant, $c = 4$. For $n = 10$, the one-wild efficiency is generally unavailable. However, as for $n = 20$ and also as in Chapter 10, we expect that the triefficiency is the minimum of the Gaussian and slash efficiencies, which are shown in Table 11-10. From Table 11-9 we have 80.1% trief-

TABLE 11-8.   **Percentage efficiencies of selected estimators, relative to the reference estimators specified in Table 11-5, for the selected situations, sample size $n = 20$.**

Estimator	Type	Scale	Tuning Constant(s)	Situation		
				Gauss	One-Wild	Slash
Mean				100.0	17.3	0
Median				66.8	72.3	84.1
Huber	m	Normalized MAD	1.5	95.1	92.1	63.1
	M		1.5	95.2	92.1	63.5
	M		2.0	98.1	88.4	52.8
	M	Simultaneous[a]	1.0	89.8	91.9	74.0
	M		1.5	96.5	92.7	48.7
	M		2.0	99.1	87.8	30.2
Hampel	M	MAD	1.7, 3.4, 8.5	88.5	96.5	82.1
	M		2.1, 4.0, 8.2	92.5	99.0	75.2
	M		2.5, 4.5, 9.5	95.6	99.8	69.3
Wave	M	MAD[b]	2.1π	93.5	99.5	71.7
Biweight	w	MAD	4.0	64.2	77.6	90.9
	w		6.0	86.4	95.6	81.8
	w		8.8	96.1	100.0	68.4

[a] Huber Proposal 2.
[b] Updated every third iteration.

ficiency for the biweight w-estimator for $c = 6$ with samples of size 10. For $n = 5$ the triefficiency of the same estimator is 73.6%.

For samples of size 20, the maximin estimators (the estimators with highest triefficiency, 82%) are a Hampel with tuning constants 1.7, 3.4, and 8.5, and the biweight w-estimator with $c = 6$. Among Huber's estimators, the highest triefficiency is 74%, a little better than the triefficiency of the wave, 72%. The median has triefficiency 67%. For samples of size 10, the biweight w-estimator with $c = 6$ and the same Hampel have the highest triefficiencies, close to 80%. The same biweight has lost a few percent efficiency, to 74%, for samples of size 5.

Comparison of families of estimators based on very few members, as in Table 11-10, is hazardous. Using the criterion of triefficiency, one family of estimators is better than a second family if some member of the first family has higher triefficiency than any member of the second. To compare families, we need to calculate triefficiencies for very low to very high tuning constants, spaced to allow safe interpolation. The Hampels, with three tuning constants, pose a special problem. Only for the biweight w-estimators are we sure, from Table 11-10, that the maximum triefficiency occurs for a tuning constant within the range considered—the triefficiency is equal to

TABLE 11-9. Percentage efficiencies of selected estimators, relative to the reference estimators specified in Table 11-5, for the selected situations, sample sizes $n = 5$ and $n = 10$.

Estimator	Type	Scale	Tuning Constant(s)	Gauss ($n = 5$)	Gauss ($n = 10$)	Slash ($n = 10$)
Mean				100.0	100.0	0
Median				68.3	73.2	86.1
Huber	M	Normalized MAD	1.5	89.6	95.3	57.8
	M		2.0	93.1	97.8	48.3
Hampel	M	MAD	1.7, 3.5, 8.5	78.7	88.7	78.5
	M		2.1, 4.0, 8.2	81.2	91.8	71.9
	M		2.5, 4.5, 9.5	84.5	94.5	65.5
Wave	M	MAD[a]	2.1π	81.2	92.3	67.9
Biweight[b]	w	MAD	6.0	73.8	85.9	80.1

[a]Updated every third iteration.
[b]Additionally, for this biweight—one-wild ($n = 5$): 73.6; slash ($n = 5$): 76.3; one-wild ($n = 10$): 85.5.

the Gaussian efficiency for $c = 4$ and to the slash efficiency for $c = 8.8$. However, we cannot tell whether $c = 6$ is the best choice of tuning constant. In this setting, what is "best" depends on how often we expect data resembling each of the three situations to arise in practice. Bell and Morgenthaler (1981) plot Gaussian efficiency versus slash efficiency (compared to the corresponding Pitman estimators) as a function of c. For $n = 20$ the two efficiencies are equal when c is approximately 6.8.

The P-estimators, introduced by Johns (1979), are Pitman-like estimators, which may be chosen for resistance and robustness of efficiency. P-estimators do not require iterative solution, but they do involve troublesome numerical integration. Johns compares a P-estimator with triefficiency 88% to the biweight w-estimator with tuning constant 6.4 and triefficiency 85%. We have adjusted both triefficiencies for the reference estimators listed in Table 11-5.

The estimators in Table 11-10 with the highest triefficiencies tend to have relatively small tuning constants because the slash distribution has heavy

TABLE 11-10. Minimum efficiencies (percent) of selected estimators; triefficiency for $n = 20$, min(Gaussian efficiency, slash efficiency) for $n = 10$.

Estimator	Type	Scale	Tuning Constant(s)	Sample Size 10	20
Mean				0	0
Median				73.2	66.8
Huber	m	Normalized MAD	1.5		63.1
	M		1.5	57.8	63.5
	M		2.0	48.3	52.8
	M	Simultaneous[a]	1.0		74.0
	M		1.5		48.7
	M		2.0		30.2
Hampel	M	MAD	1.7, 3.4, 8.5	78.5	82.1
	M		2.1, 4.0, 8.2	71.9	75.2
	M		2.5, 4.5, 9.5	65.5	69.3
Wave	M	MAD[b]	2.1π	67.9	71.7
Biweight	w	MAD	4.0		64.2
	w		6.0	80.1	81.8
	w		8.8		68.4

[a] Huber Proposal 2.
[b] Updated every third iteration.

tails. The slash efficiencies entirely determine the poor triefficiencies of the Hubers. Simultaneous estimation of scale does not improve the performance of the Hubers. We return to the performance of monotone estimators as compared to redescending estimators in the next section.

The efficiencies of the one-step Huber in Table 11-8 are almost the same as those of the corresponding fully iterated estimator with tuning constant 1.5. This early example led the Princeton study to include a variety of one-step estimators. Tukey (1981) suggests that, to obtain a *w*-estimator with the same overall performance as a particular *W*-estimator, we simply increase the tuning constant by an amount that is roughly constant for moderate values of the tuning constant. For the biweight this amount is approximately 0.5 near $c = 6$. Thus the one-step biweight with $c = 6.5$ has roughly the same variance as the fully iterated biweight with $c = 6$ for the Gaussian and one-wild situations.

11M. COMPARISONS OF *M*-ESTIMATORS OF LOCATION

Section 11H presents successively six *M*-estimators of location. The themes of the progression from mean and median through the monotone Hubers to the redescending Hampel, wave, and biweight estimators are (a) increased resistance to outliers and correspondingly increased efficiency for heavy-tailed distributions; and (b) increased smoothness in the use of the data through smoothness in the ψ-function. Here, to compare the estimators, we consider the shapes of the ψ-functions and the assembled asymptotic and finite-sample results. Table 11-2 displays criteria based on the influence curve and thus on the shape of the ψ-function for the estimators. A summary of the resistance and robustness of estimators according to six shapes for their influence curve appears in Mosteller and Tukey (1977, page 539).

Asymptotic Results

The asymptotic theory of *M*-estimators is often tractable mathematically where the finite-sample theory is not. Numerical integration, used in calculations of the asymptotic variance from the influence curve, may have more appeal than simulation of a large number of samples. However, we are concerned with estimation for samples of moderate size, $n = 10$ to $n = 100$. Asymptotic results are useful only if they approximate these finite-sample results. Huber, in Andrews et al. (1972), notes that convergence to asymptotic behavior is rapid at the Gaussian distribution and slower elsewhere. Asymptotic results may be useful for samples of size $n = 5$ at the Gaussian and for $n = 20$ at heavier-tailed distributions.

Figures 11-6 and 11-7 show, respectively, the g.e.s. and l.s.s. plotted against the Gaussian efficiency for the Hubers, waves, and biweights. In Figure 11-6 we see that, as remarked in Section 11E, poor g.e.s. corresponds to high Gaussian efficiency, and vice versa. In Figure 11-7 we see lower l.s.s. with higher Gaussian efficiency. These relationships are consistent with the properties of the mean and median: the mean is efficient at the Gaussian and has the lowest l.s.s. but infinite g.e.s., whereas the median is inefficient at the Gaussian and has infinite l.s.s. but low g.e.s.

For convenient comparison of the estimators, we also show in Figures 11-6 and 11-7 (dashed lines) the g.e.s. and l.s.s. for the Hubers plus 10%. Close to the Gaussian, the biweight and wave estimators (which are adapted to heavier-tailed distributions) have g.e.s. and l.s.s. approximately 10% greater than the Hubers for a given efficiency.

Some desirable asymptotic features of an estimator may be unimportant for the sample estimate. Thus the computational simplicity of a Huber, or the flexibility in choice of parameters of a Hampel, may be more important than the continuity of the derivative of the biweight ψ-function. Observations occur infrequently at the rejection point of the biweight. However, extensive use of the biweight has supported the dependability of its behavior for samples. In Section 11E we remark that, for resistance to rounding and grouping errors, moderate continuity of ψ may suffice, even though the local-shift sensitivity, an asymptotic property, will not be small.

Robust Estimation

The careful user of the mean watches for pitfalls. When the data contain outliers, one approach is to remove the outliers and then to use the mean. A second approach is to use a robust and resistant estimator for that sample in place of the mean. Andrews (Andrews et al., 1972) shows that if the median is substituted for the mean whenever the difference between the two is larger than a reference distance, the Gaussian efficiency may be at least 90–95%, depending on sample size. Robust estimators provide a well-defined alternative to the carefully used mean and often have high Gaussian efficiency (Table 11-8).

Robust estimators limit the influence of extreme observations. The ψ-function of a Huber estimator, Figure 11-8, is bounded, and the weight function, Figure 11-14, decreases to zero at infinity. The ψ-function is linear in the middle to give good Gaussian efficiency and resistance to rounding and grouping errors. In Section 11H we present asymptotic arguments for the use of Huber estimators when the sample is drawn from a contaminated Gaussian distribution. Huber estimators are designed to be highly efficient

for distributions close to the Gaussian. The worst possible distribution—the least favorable distribution—has exponential tails.

The very extreme observations encountered in practice indicate that we should consider distributions with heavier tails than exponential. However, very extreme observations can be removed from the data by inspection or by reference to the physical situation. The need for data screening is reduced, but not eliminated, when we use Hubers in place of the mean.

Redescending estimators remove the influence of very extreme observations. Thus the ψ-functions of the Hampels, waves, and biweights (Figures 11-3, 11-10, and 11-11), as well as the weight functions (Figures 11-15 to 11-17), are 0 beyond the rejection point. The redescending estimators also satisfy the other criteria given in Table 11-2, as do the Hubers. Manual rejection of outliers makes the Huber estimators analogous to redescending estimators. Either procedure will remove very extreme observations; the challenge is in the observations we do not know whether to throw away. The descending part of the ψ-function of a redescending estimator resolves this difficulty in a precise way. An automatic procedure is vital when we must rapidly process a large number of samples.

We choose redescending estimators to give good overall efficiency at a subjectively chosen finite set of moderate and heavy-tailed distributions. Although any "reasonable" distribution can be regarded as a contaminated Gaussian, in practice, the collection of contaminated distributions with greater than 10% contamination contains too many unrealistic members. The slash distribution is a contaminated Gaussian with at least 10% contamination. The two approaches, (a) that of Huber and (b) assessing performance over finite sets of distributions, are therefore distinct, although the tanh estimator (Section 11H) combines the two approaches.

The best choice of redescending estimator is not clear. The Hampel ψ-functions have a piecewise-linear shape with variable proportions for the ascending, level, and descending parts. The wave and biweight have ψ-functions of fixed shape which appeal because they are smooth and which resolve the problem of choosing the proportions. Figures 11-3, 11-10, and 11-11 illustrate the differences. The shapes of the wave and biweight ψ-functions are apparently well chosen; an extensive analysis of the Hampel family should help determine this. We prefer the biweight ψ-function to the wave ψ-function for the reasons discussed in Section 11H, because the redescending part extends relatively further for the biweight.

With redescending estimators, observations beyond the rejection point may be identified for further consideration. We refer to the data for a more specific reason, however, one which concerns the role of auxiliary scale estimators. As we discuss in Chapter 12, robust estimators of scale are weak

in small samples because, when observations in the tails of the sample are not used, too little of the sample remains. Redescending estimators are particularly susceptible to the resultant underestimation of scale. A large part of the sample is ignored, and the objective function may have many local minima. In Table 11-3 we see that the asymptotic variance of the biweight at the Gaussian is large for $c = 3$. Beyond considerations of the asymptotic variance, a second reason to use a ψ-function with a relatively extended redescending part is that the rejection point is increased. When the auxiliary scale of a Huber estimator is small, the estimator behaves like the median. Therefore it is robust to underestimation of scale. In location estimation we rarely encounter the problems of underestimation of scale and multiple solutions. (We meet them more often in regression, where we may use several alternative scale estimates and multistep estimation of the regression.)

In summary, Hubers and redescending estimators—Hampels, wave, and biweight—are robust and resistant alternatives to the mean and median. We use Hubers when we are prepared to sacrifice efficiency at heavier-tailed distributions for higher efficiency near the Gaussian. For overall efficiency and resistance we choose a redescending estimator. When we know little about the underlying distribution, we should check the sample for extreme observations before calculating a Huber. When we use a redescending estimator, we must be wary of unduly small estimates of scale and, possibly, multiple solutions.

REFERENCES

Andrews, D. F., Bickel, P. J., Hampel, F. R., Huber, P. J., Rogers, W. H., and Tukey, J. W. (1972). *Robust Estimates of Location: Survey and Advances*. Princeton, NJ: Princeton University Press.

Barnett, V. D. (1966). "Evaluation of the maximum likelihood estimator where the likelihood equation has multiple roots," *Biometrika*, **53**, 151–165.

Beaton, A. E. and Tukey, J. W. (1974). "The fitting of power series, meaning polynomials, illustrated on band-spectroscopic data," *Technometrics*, **16**, 147–185.

Bell, K. and Morgenthaler, S. (1981). "Comparison of the bioptimal curve with curves for two robust estimates." Technical Report No. 195, Series 2, Department of Statistics, Princeton University.

Billingsley, P. (1968). *Convergence of Probability Measures*. New York: Wiley.

Birch, J. B. (1980). "Some convergence properties of iterated reweighted least squares in the location model," *Communications in Statistics*, **B9**, 359–369.

Collins, J. R. (1976). "Robust estimation of a location parameter in the presence of asymmetry," *Annals of Statistics*, **4**, 68–85.

David, H. A. (1981). *Order Statistics*, second edition. New York: Wiley.

Gross, A. M. (1976). "Confidence interval robustness with long-tailed symmetric distributions," *Journal of the American Statistical Association*, **71**, 409–416.

Hampel, F. R. (1968). "Contributions to the theory of robust estimation." Ph.D. thesis, University of California, Berkeley.

——— (1971). "A general qualitative definition of robustness," *Annals of Mathematical Statistics*, **42**, 1887–1896.

——— (1974). "The influence curve and its role in robust estimation," *Journal of the American Statistical Association*, **69**, 383–393.

Hogg, R. V. (1974). "Adaptive robust procedures: a partial review and some suggestions for future applications and theory," *Journal of the American Statistical Association*, **69**, 909–927.

——— (1979). "Statistical robustness: one view of its use in applications today," *The American Statistician*, **33**, 108–115.

Huber, P. J. (1964). "Robust estimation of a location parameter," *Annals of Mathematical Statistics*, **35**, 73–101.

——— (1972). "Robust statistics: a review," *Annals of Mathematical Statistics*, **43**, 1041–1067.

——— (1977). *Robust Statistical Procedures*. Philadelphia: Society for Industrial and Applied Mathematics.

——— (1980). "Current issues in robust statistics." In *Proceedings of the Symposium on Recent Advances in Statistics*, Lisbon: Portuguese Academy of Sciences.

——— (1981). *Robust Statistics*. New York: Wiley.

Johns, M. V. (1979). "Robust Pitman-like estimates." In R. L. Launer and G. N. Wilkinson (Eds.), *Robustness in Statistics*. New York: Academic.

Kendall, M. G. and Stuart, A. (1977). *The Advanced Theory of Statistics*, Vol. 1 (*Distribution Theory*), fourth edition. London: Charles Griffin and Company Limited.

Mosteller, F. and Tukey, J. W. (1977). *Data Analysis and Regression*. Reading, MA: Addison–Wesley.

Relles, D. A. and Rogers, W. H. (1977). "Statisticians are fairly robust estimators of location," *Journal of the American Statistical Association*, **72**, 107–111.

Silvey, S. D. (1970). *Statistical Inference*. London: Chapman and Hall.

Smith, R. H. (1888). "True average of observations?" letter to the editor, March 15, *Nature*, **37**, 464.

Stigler, S. M. (1980). "Studies in the history of probability and statistics XXXVIII. R. H. Smith, a Victorian interested in robustness," *Biometrika*, **67**, 217–221.

Tukey, J. W. (1960). "A survey of sampling from contaminated distributions." In I. Olkin, S. G. Ghurye, W. Hoeffding, W. G. Madow, and H. B. Mann (Eds.), *Contributions to Probability and Statistics, Essays in Honor of Harold Hotelling*. Stanford, CA: Stanford University Press, pp. 448–485.

——— (1981). Personal communication.

Additional Literature (See also additional literature for Chapter 10.)

Barr, G. D. I., Money, A. H., Affleck-Graves, J. F. and Hart, M. L. (1981). "L_p-norm estimation of the location parameter of a symmetric distribution," *South African Statistical Journal*, **15**, 85–96.

Bickel, P. J. (1975). "One-step Huber estimates in the linear model," *Journal of the American Statistical Association*, **70**, 428–434.

Birch, J. B. (1980). "Effects of the starting value and stopping rule on robust estimates obtained by iterated weighted least squares," Communications in Statistics, **B9**, 141–154.

Boos, D. D. and Serfling, R. J. (1980). "A note on differentials and the CLT and LIL for statistical functions, with applications to M-estimates," Annals of Statistics, **8**, 618–624.

Brown, B. M. and Kildea, D. G. (1979). "Outlier-detection tests and robust estimators based on signs of residuals," Communications in Statistics, **A8**, 257–269.

Collins, J. R. (1977). "Upper bounds on asymptotic variances of M-estimators of location," Annals of Statistics, **5**, 646–657.

Hampel, F. R., Rousseeuw, P. J., and Ronchetti, E. (1981). "The change-of-variance curve and optimal redescending M-estimators," Journal of the American Statistical Association, **76**, 643–648.

Jurečková, J. (1981). "Tail-behavior of location estimators," Annals of Statistics, **9**, 578–585.

Maronna, R. (1976). "Robust M-estimators of multivariate location and scatter," Annals of Statistics, **4**, 51–67.

Miller, R. G. and Halpern, J. W. (1980). "Robust estimators for quantal bioassay," Biometrika, **67**, 103–110.

Policello, G. E. II and Hettmansperger, T. P. (1976). "Adaptive robust procedures for the one-sample location problem," Journal of the American Statistical Association, **71**, 624–633.

EXERCISES

1. We have introduced three classes of location estimators: R-estimators, L-estimators, and M-estimators. To which class(es) do each of the following location estimators belong?

   (a) sample mean
   (b) sample median
   (c) 25% trimmed mean.

2. Consider the ψ-function

$$\psi(x; t) = \begin{cases} -1 & x - t < -1 \\ x - t & -1 \leqslant x - t \leqslant 1 \\ +1 & x - t > 1. \end{cases}$$

   (a) Sketch this ψ-function and compare its graph to the graphs of the ψ-functions shown in Figures 11-1 and 11-2.
   (b) Determine the corresponding ρ-function, sketch its graph, and compare it to the ρ-functions shown in Figures 11-1 and 11-2.
   (c) Discuss qualitatively the ways in which the estimator based on this ψ-function incorporates data on location. Comparison with the ψ-functions of Figures 11-1 and 11-2 may again be useful.

3. A ρ-function is given by

$$\rho(u) = \begin{cases} \frac{1}{6} & |u| > 1 \\ \frac{1}{6}|u| & |u| \leqslant 1. \end{cases}$$

(a) Sketch this function and compare it to the ρ-function for the biweight.
(b) Give the corresponding ψ-function and sketch its graph.
(c) Compare and contrast the characteristics of this objective function with those shown in Figures 11-1, 11-2, and 11-3.
(d) What is the rejection point of the estimator that corresponds to this ρ-function?

4. We have discussed notions of location-invariance, location-equivariance, and location-and-scale-equivariance. Which of these notions apply to the following estimators?
(a) Sample mean
(b) Sample median
(c) Sample standard deviation
(d) Fourth-spread
(e) Median absolute deviation from the median,

$$\text{MAD} = \underset{j}{\text{med}} |x_j - M| \qquad \text{with} \qquad M = \underset{i}{\text{med}} \{x_i\}.$$

In each case, use definitions to show algebraically that your answer is correct.

5. Section 11D discusses the sensitivity curve for the sample median.
(a) Use basic definitions to verify that the formulas given for $SC(x)$ are correct when $n = 2m + 1$ is odd and the estimator is the median.
(b) Find $SC(x)$ in the case when $n = 2m$ is even.

6. (a) Find the expression for the sensitivity curve of the sample mean based on n observations.
(b) Sketch the sensitivity curve and compare your sketch to that shown in Figure 11-4 for the median.
(c) From graphs you compared in part (b), what can you say about the effects on each location estimator of adding a single wild point to the sample? For the two estimators, what can you conclude about the effects of rounding errors?

7. R. H. Smith (1888) proposed an estimator of location that has the basic ψ-function

$$\psi(u) = \begin{cases} u(1 - u^2) & |u| \leqslant 1 \\ 0 & |u| > 1. \end{cases}$$

  (a) Sketch this ψ-function.
  (b) Find the associated ρ-function and sketch its graph.
  (c) Compare the qualitative properties of this estimator to those of the biweight.

8. For the ψ-function of Smith, defined in the previous exercise,
  (a) Give the ψ'-function and sketch its graph.
  (b) Give the weight function and sketch its graph.
  (c) Compare the results of parts (a) and (b) to those shown for six location estimators in Figure 11-13.

9. Show that, for a symmetric estimator of location, a breakdown bound of $\frac{1}{2}$ for even n or $\frac{1}{2} + 1/(2n)$ for odd n is impossible. Deduce that the breakdown bound of the median, $\frac{1}{2} - 1/n$ for even n or $\frac{1}{2} - 1/(2n)$ for odd n, is as large as possible. *Hint:* Change every second observation to produce a sample that is symmetric around an arbitrary number Q.

10. The sample version of the g.e.s. is the maximum of the sensitivity curve and, for an M-estimator based on $\psi[(x - T)/(cS)]$, will be determined by the quotient of the maximum value of $|\psi|$ and the sum of the ψ'. By convention, $\psi'(0) = 1$. If we assume that $\psi'(u)$ is close to 1 for most observations, then a fair idea of the sample version of the g.e.s. is

$$\max_{i=1,\ldots,n} |\psi(u_i)|.$$

    What is the analogous approximation to the sample version of the l.s.s.? What is a lower bound on this statistic? When does the statistic equal the lower bound and for which estimators?

11. Verify, using the equation

$$\psi(x; t) = -\frac{d}{dt}[\log f(x; t)],$$

that the maximum-likelihood estimators for the Gaussian, double-

exponential, and least-favorable distributions are, respectively, the mean, the median, and Huber's estimator. Now attempt to find M-estimators that are maximum-likelihood estimators at the uniform, logistic, Student's t, and Cauchy distributions. Repeat for mixtures of normal distributions and for other distributions of your choice. How robust are the M-estimators you find?

Now construct a ψ-function, using the principles described in the chapter. How robust is your M-estimator? Does it have a target distribution? (Remember that redescending estimators do not have target distributions.)

12. Verify that the formula in equation (20),

$$\frac{2\phi(k)}{k} - 2\Phi(-k) = \frac{\varepsilon}{1 - \varepsilon},$$

ensures that the least-favorable distribution has total mass 1. Calculate ε for k between 0 and 3. Construct a graph for determining the appropriate k for given contamination ε.

13. Construct Gaussian probability plots of the least-favorable distribution for various values of k. Compare the empirical distribution function of some data to the least-favorable distributions: (1) graphically, (2) using the Kolmogorov–Smirnov statistic. Take as data either a real data set, a haphazardly constructed data set, or several data sets constructed by adding contamination to a Gaussian distribution. The contamination should be placed (a) according to a Gaussian distribution with higher variance (to produce a Gaussian mixture) and (b) at 0, ∞, and $-\infty$.

14. Discuss how the number of solutions for a redescending M-estimator increases as the scale or tuning constant decreases. Illustrate your discussion with numerical examples. You may find the computations easiest for Hampel's 3-part estimator.

CHAPTER 12

Robust Scale Estimators and Confidence Intervals for Location

Boris Iglewicz
Temple University

The standard deviation is the most common estimator of scale for a batch of data; but, like the sample mean, it lacks resistance and robustness. In this chapter we discuss robust methods of estimating the scale of a symmetric distribution. Robust scale estimation has not yet been studied as carefully as robust location estimation, so we are able to present only partial results in an emerging understanding of methods for this estimation problem.

Besides the standard deviation, we focus on several other scale estimators:

The mean absolute deviation from the sample median,

The median absolute deviation from the sample median,

An estimator related to the wave estimators of location,

An estimator related to the biweight estimators of location, and

The fourth-spread.

We compare the performance of these scale estimators for three symmetric situations: Gaussian, one-wild, and slash.

Two separate comparisons correspond to the two main applications of scale estimators: as measures of spread of a sample and in setting confidence intervals for a population location parameter. We show that the same

404

basic approach provides good robust estimators of location, robust estimators of scale, and confidence intervals for location. In addition, one of these robust estimators yields a relatively powerful test for departures from the Gaussian shape. We include several tables to facilitate the computation of robust confidence intervals.

12A. DESIRABLE PROPERTIES

Assume that we have n independent observations from a symmetric distribution. We have already seen (in Chapters 10 and 11) that the sample mean, $\bar{x}$, has relatively low efficiency as a robust estimator of the population location and that other estimators, such as the biweight, do far better in this respect. In this chapter we examine the most common measure of scale, the sample standard deviation, defined by

$$s = \sqrt{\Sigma_{i=1}^{n} (x_i - \bar{x})^2 / (n - 1)},$$

and compare this measure with alternative estimators. For independent Gaussian observations, s^2 is the minimum-variance unbiased estimator of the population variance σ^2; thus s^2 is the most efficient unbiased estimator of σ^2 for Gaussian data. For this reason, s has been the most commonly used measure of scale.

In the traditional setting, then, "scale" is almost synonymous with "standard deviation." More technical discussions of estimation deal with a scale parameter σ (not necessarily the standard deviation) of a family of distributions—most often a "location-scale family," in which the "standard" probability density function is f_0 and the location parameter θ and the (positive) scale parameter σ enter into the general density f through

$$f(x) = \frac{1}{\sigma} f_0\left(\frac{x - \theta}{\sigma}\right).$$

As soon as we consider estimating scale robustly, however, we are forced to realize that the scale parameter need not have the same meaning from one family to another. In fact, even within a family of distributions the scale parameter is actually quite arbitrary and is usually chosen to make the functional form of f_0 simple. Technically, for any fixed positive constant k, $\tau = k\sigma$ is as much a scale parameter as σ is; we need only absorb a factor of $1/k$ into f in the right places. In a sense, we are only changing the units, as one might change feet to meters.

This arbitrariness of scale parameters serves to emphasize that scale is a vague concept (Mosteller and Tukey, 1977, Section 1F) and can be made precise in many ways. We know from experience that some distributions and some samples are more spread out than others. To translate this into numerical terms, we must adopt a specific measure of spread. This is why we encounter a variety of words aimed at the vague concept: spread, scale, dispersion, variability, and width, for example. Some authors have given specific meanings to some of these same terms. For example, Bickel and Lehmann (1976) have defined "dispersion" in terms of the absolute deviation of the random variable from the parameter, and they also (1979) have defined "spread" in terms of differences between percentage points. For the rest of this chapter we adopt the term "scale" for the general notion.

We noted that s^2 is the minimum-variance unbiased estimator of σ^2 for data from a Gaussian distribution. How efficient is this estimator when the data come from an "almost Gaussian" distribution? This question is answered in a dramatic example given by Tukey (1960) and discussed by Huber (1977). They compare s with the mean absolute deviation

$$d_n = \frac{1}{n} \sum_{i=1}^{n} | x_i - \bar{x} | .$$

For Gaussian observations the means and variances of s and d_n are known functions of n [see, for example, Johnson and Kotz (1970, pp. 62–64)].* To simplify discussion, we consider their means and variances as $n \to \infty$. Then $E(s) \to \sigma$ and $E(d_n) \to \sigma\sqrt{\pi/2}$. Letting $g_n = \left(\sqrt{\pi/2}\right)^{-1} d_n$, we can compare s and g_n in terms of the ratio of their variances with var(s) placed in the numerator. For Gaussian(μ, σ^2) observations this ratio equals 0.876. Thus as expected, s is a more efficient estimator for Gaussian data.

Our next step is to compare the same two estimators using data from a slightly contaminated Gaussian distribution. Specifically, we assume that each observation comes from Gaussian (μ, σ^2) with probability $1 - \varepsilon$ and from Gaussian ($\mu, 9\sigma^2$) with probability ε. Also we make allowance for the relationship between g_n and d_n in this situation. Choosing ε as low as 0.002 then leads, surprisingly, to a ratio of 1.016, and this ratio increases to 2.035 for $\varepsilon = 0.05$. These large ratios show that the mean absolute deviation is preferable to the standard deviation for some contaminated distributions.

We do not conclude from this example that we should use d_n as a measure of scale, because we will identify better robust measures. The key

---

*To simplify notation, the same lower-case letters will be used to represent estimates and estimators.

point is that estimators that perform well under highly restrictive distributional assumptions may cease to do so in the face of slight deviations from these assumptions. It is precisely for this reason that we hesitate to assume exact knowledge of the distribution from which the sample comes. As an alternative, we now discuss some reasonable properties of scale estimators, define a measure of efficiency, and compare a number of scale estimators in terms of this measure of efficiency, for a variety of symmetric distributions.

Up to now, we have not actually defined a scale estimator, and so we begin with a definition.

DEFINITION: A *scale estimator* w is a nonnegative-valued function of the sample, $w(x_1, x_2, \ldots, x_n)$, such that

$$w(a + bx_1, \ldots, a + bx_n) = |b| w(x_1, \ldots, x_n).$$

Thus a scale estimator ignores changes in the location of the sample, and it responds as one would want to uniform changes in spread. In the language of Chapter 11, it is location-invariant and scale-equivariant.

Any function that satisfies the definition qualifies as a scale estimator, but some are more desirable than others. From an exploratory point of view, one important property is *resistance*; that is, w should not be greatly affected by a relatively small number of outlying values, no matter how extreme they may be.

An example easily shows that the sample standard deviation is not resistant. Let $x_1 = x_2 = \cdots = x_{n-1} = y$ and $x_n = y + na$ ($a \geq 0$). Then $\bar{x} = y + a$ and

$$s = \sqrt{\frac{(n-1)a^2 + (n-1)^2 a^2}{n-1}} = a\sqrt{n}.$$

The point is not that a nondegenerate continuous distribution is likely to produce a sample of many identical values. Instead, if most of the x_i are quite close together and one is very different, then the standard deviation is controlled primarily by the different one.

The estimators that we will recommend as being efficient robust estimators are all highly resistant. The fact that s can be so easily influenced by an outlier is one more reason for considering alternative measures of scale.

12B. SEVERAL SIMPLE SCALE ESTIMATORS

In this section, we consider four estimators of scale. The reader may be familiar with some, if not all, of these because they are frequently used and

are relatively simple to compute. These four estimators are defined for the n observations $x_1, x_2, \ldots, x_n$ as follows:

Standard deviation

$$s = \sqrt{\Sigma_{i=1}^{n}(x_i - \bar{x})^2 / (n-1)}, \quad \text{where } \bar{x} \text{ is the sample mean;}$$

Mean absolute deviation from the sample median

$$\text{AD} = \frac{1}{n}\sum_{i=1}^{n}|x_i - M|, \quad \text{where } M \text{ is the sample median;}$$

Median absolute deviation from the sample median

$$\text{MAD} = \underset{i}{\text{median}}\{|x_i - M|\};$$

Fourth spread (F-spread), which is the difference between the upper and lower fourths (see Section 2C)

$$d_F = F_U - F_L.$$

TABLE 12-1. Samples of SAT scores.

	Rural Students				Urban Students		
i	x_i	$x_{(i)}$	$|x_{(i)} - M|$	i	x_i	$x_{(i)}$	$|x_{(i)} - M|$
1	800	500	312	1	900	675	225
2	974	700	112	2	803	751	149
3	500	725	87	3	1145	765	135
4	725	765	47	4	900	803	97
5	812	794	18	5	1225	825	75
6	794	800	12	6	751	850	50
7	765	812	0	7	825	900	0
8	900	826	14	8	1070	900	0
9	826	850	38	9	1128	1070	170
10	700	850	38	10	1080	1080	180
11	850	900	88	11	675	1128	228
12	945	945	133	12	850	1145	245
13	850	974	162	13	765	1225	325

$\bar{x} = 803.15$	$M = 812$	AD $= 81.62$		$\bar{x} = 932.08$	$M = 900$	AD $= 144.54$	
$s = 120.37$	MAD $= 47$	$d_F = 85$		$s = 176.58$	MAD $= 149$	$d_F = 277$	

Source: P. Nemenyi, S. K. Dixon, N. B. White, and M. L. Hedstrom (1977). *Statistics from Scratch.* San Francisco: Holden–Day, Inc., p. 240.

EXAMPLE: SAT SCORES

For a simple numerical example throughout this chapter, we consider two samples of SAT scores given by Nemenyi et al. (1977). The first sample consists of rural students and the second sample of urban students; the data are given in Table 12-1. For this example, $\bar{x}$ and s are computed in the usual fashion, M equals $x_{(7)}$, AD is the average of the $|x_i - M|$, and MAD is the median of $|x_i - M|$. Because $([(13 + 1)/2] + 1)/2 = 4$, using $[x]$ to indicate the largest integer not exceeding x, the F-spread equals $850 - 765 = 85$ for the rural students and $1080 - 803 = 277$ for the urban students.

Before interpreting these scale computations, we briefly summarize the two samples through the use of boxplots. Since we have already computed

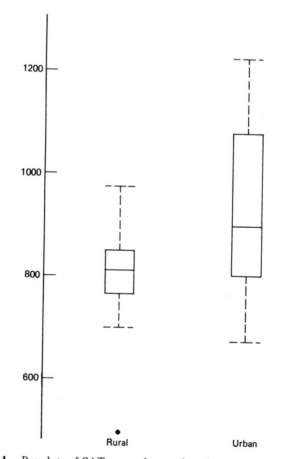

Figure 12-1.   Boxplots of SAT scores for rural students and urban students.

the medians and F-spreads, we can readily obtain the boxplots as shown in Figure 12-1. Inspection reveals that one rural SAT score is a low outlier and that the urban scores have more spread than do the rural scores. In fact, the ratio of the length of the boxplots is $\frac{1225 - 675}{974 - 700} = 2.01$. Thus there seems to be twice as much dispersion for the urban scores as for the rural. The lack of resistance of the standard deviation is clearly illustrated: if we set aside the outlier from the rural scores, the sample standard deviation changes from $s = 120.37$ to $s' = 82.20$.

The values of the four different scale estimators and of s' are given in Table 12-2, whose last column consists of the ratio of the urban score estimate to the rural score estimate. These ratios are always greater than one, indicating that, for all these ways of measuring scale, the urban students' scores are more dispersed than the rural students' scores. At the same time, the ratios differ, and s has the smallest ratio. This is primarily due to the one outlying rural observation. The F-spread and MAD lead to ratios that are substantially higher than the others. In this example, trimming 50% of the observations may be too much, or the fourths may reflect local irregularities in the data.

An appropriate choice of scale estimators can become even more crucial in other situations. Consider the two hypothetical samples,

Sample 1	Sample 2
0	0
1	0
2	2
3	3
10	4

for which the MAD estimates are 1 and 2 and the sample standard deviations are 3.96 and 1.79, respectively. That is, MAD indicates that

TABLE 12-2. **Comparison of four different scale estimates plus s' for the two samples of SAT scores.**

	Rural Students (1)	Urban Students (2)	(2)/(1)
s	120.37	176.58	1.47
AD	81.62	144.54	1.77
MAD	47	149	3.17
d_F	85	277	3.26
s'	82.20	176.58	2.15

Sample 2 has twice as much dispersion as Sample 1, whereas s states the opposite. Again, the one large value, 10, greatly influences s in the first sample.

12C. EFFICIENCY OF THE SIMPLE SCALE ESTIMATORS

We turn next to the efficiency and robustness of the four scale estimators. Our discussion concentrates on data from three symmetric unimodal situations (discussed in Chapter 10):

Gaussian(0, 1);

"One-wild": exactly one of each 20 observations comes from Gaussian (0, 100), and the other 19 observations come independently from Gaussian(0, 1);

"Slash": the distribution of the ratio of a Gaussian(0, 1) random variable to an independent uniform(0, 1) random variable.

These three situations represent increasing amounts of heavy-tailedness, with one-wild being heavier-tailed than Gaussian and slash being very heavy-tailed. Many heavier-tailed symmetric distributions have tail weights between Gaussian and slash.

Lax (1975) reports on an extensive simulation study of scale estimators in these three situations. We use his numerical results in this section and the next. We also incorporate new simulation results for the F-spread.

Table 12-3 contains the average values of s, MAD, and F-spread for the three chosen situations. (Because AD is seldom used and offers no resistance, we have not included it.) The exact expected values for some of these entries are available as a check on the simulation results. For example, for data from the Gaussian(0, 1) distribution, it is known (see, for example, Johnson and Kotz, 1970, p. 62) that

$$E(s) = \left[\left(\frac{2}{n-1} \right)^{1/2} \Gamma \left(\frac{1}{2} n \right) \right] \Big/ \Gamma \left(\frac{1}{2} n - \frac{1}{2} \right),$$

where $\Gamma(x)$ is the gamma function. For $n = 20$, this expression yields 0.98, which is the same as the value in Table 12-3.

Two features of Table 12-3 deserve special notice. First, the estimators do not have the same expected value. For example, for the Gaussian distribution, $E(s) = 0.98$, whereas $E(\text{MAD}) = 0.64$. Because the variability of a

TABLE 12-3. Average values from simulation of three simple scale estimators for sample size 20.[a]

Estimator	Situation		
	Gaussian	One-Wild	Slash
s	0.98	2.23	23.26
MAD	0.64	0.68	1.51
d_F	1.35	1.41	3.25

[a]Entries for s and MAD are based on results given by Lax (1975). Entries for d_F are based on 8000 replications generated using subroutines from the IMSL Library on the CDC CYBER-174 at Temple University.

scale estimator probably depends on its mean, it would be unwise to use a measure of efficiency based directly on the variance of the scale estimators. Second, the entries differ more for some estimators than for others. For example, $E(s) = 0.98$ for Gaussian and 23.26 for slash, whereas $E(\text{MAD})$ equals 0.64 and 1.51, respectively, for the same distributions. This gives an indication that s is more sensitive to heavy tails than is MAD.

We also note that $E(s)$ is greatly affected by one wild observation. The other entries in the one-wild column of Table 12-3 are close to the corresponding Gaussian entries.

How does one compare scale estimators whose expected values differ? One approach is based on adjusting for the expected values. We prefer an alternative approach which does not depend on such adjustments. For any scale estimator w, our measure of performance is based on $\text{var}\{\ln(w)\}$. The advantage is that $\text{var}\{\ln(w)\}$ is not affected by a scale factor, because

$$\text{var}\{\ln(kw)\} = \text{var}\{\ln(w) + \ln(k)\} = \text{var}\{\ln(w)\}$$

for any positive constant k.

The use of $\text{var}\{\ln(w)\}$ leads to some helpful simplifications. For example, $\text{var}\{\ln(s)\}$ is the same whether s^2 has n or $n - 1$ in its denominator. Furthermore, $\text{var}\{\ln(s^2)\} = \text{var}\{2 \times \ln(s)\} = 4\,\text{var}\{\ln(s)\}$, so that one can obtain $\text{var}\{\ln(s^2)\}$ directly from $\text{var}\{\ln(s)\}$.

Table 12-4 gives the values of $\text{var}\{\ln(w)\}$ for the four simple estimators, as well as the lowest attained variance as given by Tukey et al. (1977). These lowest attained variances are the known minimum value for the Gaussian and the lowest values found through simulation for one-wild and slash.

TABLE 12-4. var{ln(w)} for sample size 20.[a]

Estimator	Situation		
	Gaussian	One-Wild	Slash
s	0.026	0.271	1.1
AD	0.032	0.085	0.634
MAD	0.074	0.071	0.105
d_F	0.063	0.062	0.115
lowest attained variance[b]	0.026	0.029	0.099

[a]Entries for s, AD, and MAD are based on results given by Lax (1975). See Table 12-3.
[b]From Tukey, Braun, and Schwarzschild (1977, Table 1).

Table 12-5 gives the *efficiencies*, which are computed by taking, for each situation, the lowest attainable variance divided by var{ln(w)} and multiplied by 100. Table 12-5 also gives the *triefficiencies*, which are defined as the lowest efficiency attained by the estimator for any of the three distributions. Since the three distributions have varying degrees of heavy-tailedness, the triefficiency gives an indication of the smallest efficiency that one might experience through the use of the estimator. An inspection of the last column of Table 12-5 reveals that none of the simple scale estimators has a high triefficiency. In particular, s has quite poor performance for the two nonGaussian situations. Of special importance is the performance of the F-spread, which has the highest triefficiency among these four estimators. The F-spread is simple to compute and has been extensively used in Chapters 2 and 3. Its triefficiency now provides an added rationale for using the F-spread as a simple robust and somewhat efficient measure of scale.

TABLE 12-5. Efficiencies corresponding to the entries of Table 12-4.

Estimator	Situation			Triefficiency (%)
	Gaussian (%)	One-Wild (%)	Slash (%)	
s	100	11	9	9
AD	81	34	16	16
MAD	35	41	94	35
d_F	41	47	86	41

Other, more complicated, estimators can offer higher triefficiencies than those recorded in Table 12-5. In the next section we discuss a promising class of robust scale estimators.

12D. SCALE ESTIMATORS BASED ON *M*-ESTIMATORS OF LOCATION

Although such simple scale estimators as the MAD and the fourth-spread are far from disastrously inefficient, we should expect to do much better. From Chapters 10 and 11 we recall that high-performance *M*-estimators of location offer substantial improvements over the simple estimators and also leave little room for further practical improvement in triefficiency. By analogy, then, we should consider *M*-estimators of scale as a possible source of higher performance. In fact, we pursue an alternative. First, we briefly sketch *M*-estimation of scale.

If scale is the only unknown parameter (for example, because the location parameter is zero or some other known value), then the *M*-estimator of scale w_n based on the function χ is determined by the equation

$$\sum_{i=1}^{n} \chi\left(\frac{x_i}{w_n}\right) = 0. \tag{1}$$

Usually χ is an even function; that is, $\chi(-u) = \chi(u)$.

For a simple example, we recall the connection between *M*-estimation and maximum likelihood. In a sample of n observations from a Gaussian distribution with mean 0 and variance σ^2, the likelihood (as a function of σ) is

$$\prod_{i=1}^{n} \left(\frac{1}{\sigma\sqrt{2\pi}}\right) e^{-(x_i/\sigma)^2/2}.$$

Taking logarithms, differentiating with respect to σ, and equating the derivative to 0 yield

$$-\frac{n}{\sigma} + \frac{1}{\sigma}\sum_{i=1}^{n}\left(\frac{x_i}{\sigma}\right)^2 = 0.$$

Arranging this in the form of equation (1), we see that the χ-function corresponding to the maximum-likelihood estimator of scale in a Gaussian

distribution is

$$\chi(u) = u^2 - 1.$$

A χ-function generally involves a constant term in this way because the constant belongs more naturally in the χ-function than on the right-hand side of equation (1).

Ordinarily, we estimate both location and scale, and we need a definition that covers simultaneous M-estimators.

DEFINITION: A location estimator T_n and a scale estimator w_n are said to be simultaneous *M-estimators of location and scale* in the sample $x_1, \ldots, x_n$ if they satisfy the pair of equations

$$\sum_{i=1}^{n} \psi\left(\frac{x_i - T_n}{cw_n}\right) = 0 \qquad (2a)$$

$$\sum_{i=1}^{n} \chi\left(\frac{x_i - T_n}{cw_n}\right) = 0. \qquad (2b)$$

For symmetric situations, ψ is an odd function and χ is an even function [i.e., $\psi(-u) = -\psi(u)$ and $\chi(-u) = \chi(u)$, as discussed in Chapter 11]. The constant c is the tuning constant.

In estimating location and scale simultaneously, equation (2b) keeps w_n comparable to the data. Without such a constraint many ψ-functions would permit an absurd solution for T_n in equation (2a) when w_n is sufficiently small that none of the observations lie on the central (linear) part of the ψ-function. Huber (1981, Chapters 5 and 6) discusses M-estimators of scale as well as L-estimators and R-estimators.

Because we usually estimate location whenever we are estimating scale for a sample, we could use equations (2a) and (2b); but we have available an alternative approach which avoids the combined iteration linking (2b) to (2a) and capitalizes on the way that M-estimators will often be implemented. This approach recognizes that the formula for the asymptotic variance of an M-estimator of location can be applied to a sample and the square root of the result used as an estimator of scale. If the data come from distribution F, we denote the population values of location and scale by $T(F)$ and $w(F)$. Here $w(F)$ does not correspond to w_n in equation (2b); instead it is the population value for the auxiliary scale estimator (such as MAD) that we are using in calculating T_n. As Section 11D explains, the

asymptotic variance of T_n—that is, the variance of the limiting distribution of $\sqrt{n}\,[T_n - T(F)]$—is given by

$$A(F, T) = \frac{c^2 w^2(F) \int \psi^2\left[\dfrac{x - T(F)}{cw(F)}\right] f(x)\, dx}{\left\{\int \psi'\left[\dfrac{x - T(F)}{cw(F)}\right] f(x)\, dx\right\}^2}, \tag{3}$$

where f is the density function corresponding to F. The notation $A(F, T)$ emphasizes that the asymptotic variance depends on the underlying distribution as well as on T.

To form a scale estimator, we approximate $A(F, T)$ from the sample and then take the square root. This requires that we replace, for example, $w(F)$ by MAD, $T(F)$ by M, $f(x)$ by $1/n$, and integration by summation over the sample. Letting

$$u_i = \frac{x_i - M}{c\text{MAD}},$$

we obtain the estimator of scale

$$s_T = \frac{(c\text{MAD})n^{1/2}\left[\sum_{i=1}^{n} \psi^2(u_i)\right]^{1/2}}{\left|\sum_{i=1}^{n} \psi'(u_i)\right|}. \tag{4}$$

We refer to such estimators of scale as *A-estimators*.*

We consider two ψ-functions in this discussion. First,

$$\psi(u) = \begin{cases} \sin(\pi u) & \text{for } |u| < 1 \\ 0 & \text{for } |u| \geqslant 1 \end{cases}$$

leads to the scale estimator

$$s_{wa} = \frac{(c\text{MAD})n^{1/2}\left[\sum_{|u_i| < 1} \sin^2(\pi u_i)\right]^{1/2}}{\pi\left|\sum_{|u_i| < 1} \cos(\pi u_i)\right|},$$

based on the wave (Andrews sine) estimator of location. We actually use a

---

*This term was introduced by David A. Lax early in 1982.

version of s_{wa} that performs slightly better. This is the modified wave estimator

$$s_{mw} = (c\text{MAD})n^{1/2}\tan^{-1}\frac{\left[\Sigma_{|u_i|<1}\sin^2(\pi u_i)\right]^{1/2}}{\pi\left|\Sigma_{|u_i|<1}\cos(\pi u_i)\right|}.$$

We also consider the biweight ψ-function

$$\psi(u) = \begin{cases} u(1-u^2)^2 & \text{for } |u| < 1 \\ 0 & \text{for } |u| \geq 1. \end{cases}$$

Then $\psi'(u) = (1-u^2)(1-5u^2)$ for $|u| < 1$, and the corresponding *A*-estimator of scale is

$$s_{bi} = \frac{n^{1/2}\left[\Sigma_{|u_i|<1}(x_i - M)^2(1-u_i^2)^4\right]^{1/2}}{\left|\Sigma_{|u_i|<1}(1-u_i^2)(1-5u_i^2)\right|},$$

based on the biweight estimator of location.*

Good choices for the constant c depend on the sample size and the ψ-function. A clearer picture of the role of c comes from considering the Gaussian case, for which $E(\text{MAD}) \approx \frac{2}{3}\sigma$. Thus a biweight estimator with $c = 9$ means that observations more than $(\frac{2}{3})(9) = 6$ standard deviations away from the median will be given zero weight. Another popular choice for the constant in the biweight is $c = 6$, which gives zero weight to observations more than 4 standard deviations away from the median. Choosing $c = 9$ for the biweight and $c = 2.1\pi$ for the wave estimator, respectively, yields estimators of scale with relatively high triefficiencies, although other choices of c may slightly increase the triefficiencies for some sample sizes.

Table 12-6 repeats the efficiency values from Table 12-5 and adds results for s_{mw} and s_{bi}. Notice the relatively high triefficiency of these two *A*-estimators. In particular, the triefficiency of s_{bi} is 86%.

The stated efficiency results apply only for sample size 20. Additional simulations for other sample sizes have produced similar patterns of triefficiency. In summary, s_{mw} and s_{bi} have high efficiency under a number of

---

*Kafadar (1979) has illustrated the advantages of replacing the denominator above by $[(\text{denominator})(-1 + \text{denominator})]^{1/2}$.

TABLE 12-6. Efficiencies and triefficiencies, based on var$\{\ln(w)\}$, for the scale estimators with $n = 20$.[a]

	Situation			
Estimator	Gaussian (%)	One-Wild (%)	Slash (%)	Triefficiency (%)
s	100	11	9	9
AD	81	34	16	16
MAD	35	41	94	35
d_F	41	47	86	41
s_{bi}	87	86	91	86
s_{mw}	82	90	97	82

[a]Entries for s, AD, MAD, s_{bi}, and s_{mw} are based on results given by Lax (1975). See Table 12-3.

distributional assumptions, and s_{bi} can be recommended as a robust measure of scale.

Returning to the SAT scores example, we obtain $s_{bi} = 98.14$ and 178.99 for the rural and urban students' scores, respectively. This indicates $\frac{178.99}{98.14} = 1.82$ times as much dispersion for the urban scores as compared to the rural scores. This ratio is similar to that obtained using AD.

As a robust measure of scale, s_{bi} has potential for many applications. Later in this chapter we discuss the use of this estimator in obtaining robust confidence intervals and in testing for Gaussian shape.

12E. PSEUDOVARIANCES

In the previous sections we investigated a number of scale estimators w and compared performance by using var$\{\ln(w)\}$. The var$\{\ln(w)\}$ is a good measure of performance when $\ln(w)$ is almost Gaussian, but it is a poor measure for highly skewed distributions of $\ln(w)$. In order to investigate further the distribution of $\ln(w)$, we can use the pseudovariance (also mentioned in Sections 2C and 10C).

DEFINITION: Let y be a random variable, G its distribution function, Φ the standard Gaussian distribution, and $0 < p < \frac{1}{2}$. Then the *100p% pseudovariance* of y is defined as

$$v(p) = \left(\frac{G^{-1}(1-p) - G^{-1}(p)}{\Phi^{-1}(1-p) - \Phi^{-1}(p)} \right)^2.$$

TABLE 12-7. Pseudovariance divided by variance of ln(w) for four estimators.[a]

Estimator	Tail Area			
	0.1%	1%	4.2%	25%
Gaussian distribution				
s	1.09	1.07	1.05	1.03
MAD	1.05	1.04	1.01	0.98
$s_{bi}(c = 9)$	1.12	1.07	1.04	1.01
$s_{mw}(c = 2.1\pi)$	1.10	1.07	1.04	1.01
One-wild situation				
s	0.64	0.77	0.91	1.36
MAD	1.00	1.03	1.02	1.00
$s_{bi}(c = 9)$	1.11	1.07	1.05	1.02
$s_{mw}(c = 2.1\pi)$	1.08	1.06	1.05	1.03
Slash distribution				
s	large	large	large	0.88
MAD	1.04	1.00	0.98	0.96
$s_{bi}(c = 9)$	1.06	1.03	1.00	0.93
$s_{mw}(c = 2.1\pi)$	1.02	1.00	0.98	0.95

[a]Pseudovariance and variance entries obtained from Lax (1975).

Here $v(p)$ is the square of a percentile spread of the distribution of y divided by the corresponding percentile spread of the standard Gaussian. Notice that if y follows a Gaussian distribution, then $v(p) = \text{var}(y)$ for all p. For heavy-tailed symmetric distributions, $v(p)$ will tend to increase as $p \to 0$. Thus if $v(p)$ is almost constant for a number of choices of p, it indicates that y is close to Gaussian.

Further discussions of pseudovariances appear in Andrews et al. (1972) and Huber (1977). In particular, Andrews et al. (p. 167) state that the 4.2% pseudovariance stays almost constant for members of the Pearson system of distributions. For a discussion of the Pearson system of curves see, for example, Johnson and Kotz (1970, pp. 9–15). Because the Pearson system includes many of the common continuous distributions, the 4.2% pseudovariance may be a more satisfactory measure than the variance for comparing estimators.

Table 12-7 shows the 0.1, 1, 4.2, and 25% pseudovariances of ln(w), each divided by the variance of ln(w), as calculated by Lax (1975). We have not performed the corresponding computations for the F-spread. Notice that the 4.2% pseudovariances are, with one exception (s for slash), almost equal to the variances. The other entries in Table 12-7, excluding those for s, are also

close to the value 1. Thus the distribution of $\ln(w)$ is close enough to Gaussian that using pseudovariances instead of variances would cause only slight changes in the triefficiencies.

12F. ROBUST CONFIDENCE INTERVALS

Given n independent observations, the most common technique for finding a $100(1 - \alpha)\%$ confidence interval for the center of a symmetric distribution consists of computing $\bar{x} \pm ts/\sqrt{n}$, where t is the $100(1 - \alpha/2)$ percentage point of the t distribution on $n - 1$ degrees of freedom. That is, the confidence interval is based on the most efficient location and scale estimators for the Gaussian distribution.

What would happen if the data did not come from a Gaussian distribution, but from one with heavier tails? Because both $\bar{x}$ and s have low triefficiency, the interval may vary unnecessarily from one sample to the next. Furthermore, the average value of s may be quite large, and this would tend to give relatively long intervals. For these reasons, we introduce an alternative approach for finding robust and efficient confidence intervals.

The Gaussian confidence interval is $\bar{x} \pm ts/\sqrt{n}$. Using this as a model, Gross (1976) investigates the properties of robust confidence intervals of the form $T \pm t^*w/\sqrt{n}$, where T and w are a pair of robust estimators of location and scale, respectively, and t^* is a constant conservatively chosen in order to make the confidence level of the interval at least $100(1 - \alpha)\%$ at each of the "three corners." Gross makes an extensive study of robust confidence intervals for sample sizes 10 and 20. In this section we give a brief summary of his results for sample size 20. To Gross's results we have added our own for the F-spread.

In order to construct a robust confidence interval, one needs both a location estimate and a scale estimate. We consider only the following five pairs of estimators:

$\bar{x}$ and s

M and MAD

M and d_F

The wave interval with

$$T_{wa} = M + (c\text{MAD})\tan^{-1}\left[\frac{\Sigma_{|u_i|<1}\sin(\pi u_i)}{\Sigma_{|u_i|<1}\pi\cos(\pi u_i)}\right]$$

and s_{wa} as defined in Section 12D. Here $u_i = (x_i - M)/c\mathrm{MAD}$ and, following Gross, we use $c = 2.4\pi$. (The $\tan^{-1}$ serves to accelerate the convergence of the M-estimator.)

The biweight interval with

$$T_{bi} = M + \frac{\Sigma_{|u_i|<1}(x_i - M)(1 - u_i^2)^2}{\Sigma_{|u_i|<1}(1 - u_i^2)^2}$$

and s_{bi} as defined in Section 12D. Here again $u_i = (x_i - M)/c\mathrm{MAD}$ and we use $c = 9$.

Table 12-8 gives the t values for 95% confidence intervals for the Gaussian, one-wild, and slash situations. The last column of this table consists of the maximum value for each row. Notice that for each of our intervals the maximum value of t comes from the Gaussian distribution. Thus we get a conservative value of t by considering only the Gaussian distribution. This need not always be true, but the Gaussian t is usually close to the maximum t.

An interval based on the maximum t would be at least a 95% confidence interval for the location of a Gaussian, one-wild, or slash distribution. Because these three situations contain varying degrees of heavy-tailedness,

TABLE 12-8. Selected t-values for conservative 95% confidence
intervals for $n = 20$.[a]

Location and Scale Estimators	Situation			Maximum
	Gaussian	One-Wild	Slash	
$\bar{x}, s$	2.10	1.77	1.80	2.10
M, MAD	4.29	3.98	3.55	4.29
M, d_F	1.95	1.84	1.71	1.95
Biweight location, s_{bi}	2.19	2.15	2.18	2.19
Wave location, s_{wa}	2.20	2.16	2.19	2.20

[a]Entries from Gross (1976). The M, MAD and M, d_F values were computed using the Temple University CDC CYBER-174 computer and a technique similar to that used by Gross.

such an interval would be a conservative 95% confidence interval for the location of most symmetric distributions.

Having decided to use the maximum value of t for finding the conservative confidence interval, we may wish to know the resulting average confidence interval length. Because the average lengths are proportional to $2tE(w)$, we compute only those values. For Gaussian observations with $\sigma^2 = 1$, $E(s) = 0.985$ so that $2tE(s) = 2(2.10)(0.985) = 4.14$. Gross (1976) obtains such average confidence interval lengths for 25 pairs of estimators. To his results we add those corresponding to the median and F-spread pair. In order to relate interval length to variance (a quadratic measure), we define length efficiency corresponding to a specific distribution as

$$\left(\frac{\text{shortest average interval length found}}{\text{average interval length for pair of estimators}} \right)^2 100\%.$$

For example, under the Gaussian distribution the shortest average length is 4.14, and the average length for the M and MAD pair is 5.51. This leads to an efficiency value of $(4.14/5.51)^2 100\% = 56\%$. The triefficiency is again defined as the lowest efficiency for the three situations used.

Table 12-9 contains the efficiencies corresponding to the Gaussian, one-wild, and slash situations and the five pairs of estimators. The median and F-spread have the largest triefficiency among the pairs of simple estimators. Far better results are obtained for the two pairs based on M-estimators of location, both of which have triefficiency above 90%. Although the wave has a slightly higher triefficiency, many will prefer the

TABLE 12-9. Length efficiencies and triefficiencies of confidence intervals.[a]

Location and Scale Estimators	Situation			Triefficiency (%)
	Gaussian (%)	One-Wild (%)	Slash (%)	
$\bar{x}, s$	100	23	1	1
M, MAD	56	58	70	56
M, d_F	65	66	74	65
Biweight location, s_{bi}	94	100	91	91
Wave location, s_{wa}	93	99	93	93

[a]All rows except the third are based on values from Gross (1976).

TABLE 12-10. *t* values required for the construction of robust confidence intervals and approximations to these values.

Sample Size	(T_{bi}, s_{bi})	$t_{.7(n-1)}$	(M, d_F)	$t_{n-1}/1.075$	(M, MAD)	(M, s_{bi})
10	2.57	2.45	2.18	2.10	4.94	2.79
20	2.18	2.16	1.94	1.94	4.22	2.52
30	2.09	2.09	1.92	1.91	3.98	2.48
40	2.05	2.05	1.88	1.88	3.89	2.47
50	2.03	2.03	1.87	1.87	3.80	[a]
100	1.99	1.99	1.84	1.84	3.72	[a]

[a] Not computed.

biweight pair of estimators because they involve simple weights and have easily approximated *t* values.

The use of conservative confidence intervals leads to reasonable confidence levels for the robust pairs of estimators. For example, the biweight pair of estimators has true levels 5%, 4.7%, and 4.9% under the Gaussian, one-wild, and slash situations, respectively. These values are very close to the nominal 5%.

A further simulation obtained the conservative *t* values for a variety of sample sizes. We used the Monte Carlo swindle discussed by Gross (1973) for three pairs of estimators—M, MAD; M, d_F; T_{bi}, s_{bi}—under the Gaussian, one-wild, and slash situations. The largest *t* values always came from the Gaussian distribution; these are recorded in Table 12-10 for sample sizes 10, 20, 30, 40, 50, and 100.

Mosteller and Tukey (1977, p. 209) suggest that the percentage points of the *t* distribution with $0.7(n-1)$ degrees of freedom* provide a good approximation for the conservative *t* values when using the biweight pair of estimators. Table 12-10 also shows that the values of $t_{.7(n-1)}$ are in excellent agreement with the *t* values found through simulation. Several additional *t* values were simulated for a 90% confidence interval, and these are also in excellent agreement with those given by $t_{.7(n-1)}$. From this evidence we believe that the conservative *t* values required for using the biweight pair of estimators when $n \geq 20$ are very close to $t_{.7(n-1)}$.

Table 12-10 also contains the values of $t_{n-1}/1.075$, which are in close agreement with the required *t* for a confidence interval using M and d_F. The value 1.075 was estimated from the simulated *t* values. The last column in

---

*More precisely, if $0.7(n-1)$ is not an integer, one can use the next smaller integer number of degrees of freedom, but linear interpolation in "1/(degrees of freedom)" is presumably better.

Table 12-10 contains the conservative t values using M and the biweight A-estimator of scale. Notice the considerable difference between the t values required when using M and s_{bi} and those for T_{bi} and s_{bi}, an indication that different choices for the location estimator require different t values.

We can now recommend relatively simple procedures for finding robust confidence intervals. For hand computation we recommend

$$M \pm \frac{t_{n-1}(d_F)}{1.075\sqrt{n}},$$

which yields the approximate 95% confidence interval for the center of the distribution. A more efficient robust interval is

$$T_{bi} \pm t_{.7(n-1)} \frac{s_{bi}}{\sqrt{n}},$$

TABLE 12-11.   The 95% confidence intervals for the student SAT scores example.

Estimates and Confidence Intervals	Rural Students' Scores	Urban Students' Scores
$\bar{x}$	803	932
M	812	900
T_{bi}	821	931
s	120	177
d_F	85	277
s_{bi}	98	179
$\dfrac{t_{n-1}s}{\sqrt{n}}$	73	107
$\dfrac{t_{n-1}(d_F)}{\left(1.075\sqrt{n}\right)}$	48	156
$\dfrac{t_{.7(n-1)}s_{bi}}{\sqrt{n}}$	63	115
$\left(\bar{x} - \dfrac{t_{n-1}s}{\sqrt{n}}, \bar{x} + \dfrac{t_{n-1}s}{\sqrt{n}}\right)$	(730, 876)	(825, 1039)
$\left(M - \dfrac{t_{n-1}(d_F)}{(1.075)\sqrt{n}}, M + \dfrac{t_{n-1}(d_F)}{(1.075)\sqrt{n}}\right)$	(764, 860)	(744, 1056)
$\left(T_{bi} - \dfrac{t_{.7(n-1)}s_{bi}}{\sqrt{n}}, T_{bi} + \dfrac{t_{.7(n-1)}s_{bi}}{\sqrt{n}}\right)$	(758, 884)	(816, 1045)

where T_{bi} is the biweight location estimate and s_{bi} is the square root of the sample estimate of the asymptotic variance of T_{bi}.

Let us again return to the SAT scores example and compute the confidence intervals for the following pairs of estimators: $\bar{x}, s$; M, d_F; T_{bi}, s_{bi}. Remember that we found one potential outlier among the rural students' scores. Table 12-11 contains the computed estimates and the 95% confidence intervals based on the above three pairs of estimators. The biweight confidence interval is considerably shorter, as compared to the interval using $\bar{x}$ and s, for the rural scores and somewhat longer for the urban scores. In the following section we show that the urban scores seem to have a Gaussian shape. This example illustrates the tradeoff between using robust versus standard procedures. For Gaussian observations the robust intervals will tend to be longer, whereas for nonGaussian data they can be considerably shorter and still maintain the desired confidence level.

Although we have concentrated on confidence intervals, the results are directly applicable to testing hypotheses on the location parameter. For example, for testing $H_0: \mu = \mu_0$ versus $H_a: \mu > \mu_0$, one can use the critical region

$$\frac{T_{bi} - \mu_0}{s_{bi}/\sqrt{n}} > t_{.7(n-1)}.$$

12G. A TEST FOR DEPARTURES FROM GAUSSIAN SHAPE

We have seen that under the Gaussian distribution both s and s_{bi} are highly efficient estimators of scale. The estimator s_{bi} remains highly efficient for heavy-tailed symmetric distributions, whereas s becomes very inefficient. It thus becomes tempting to use s^2/s_{bi}^2 as a test statistic for detecting departures from the Gaussian shape. An investigation of the properties of this statistic reveals that it is more powerful than the usual competitors for detecting heavy-tailed symmetric distributions. However, it is somewhat less effective in detecting highly skewed distributions. As an overall test statistic,

$$\frac{\sum_{i=1}^n (x_i - M)^2}{(n-1)s_{bi}^2}$$

performs far better. For this reason, we discuss this test statistic in some detail.

As a preliminary, we briefly review the rationale of testing for Gaussian shape, especially in the context of exploratory data analysis. First, such a

test represents an exploratory step because evidence of a substantial departure from Gaussian shape requires care in the use of classical confirmatory techniques. In addition, continued use of tests for departures from Gaussian shape would help to convince practitioners that "normal" data often do not have Gaussian distributions. This discovery should lead to a greater awareness of the need for robust methods.

Also, some exploratory techniques use the Gaussian shape as an ideal standard for comparison. Two examples are the rule of thumb (discussed in Chapter 2) for identifying possible outliers and the suspended rootogram (Tukey, 1972; Velleman and Hoaglin, 1981). The rule of thumb for outliers is designed to find only a few "false positives" when the data are well behaved (i.e., Gaussian). Hoaglin, Iglewicz, and Tukey (1981) show that it does this and that it finds many more outliers when the data come from heavy-tailed distributions.

Another important application of tests for Gaussian shape occurs in the investigation of residuals in regression analysis (see Section 7B). Rejection of the Gaussian hypothesis may indicate the need for a data transformation, the requirement of additional explanatory variables, or the use of a resistant fit in order to reduce the effects of potential outliers.

Let us return now to the discussion of the use of

$$I = \frac{\sum_{i=1}^{n} (x_i - M)^2}{(n-1)s_{bi}^2} \tag{5}$$

as a test for departures from Gaussian shape. This statistic has been investigated by Martinez and Iglewicz (1981), who find through extensive simulations that the 100β percentage point, I_β, can be very accurately approximated by working in the log scale with $\tilde{I}_\beta = \log_{10}(I_\beta - 0.982)$ and $\tilde{n} = \log_{10}(n-1)$. For $\beta = .90$ and $\beta = .95$ they use a data-analytic approach to obtain the formulas

$$\tilde{I}_{.90} = 0.6376 - 1.1535\tilde{n} + 0.1266(\tilde{n}^2)$$

and

$$\tilde{I}_{.95} = \begin{cases} 1.9065 - 2.5465\tilde{n} + 0.5652(\tilde{n}^2) & \text{for } n < 50 \\ 0.7824 - 1.1021\tilde{n} + 0.1021(\tilde{n}^2) & \text{for } n \geqslant 50. \end{cases}$$

Comparisons of this test with several well-known alternative tests of departure from Gaussian shape indicate that it is more powerful for heavy-tailed symmetric distributions and that it performs well for a wide variety of situations.

Returning to the SAT scores example, we find that $I = 1.51$ and 1.01 for the rural and urban observations, respectively. The critical value for $\alpha = 0.10$ and $n = 13$ equals 1.329, so that we would reject the hypothesis of Gaussian shape for the rural data. When we remove the outlying observation, 500, from the rural sample, the remaining 12 observations yield a statistically nonsignificant I value of 1.02.

12H. SUMMARY

Even in a symmetric distribution, robust estimation of scale is not as straightforward as robust estimation of location, in part because different distributions do not share a readily agreed-upon parameter to estimate. This technical obstacle does not hamper comparisons of scale among samples that are believed to come from the same basic distribution, but it does complicate comparisons across distributions in terms of the usual measures of efficiency. We avoid the difficulty by accepting $\text{var}\{\ln(w)\}$ as the basis for comparisons.

The classical simple estimators, such as the standard deviation and the mean deviation, rapidly lose efficiency when one moves away from the common but unrealistic assumption of Gaussian data and toward heavier-tailed contamination or a heavy-tailed distribution. Although they are not highly efficient for near-Gaussian data, such simple resistant estimators as the fourth-spread and the MAD perform well for heavy-tailed distributions and have adequate triefficiency for exploratory work.

For good overall performance and robustness—in terms of triefficiency—we recommend selected estimators based on the formula for the asymptotic variance of an M-estimator of location. Two of these A-estimators, s_{bi} and s_{wa}, show considerable promise, both in estimating scale for its own sake and in forming robust confidence intervals for the center of a symmetric distribution. Also, s_{bi} serves as the basis for an effective new test for departures from Gaussian shape.

REFERENCES

Andrews, D. F., Bickel, P. J., Hampel, F. R., Huber, P. J., Rogers, W. H., and Tukey, J. W. (1972). *Robust Estimates of Location: Survey and Advances*. Princeton, NJ: Princeton University Press.

Bickel, P. J. and Lehmann, E. L. (1976). "Descriptive statistics for nonparametric models. III. Dispersion," *Annals of Statistics*, **4**, 1139–1158.

——— (1979). "Descriptive statistics for nonparametric models IV. Spread." In J. Jurečková (Ed.), *Contributions to Statistics, Jaroslav Hajek Memorial Volume*. Prague: Academia, pp. 33–40.

Gross, A. M. (1973). "A Monte Carlo swindle for estimators of location," *Applied Statistics*, **22**, 347–353.

———— (1976). "Confidence interval robustness with long-tailed symmetric distributions," *Journal of the American Statistical Association*, **71**, 409–416.

Hoaglin, D. C., Iglewicz, B., and Tukey, J. W. (1981). "Small-sample performance of a resistant rule for outlier detection." *1980 Proceedings of the Statistical Computing Section*. Washington, DC: American Statistical Association, pp. 148–152.

Huber, P. J. (1977). *Robust Statistical Procedures*. Philadelphia: Society for Industrial and Applied Mathematics.

Huber, P. J. (1981). *Robust Statistics*. New York: Wiley.

Johnson, N. L. and Kotz, S. (1970). *Distributions in Statistics—Continuous Univariate Distributions—1*. Boston: Houghton Mifflin.

Kafadar, K. (1979). "Robust confidence intervals for the one- and two-sample problems." Ph.D. dissertation, Princeton University.

Lax, D. A. (1975). "An interim report of a Monte Carlo study of robust estimators of width." Technical Report 93, Series 2, Department of Statistics, Princeton University.

Martinez, J. and Iglewicz, B. (1981). "A test for departure from normality based on a biweight estimator of scale," *Biometrika*, **68**, 331–333.

Mosteller, F. and Tukey, J. W. (1977). *Data Analysis and Regression*. Reading, MA: Addison-Wesley.

Nemenyi, P., Dixon, S.K., White, N. B., and Hedstrom, M. L. (1977). *Statistics from Scratch*. San Francisco: Holden–Day.

Tukey, J. W. (1960). "A survey of sampling from contaminated distributions." In I. Olkin, S. Ghurye, W. Hoeffding, W. Madow, and H. Mann (Eds.), *Contributions to Probability and Statistics*. Stanford, CA: Stanford University Press, pp. 448–485.

Tukey, J. W. (1972). "Some graphic and semigraphic displays." In T. A. Bancroft (Ed.), *Statistical Papers in Honor of George W. Snedecor*. Ames, IA: Iowa State University Press, pp. 293–316.

Tukey, J. W., Braun, H. I., and Schwarzschild, M. (1977). "Further progress on robust/resistant widthing." Technical Report 129, Series 2, Department of Statistics, Princeton University.

Velleman, P. F. and Hoaglin, D. C. (1981). *Applications, Basics, and Computing of Exploratory Data Analysis*. Boston: Duxbury Press.

Additional Literature

We list a number of additional references related to topics discussed in this chapter, and we comment on some of these. No attempt has been made to exhaust the literature.

Boos (1980), Maritz (1979), and Prescott (1975) use mathematical tools to obtain robust confidence intervals. The articles by Budescu (1980) and Healy (1978) deal with Gini's mean difference and related estimators, which a number of researchers have recommended as robust measures of scale. Carroll (1979) and Thall (1979) investigate robust scale estimators for asymmetric distributions. Considerable work has also focused on adaptive robust estimators. The papers by De Wet and van Wyk (1979) and Harter et al. (1979) deal with adaptive scale estimators. Shoemaker and Hettmansperger (1982) approximate cs_{bi}^2, c being the approximately chosen constant, by a chi-squared distribution and show how to use the data to estimate the number of degrees of freedom. Also, the article by Green (1976) gives a more formal treatment

of heavier-tailed distributions. Finally, the paper by Pearson et al. (1977) is representative of the many articles dealing with tests for departure from Gaussian shape.

Boos, D. D. (1980). "A new method for constructing approximate confidence intervals from M estimates," *Journal of the American Statistical Association*, **75**, 142–145.

Budescu, D. V. (1980). "Approximate confidence intervals for a robust scale parameter," *Psychometrika*, **45**, 397–402.

Carroll, R. J. (1979). "On estimating variances of robust estimators when the errors are asymmetric," *Journal of the American Statistical Association*, **74**, 674–679.

De Wet, T. and van Wyk, J. W. J. (1979). "Efficiency and robustness of Hogg's adaptive trimmed means," *Communications in Statistics*, **A8**, 117–128.

Green, R. F. (1976). "Outlier-prone and outlier-resistant distributions," *Journal of the American Statistical Association*, **71**, 502–505.

Harter, H. L., Moore, A. H., and Curry, T. F. (1979). "Adaptive robust estimation of location and scale parameters of symmetric populations," *Communications in Statistics*, **A8**, 1473–1491.

Healy, M. J. R. (1978). "A mean difference estimator of standard deviation in symmetrically censored normal samples," *Biometrika*, **65**, 643–646.

Lemmer, H. (1978). "A robust test for dispersion," *Journal of the American Statistical Association*, **73**, 419–421.

Maritz, J. S. (1979). "A note on exact robust confidence intervals for location," *Biometrika*, **66**, 163–166.

Maronna, R. (1976). "Robust M-estimators of multivariate location and scatter," *Annals of Statistics*, **4**, 51–67.

Pearson, E. S., D'Agostino, R. B., and Bowman, K. O. (1977). "Tests for departure from normality: comparison of powers," *Biometrika*, **64**, 231–246.

Prescott, P. (1976). "A simple alternative to Student's t," *Applied Statistics*, **24**, 210–217.

Shoemaker, L. H. and Hettmansperger, T. P. (1982). "Robust estimates and tests for the one- and two-sample scale models," *Biometrika*, **69**, 47–53.

Thall, P. F. (1979). "Huber-sense robust M-estimation of a scale parameter, with application to the exponential distribution," *Journal of the American Statistical Association*, **74**, 147–152.

Wainer, H. and Thissen, D. (1976). "Three steps towards robust regression," *Psychometrika*, **41**, 9–34.

EXERCISES

1. Table 1-1 gives the mean menstrual cycle length in days for 21 women.

   (a) Construct a boxplot for this data set. Which values, if any, are outliers?

   (b) Calculate $\bar{x}$, s, M, AD, MAD, and d_F for this batch. For a batch of this size, which of the four scale measures is easiest to obtain by hand?

   (c) Discuss the impact of any outliers on each of the four simple scale measures. You may want to recalculate the measures after removing the outlier(s).

2. Give sketches of symmetric distributions of nine points with

    (a) MAD > AD
    (b) AD > MAD
    (c) MAD = AD.

    For your three illustrations, how do the three fourth-spreads compare with each other?

    The 18 most populated places in Massachusetts and Pennsylvania in 1970 are listed below, along with their population according to the 1970 U.S. Census.

Pennsylvania		Massachusetts	
City	Population	City	Population
Philadelphia	1949996	Boston	641071
Pittsburgh	520117	Worcester	176572
Erie	129231	Springfield	163905
Allentown	109527	New Bedford	101777
Scranton	103564	Cambridge	100361
Reading	87643	Fall River	96898
Bethlehem	72686	Lowell	94239
Harrisburg	68061	Newton	91066
Altoona	63115	Lynn	90294
Wilkes-Barre	58856	Brockton	89040
Lancaster	57690	Somerville	88779
Chester	56331	Quincy	87966
York	50335	Lawrence	66915
Johnstown	42476	Chicopee	66676
New Castle	38559	Medford	64397
Norristown	38169	Framingham	64048
McKeesport	37977	Waltham	61582
Williamsport	37918	Brookline	58886

Source: *1970 Census of Population*, Volume 1: Characteristics of the Population, Part A (Number of Inhabitants). U.S. Government Printing Office, Washington, DC, May 1972.

Use these two data sets for Exercises 3 through 5.

3. (a) Draw boxplots of the data.
    (b) Will a power transformation promote stability of spread or symmetry of the two batches? If so, transform the data accordingly and make new boxplots.

4. Compare the spread of the two batches in terms of s, AD, MAD, and d_F. (If you transformed in Exercise 3, use the transformed data.)

5. (a) Apply the computations of Table 12-11 to the (transformed) data.
   (b) Test for departure from Gaussian shape by using the statistic I in equation (5) and $\alpha = 0.10$.

6. Section 12A discusses the comparison of the variance of s with that of a scale-adjusted mean absolute deviation for slightly contaminated Gaussian distributions. Verify that the ratio of the adjusted variances is 1.016 for $\varepsilon = 0.002$ and 2.035 for $\varepsilon = 0.05$.

7. Section 12F introduces the confidence interval

$$M \pm \frac{t_{n-1}d_F}{1.075\sqrt{n}}$$

Verify that this is a 95% confidence interval for large sample sizes. Find var(M) and use matched re-expression.

8. Devise two sets of numbers such that $\frac{1}{2}d_F$ is larger than the MAD for the first set and smaller than the MAD for the second set.

*9. For n ordered observations, $x_1 \leqslant x_2 \leqslant \cdots \leqslant x_n$,

$$s^* = \frac{2\sqrt{\pi}}{n(n-1)} \sum_{i=1}^{n} \left[i - \frac{1}{2}(n+1)\right]x_i$$

has been recommended as a robust scale estimator. This estimator has $E(s^*) = \sigma$ for independent Gaussian observations and is equal to $\frac{1}{2}\sqrt{\pi}\, G$, where G is Gini's mean difference. Simulate var$\{\ln(s^*)\}$, for $n = 20$, and show that the triefficiency is approximately 12%.

10. Calculate s^* (defined in Exercise 9) for the Pennsylvania and Massachusetts population data used in Exercises 3 through 5.

11. Generate samples of size $n = 20$ and $n = 50$ from the Gaussian(0, 1) and uniform(0, 1) distributions.
   (a) Complete the calculations in Table 12-11 for these four samples.
   (b) Compare the results for the two Gaussian samples to those for the two uniform samples.

Index